BLACK AND WHITE BABY

BLACK

AND

WHITE

BABY

bobby short

ILLUSTRATED WITH PHOTOGRAPHS

DODD, MEAD & COMPANY   *NEW YORK*

ISBN 0-396-06348-9
Library of Congress Catalog Card Number: 70-150167

Printed in the United States of America
by The Cornwall Press, Inc., Cornwall, N. Y.

*To Myrtle, Na, Tid
and Barbara*

I am most grateful to Winneta Rachels Thomas, Sister M. Eugene, Marian Campbell Sheehan, Leona Rouse Morris, and Mildred Short Stratton for their many suggestions as well as kind words of encouragement. And I am particularly appreciative to Merrill Faulk for his considerable help. To Elaine Kaufman who suggested the book's title with an assist from Cole Porter, and to all my friends in Danville, warm thanks. While to Mary Durant—who questioned thoughtfully, worked together with me patiently, and was always sensitive—my profound indebtedness and lasting affection.

CONTENTS

DANVILLE

I

I am a Negro who has never lived in the South, thank God, nor was I ever trapped in an urban ghetto. I grew up in Danville, Illinois, where my family always lived on a pleasant street, in a pleasant neighborhood where the houses had front yards and back yards, with flower beds and vegetable gardens. Many of our neighbors were white. This book is a collection of memories from those days and from the two years when I was a child star on the vaudeville and nightclub circuit, out on stage in a white suit of tails, playing the piano and singing. "Sell it, sell it, sell it! Smile, smile, smile!" That was my manager in the wings, just out of sight offstage. Some of my memories are bitter, some are barbed, but most, when all is said and done, are sentimental recollections about my family, my home town, and my childhood stint in show business.

The family, on both sides, had been part of the great Negro migration that beat it out of Kentucky and points south at the turn of the century, moving up into the midwestern states. They were small-town and country people who did not choose to head for the melting pots, the big cities with their vicious racial and labor conflicts: niggers against rednecks, hunkies against polacks, dagoes against krautheads against micks against kikes, and on and on and on. Americans probably have more derisive names for their fellow citizens than does any other country in the world.

My relatives chose to settle in Danville, a town that was classically midwestern. It was Heartland, USA—predominantly white, predominantly Protestant, a town founded on the site of an Indian village called Piankeshaw and renamed Danville after one Dan Beckwith, a trader, who built a cabin there in 1824. (Good-bye, Piankeshaw. Welcome, o pioneers.) This was prairie country, Lincoln country. In the old section of town near the river there still stands the house, with its balcony, from which Lincoln spoke during a campaign tour.

When I was a child, Danville sported two homegrown celebrities—Joseph G. Cannon and Helen Morgan. "Uncle Joe" Cannon, Speaker of the House early in the 1900's, whose politics had been less than noble, died in 1926. But no matter. He continued as a local celebrity, and we knew his name. His daughters still reigned from the Cannon mansion in the middle of town, a Victorian castle bristling with towers and balconies and little catwalks, and with deep lawns that rolled down to Vermilion Street. I thought it was the most beautiful building in Danville.

Helen Morgan, then in her heyday, was sitting up on that piano singing "My Bill" and "Can't Help Loving That Man of Mine," her hits from *Showboat,* in which she'd starred as Julie La Verne, the doomed octoroon, too white to be colored, too colored to be white. I saw Helen Morgan once in New York in 1938, a small, forlorn person in heavy dark glasses. She was crossing from her limousine to the French Casino for a rehearsal, but I didn't run up to her and say, "Hello, Miss Morgan. I'm from Danville, too." Miss Morgan didn't look as if she could handle an unexpected confrontation with a young boy. I just stood on the sidewalk and stared.

All told, Danville was an attractive town. It still is an attractive town, and the drive down from Chicago on a spring morning is an impressive journey through mile after mile of well-tended prairie farmlands and sudden sweeping areas of trees. Danville has green everywhere—parks and woodlands with brooks and creeks. The appearance of the town has never been dominated by the local industries—the brickyards, zinc smelters, and coal mines, where my father and my mother's father worked for so many years.

When I was born, Danville had a population of about 34,000. Of this number a scant thirteen percent was listed by the census as Negroes and foreign-born (mostly white, some yellow). The remaining eighty-seven percent was described as "native-born whites." As a matter of fact, I was included among the lily-pure eighty-seven percent for a number of years. My birth certificate had been filed as follows: *Robert Waltrip Short, born September 15, 1924, to Myrtle Render Short and Rodman Jacob Short, 1034 North Robinson Street.* All correct, so far. And then: *Color—White.* I don't know who was responsible for this, Dr. McCaughey, the white physician who delivered me, or the registrar in the Danville city hall, but I discovered the mistake early in the 1950's when I applied for my first passport. So much for official documents.

But the official fact of a Negro minority was real. We were

so much in the minority that white Danville did not feel endangered by our presence, and because they felt no danger, few open conflicts arose. There were not enough of us to rock the boat, not enough of us to threaten the labor market, real-estate prices, or city hall. (Nor were there enough of us to seduce all their daughters.) The colored community was discriminated against, of course. Theaters, restaurants, social organizations—all had clearly-defined boundaries that we could not step over. But the injustices leveled against us were petty. And I use the word petty, much as these discriminations rankled, because they were as nothing compared to the violence and terrorization to which Negroes were subjected in so many other sections and cities of America.

As for me, living in Danville, I remember only one moment of alarm, and that happened when I was in high school, coming home late one evening from my job at a local nightclub. A gang of white, middle-aged drunks reeled out of a corner tavern on Washington Avenue, a predominantly Negro neighborhood, and headed toward me:

"There's a nigger. Let's get him!"

I knew that paralyzing split second of fear, when your blood does indeed run cold and your fingers and feet prickle. But nothing happened, nothing more was said. They shouted and hooted and staggered on past me down the street. It was the only time I was ever called a nigger on the streets of Danville. And I never heard the word at school.

However, the midwest as a whole seethed with prejudice in those days. The Negro, of course, was at the bottom of just about everyone's list, but the Jews and the Catholics got their lumps, too. In Detroit, Henry Ford published an exposé of an international Jewish conspiracy. The Jews were blamed for everything, from the shortage of farmhands, to jazz, short skirts, high rents, gambling, and loose morals. (On the other hand, Ford hired more Negroes for his plant than any other industrialist in America.) In the 1930's, Father Coughlin made a name for himself with his anti-Semitic broadcasts from Detroit. As for the Catholics, untold numbers of midwestern Protestants firmly believed that given half a chance the Vatican would take over the U.S.A., lock, stock, and barrel. And God help us if Al Smith made it to the White House.

Most people think of the Klu Klux Klan as a strictly southern outfit, but in the 1920's and early 30's, the Klan was very strong in the midwest. And they took off against anyone who wasn't white, native-born, and Protestant. In other words, Negroes, Jews, Catholics, and the foreign-born. Danville had a branch of the KKK. It was no secret; their activities were well publicized in the Danville *Commercial News*—after-dark rallies in open fields with large electric-lit K's in red, white, and blue. Prayer meetings in a Danville park with scripture lessons, "Onward, Christian Soldiers," and "Nearer, My God, to Thee." The public was cordially invited to attend, barbecued meat and refreshments were served. A three day "Klantauqua" (entertainment and speeches) was held at Lincoln Park, just a few blocks up the street from where we lived. And a statewide "reunion" was held at the Danville fairgrounds with special trains to accommodate the out-of-town Klansmen—something like 15,000 of them.

I've been told since then that some local people opposed all this, but on the whole the Klan was accepted. The Danville KKK seemed to be fairly content with prayer meetings and barbecues. I know of only one incident when they resorted to terrorizing tactics. In 1936 or 1937, when I was away

7

from home on my show-business stint, a cross was burned
on the front lawn of one of our neighbors, a colored man who
was highly successful in his business ventures and, sin of sins,
was rumored to have a white mistress. Either of these facts
alone would be mighty upsetting to any self-respecting
White Supremacist. But when I came back to Danville after
my two years on the road, the fiery cross on the neighbor's
lawn was never mentioned, and I was dumbfounded when I
at last heard about it, twenty-five years later. This hadn't
been the silence of fear, but the silence of indifference. Klan
activities had evidently been dismissed as nonsense and forgotten.

Shortly after I was born, for example, my mother took me
to a baby meet (I don't know what else to call it), where
your child's sight, hearing, intelligence, and general alertness
were tested by experts, and you were given a chart, like an
achievement test, that rated your child's health and wits. It's
not a question of how I fared on the test, but that the test was
given at the fairgrounds, the self-same fairgrounds that had
been staked out as Klan territory during their statewide reunion. My mother was not the least bit intimidated by any
of this, but bustled me out to the baby meet, and the devil
with those fool peckerwoods and their sheets and crosses.

Meantime, despite all the racial and religious thunder rumbling on the horizon, we too were midwesterners. And not
only were we midwesterners, we too belonged to the Protestant American majority. Except for our color, we conformed
in almost every degree to the image of the white Anglo-Saxon
Protestant—in our manners, our mores, and our way of life.
We were, in effect, Wasps. Colored—or black, if you will—
Wasps.

Like all well-brought-up Protestant children, my brothers
and sisters and I sat in our Sunday-School classes, scrubbed
and shining, and sang: "Jesus loves me, this I know, for the
Bible tells me so." And we sang: "Jesus wants me for a sunbeam, a sunbeam, a sunbeam. I'll be a sunbeam for him."
Every Sunday morning we were given Sunday-School cards
printed in glorious technicolor with romantic views of the
Holy Land, the desert, and Gethsemane. On these cards Jesus
was always pictured as a blond with the most beautiful blue
eyes in the world, neither aggressively masculine in his appearance nor overly effeminate, but halfway between—a
neutral and neuter sort of fellow. Years later, when it was
suggested to me that Christ, as a Semite, was probably dark-
skinned, dark-eyed, and dark-haired, I was shocked. Christ
was a blue-eyed blond; I had seen his picture many, many
times.

We were raised in the old-time Protestant ethic, as our
parents had been and their parents before them. Hard work
never hurt anybody. Children should be seen and not heard.
Father knows best. Mother knows best. Pay your own way.
Do unto others as you would have others do unto you. The
road to heaven is thorny. The road to hell is a primrose
path. The Lord giveth and the Lord taketh away. God's will
be done. Amen and amen.

And as midwestern Protestants, we also fell heir to midwestern Protestant prejudices. We, too, believed that Jews
and Catholics were taboo. Judaism was a mysterious, somehow foreign entity, and Catholics were "different." Actually,
I didn't know what a Jew was until I was eleven years old
and went into show business. At that time I also got my first
inside view of Roman Catholicism. My managers, who were

Jewish, enrolled me in a parochial school in Chicago, an event that provoked a number of phone calls to my mother back in Danville, *serious* phone calls from her friends: "Myrtle, do you realize your son is in the hands of those nuns!"

Curiously, this prejudice did not extend to colored Catholics. Our neighbors the Taylors had a daughter who became a nun. The Butlers were Catholics, and so was the Hughes family, whose daughter Gertrude, a roly-poly little girl, wore her hair in sausage curls and sang Shirley Temple songs in entertainments around town. It was *white* Catholics who were different and foreign.

But there it was. Negroes had been trained as Protestants in centuries past, our American education, after all, usually having been undertaken by ardently Protestant whites. We had subscribed to the whole program—the theology, the code of manners, and the taboos. We were the Negro minority of the Protestant majority. We were full-fledged Wasps, except for that one insurmountable difference—color. Here our white brethren drew the line.

II

Father was born in Rockport, Muhlenberg County, Kentucky, in 1883. His father, John Waltrip Short, was a Negro of some means, who collected a fair amount of farm properties during his lifetime, all in Muhlenberg County. When my father finished grade school in Rockport, Grandfather Short sent him to Frankfort, Kentucky, to enter high school. Evidently there was no high-school education for the colored children of Rockport, or possibly there was no high school at all; the town of Rockport is so small, it's not always on the map. In Frankfort, my father finished his schooling, and in later years, my mother used to say that she, of course, had married an educated man. One of my fondest childhood memories is sitting across from Papa, with a book on the table in front of me and he is reading the story aloud, upside down. That delighted me. It was pure magic to a small child.

My father had one sister, Aunt Nancy, and a brother, Uncle John Will. Aunt Nancy settled in Detroit, and I've been told that from time to time in the old days, she used to whirl through Danville with a little extra money to help out my parents and their growing family. Uncle John Will, however, stayed in Kentucky for years, and my mother always felt he had got more than his share of handouts from Grandfather Short, that the old man had favored him and slighted his Danville son and Danville grandchildren. So Mother didn't care too much for Uncle John Will.

After he finished school in Frankfort, Father moved to Danville and went to work in the Little Vermilion mine. Before I was born, he quit the mines for a while and worked as a mailman. He also served as a notary public and justice of the peace and was active in the Republican Party county organization. He took a brief flier into private enterprise, an ice-cream parlor and confectionery shop, but that was abandoned for some reason or other, and he went back to mining. It was his occupation until the day he died, and mining killed him. But it was a job he liked; he really preferred working the mines.

Mother, who'd lived in Danville since she was a child, used to tell us about driving around town, as a girl, in their phaeton buggy, drawn by an old carriage horse named Nell. Mother was born in 1887 in Ohio County, Kentucky, in McHenry, another town that's not always on the map. Her mother, Mildred Elizabeth Jackson Render, died quite young, and Grandfather Render, George Washington Render, came to Danville to work in the mines and make a home for his three little children—my mother, her older sister, and her younger brother. They had been named after flowers, Mother told us. Myrtle, Rose, and William—for sweet william.

I never knew Grandfather Render. He was said to have Cherokee blood, as did so many Negroes with southern ancestry—the Cherokees having intermarried right and left with both colored and white. But we had a picture of him stowed away in a trunk in the attic—Grandfather Render with a heavy mustache, dressed in a dark suit, and laid out in his coffin, surrounded by banks of flowers. When we were children, we would go up to the attic, take out his picture, and shiver.

That trunk was a treasure trove. Besides Grandfather in his coffin, there was a revolver and a handful of shells that mysteriously were not of the same caliber as the gun. There were clippings about a scrape my father had got into at the Little Vermilion—a row with the foreman, in which Father had taken after him with a pickaxe or a wrench. The police were called, and Father was arrested. His notary seal was also packed away in the trunk, and my mother's old fox fur that my little sister wore for dress-ups. A few pieces of a uniform from Uncle Bill's days in the army were also up in the attic, and a big tin lard bucket filled to the brim with marbles, and Grandfather Render's French horn, which none of us ever learned to play.

III

Various neighborhoods within the Danville city limits had been given local nicknames in the early days, and the nicknames stuck. There was Belgium Town to the south, Rabbit Town out on the Perrysville Road, and German Town up on a hill to the east.

And down on the bottom land that bordered Stoney Creek was another neighborhood known, of course, as the Bottoms, which seems to be a universal term in America for a town slum on a river bank. The Bottoms was our town slum, the original Negro settlement, and, as in most American towns, it was on the wrong side of the tracks. In this instance, down the hill on Seminary Street and under the Wabash railroad viaduct, just like Bessie Smith's old song: "Down in Atlanta, Ga., under the viaduct every day. . . ." Along the shores of Stoney Creek, which flooded almost every year in the spring rains, were clusters of decaying shanties. Shotgun houses, we called them. A row of rooms built up off the ground, no plumbing, no utilities. Most of the streets were unpaved, a puzzling crisscross of roads, alleys (one was called Death Alley) and nameless, dusty pathways.

Long before my day, Negroes had pushed their boundaries beyond the Bottoms and ventured up onto higher ground, the east end of town, where the principal colored neighborhood was established. And the East End, like so many colored communities in America, had its Sugar Hill, where the affluent Negro families made their homes. So the East End ranged from the very worst down on the shores of Stoney Creek to the very best, up on Sugar Hill. In between were households such as my Aunt Rosie's. Aunt Rosie's husband was Uncle Arthur Reid, the first Negro policeman on the Danville force. They owned their own home on Seminary Street, a substantial house with my uncle's name on a scallop-edged plate affixed to the front door. But they had no electricity or running water. To get water, Aunt Rosie went down her back steps and into a nearby field that had a water faucet. And she always kept a covered bucket of drinking water, with a dipper, on top of the icebox out on the back porch.

My mother and father originally lived down in the East End, where they met and were married—in a double wedding in 1904. The other couple was Miss Carrie Reid (Uncle Arthur's sister) and Mr. John Phipps. Carrie had been a girlfriend of my father's for a brief spell. "But I beat her time," said Mother, at the age of eighty-three, with an enigmatic smile.

Early in their marriage, my parents left the East End and moved on through town, eventually settling in an integrated niche in the middle of the North End.

That is where I was born, the ninth child in a line of ten children. Six of us lived. Frances Naomi was the first, then Ruth, who died when she was about fifteen, then twin boys, who died at birth. Next were Mildred Elizabeth, Charles William, a little girl named Roberta, who died when she was two or three days old, then Reginald, a name that Mama said came to her in a dream. Then I was born, and last of all, Barbara Louise.

My earliest memories are a montage of little things. My father coming home from the mines and the children crowding around his dinner pail to see if there were a slice of pie or an apple left over from his lunch. Our evening meal after Father had bathed, but he never seemed to quite get all the coal dust away from around his eyes. A whist game in the living room and Mama's lady friends making fancy bids at 500. Myself, scarcely two years old, crawling into Mother's lap when she was nursing my baby sister and insisting that I be nursed, too. My big sister Mildred graduating from grade school in 1928 in a green dress ordered from old Mrs. Dowthet, a white lady who had a catalogue service for mail-order clothes; Mildred trying on the dress behind the stove in the parlor.

And I remember Ruth's dying. I must have been about three. She had been run over by a car on Main Street, near Vermilion Street. The accident injured her lungs, and she was bedridden for quite a while, unable to recover. The lung damage was at last fatal—Mother always felt obliged to explain that it was not TB because TB in those days was as dire and unmentionable as cancer. When Ruth was sick, I used to go into her room and steal fresh fruit, which was always set out at her bedside, and I'd hide under her bed eating grapes or a tangerine. Later, Mother often talked about Ruth. She was a good child and a diligent student, who never made a murmur of complaint about going to school in hand-me-downs or clothes that had been made over. She used to tell

Mama that she was going to go to college, so she could get a good job and Mama wouldn't have to work so hard. Ruth's doctor, a colored man, was a first-rate physician, but he was a blusterer who fancied himself a great wit. When Ruth would ask him if she were going to die, he'd crack one of his jokes and give her a hearty laugh, "Of course, you're going to die. Look at your fingernails. They're turning blue." My mother would find Ruth, hours later, still staring at her fingernails. After Ruth died, it was years before Mama would again have a colored doctor in the house.

Our house, my first view of the world, was a small frame building with vaguely Victorian pretensions. In the front yard when the grass was freshly mowed, you could see the foundation where my father's ice-cream parlor had stood. The building had been moved, and nothing remained of this enterprise but a few bent-metal ice-cream-parlor chairs, a couple of counter stools, and some of the spoons and ice cream scoops and sherbet dishes, all of which crept into our household furnishings. One of the stools became my own special seat at the table, and one of the spoons my own special spoon that I clamored for at every meal.

The house was choked with oak furniture—golden oak with leatherette upholstery and brass studding, the ugliest furniture in the world, on display in a million homes across America in those days. In our dining room, there was an oak buffet, a round oak dining table with expansion leaves, and a half dozen oak chairs. The living room was dominated by a davenport with massive oak arms and feet, matching chairs, an oak library table, an oak bookcase, and a standing, wind-up phonograph, also oak. At the far end of the room stood an ebony-finished upright piano. On its front, inscribed

17

in Old English gold lettering, was the name Walworth. I found the Walworth as soon as I could walk across the living room. The first song I remember playing was Jerome Kern's "Who?" from *Sunny*, which had starred Clifton Webb and Marilyn Miller, but I knew nothing of that; I was four years old. I'd heard the song on a victrola record or the radio, and I stood at the piano, played the melody through, and piped the lyrics. "Who stole my heart away? Who makes me dream all day . . . ?"

We had a fair share of musical talent in the family. Father could play a good, working, church piano, and tunes like "Marching Through Georgia." Mother played some, because when she was a girl it had been proper to have piano lessons. But she sang from morning to night. "Ten Baby Fingers and Ten Baby Toes, That Was My Mother's Rosary" ranked as one of her all-time favorites, along with "Two Little Girls in Blue," "Little Gypsy Sweetheart," and everything Victor Herbert wrote. But no spirituals, only hymns. "The Old Rugged Cross" and "In the Garden": "He walks with me, and He talks with me, and He tells me I am His own. . . ." She sang some minstrel numbers from long-forgotten revues: "My bonbon buddy, chocolate drop, a chocolate drop was he." And "J-I-M-B-O, Jimbo, Jimbo was his namey, namey, namey, namey. . . ." And another that began, "If the man in the moon was a coon, coon, coon. . . ." Best of all, a long, tragic ballad called "That is Love." The closing verse had lines about the clatter of the hooves of a maddened horse, running away with a little child who is alone in the plunging carriage. The child's father throws himself to the rescue, and

18

saves the child, "but he lay there a mangled corpse. That is love. That is love."

Grandfather Render had played the violin, as well as the French horn that was stored away in our attic. Mother's brother Bill played the mandolin and a very, very good ragtime piano. Earlier on, he'd gone off for a while as the piano player with a traveling carnival, and Bill belonged to a local outfit, the Jessie Ayres Quartet, which once shared the bill with Jack Johnson, when he came through Danville to give a campaign speech for Senator Robert La Follette. Many evenings, Uncle Bill, his wife, and Aunt Rose, with maybe a cousin or two, would come over to visit Sister Myrtle, and Uncle Bill would go into the front room and play for me. But little by little he gave up his music; he didn't seem interested anymore, but settled into his job as a presser at a Danville laundry.

Over in Terre Haute lived cousins on my mother's side. One of the boys was a fine pianist: Rudy Render (Rudolph Valentino Render, in full, and you know where *his* mother's heart lay), who eventually became Debbie Reynolds' musical director. Another cousin, Leon Morton from Dixon, Illinois, played extremely well. He didn't get to Danville too often, but when Cousin Leon came to the house, I always asked him to play for me. Yet another cousin, Aunt Rosie's son Carl Reid, had a jug band and used to think nothing at all of walking right into the Hotel Wolford, Danville's best hotel, during a convention, to set up his band in the lobby and pass the hat. He left Danville for a while to work professionally as King Tut and His Jug Band, and was recorded by Brunswick and Vocalion.

The old Walworth was kept in tune and in repair by a tall

white man, Mr. Cole, who also came to the house to give lessons to our oldest sister, Naomi. She studied for a long time with Mr. Cole, and out of all that learned to play a waltz called "The Frolic of the Frogs." My sister Mildred could pick out hymns on the piano, having learned to read notes at school. Neither of my brothers played the piano, but Reg was a wonderful whistler and had a good singing voice, which he often raised in a fine imitation of Bing Crosby. Bill sang, too, and one of his crazy songs will stick in my head forever:

> Hot tamales, get 'em red hot, a favorite dish of mine.
> Got a letter from my baby, down in Caroline.
> She's so sweet, like turkey meat,
> Great big legs and little-biddy feet.
> Hot tamales, get 'em ready, a favorite dish of mine.

IV

I was very young when Father went back to Kentucky to get a job in the mines at Lynch. The Depression had struck and there was no work for him in Danville. The thought of moving the whole family back to the South, however, was never considered. Mother once took Barbara and me down to visit, an ambitious journey in those days with two small children, but I imagine she wanted to see what was going on in Kentucky and to look into her life. Father came home to visit us in Danville when he could and did everything in his power to keep in touch. He sent birthday presents, a new set of china, new clothes for my mother, and tins of sorghum, which she loved but couldn't get in Danville. One year he sent up a Thanksgiving turkey dinner with all the trimmings, but it arrived by slow freight the day after Thanksgiving and was rotten.

He mailed home a check twice a month, sometimes for as much as twenty-five dollars, sometimes only eight or nine, depending on how many days he had got work. Mother was now working as a domestic to eke out a few extra dollars each week, and the reins of the household had been taken

21

over by Naomi, a retiring young woman who happily undertook Mother's chores. Sister Naomi, like maiden ladies of an earlier day, preferred to stay at home rather than tackle the hazards of the outside world and she was devoted to such tasks as her needlework—embroidering and monogramming hand towels, pillowcases, sheets, and table linens. She was always deeply involved with old friends and relatives, and still keeps a scrapbook of births, marriages, and deaths among people she has known during her lifetime. Gentle Naomi, who cries when she hears my voice on a phonograph record.

With Father's departure to Kentucky, we moved from 1034 North Robinson to 1135 in the next block, the last block in the neighborhood where colored families could rent or own property. I realize now that all this moving about, not only for us but for many of our friends and neighbors, was largely a matter of economics, as a family's fortunes rose or fell. We moved into a house with no plumbing, just like Aunt Rosie's down on East Seminary Street. There was a pump in the yard with sparkling cold well water—freezing cold on a winter day with snow on the ground and icicles hanging from the pump handle. And out in the backyard, next to the coal shed was the privy, or "Mrs. Hoover," as we called it during the Depression. "I'm going out back to visit Mrs. Hoover. Got to go see Mrs. Hoover."

But the house had two stories and was big enough for us all. Again it was a frame building of the Victorian school, with borders of stained glass around the front windows and with good hardwood floors inside, as Mother so often observed to her friends. And for the first time we had a staircase. The golden oak furniture had come along with us, pongee curtains hung at the windows, and the Walworth upright stood in the parlor.

On the walls were a framed illuminated poem, "To Mother," a print of Fraser's "End of the Trail," a sepia of a winged cherub, a pastoral scene of trees in bloom, and a bust of Hiawatha, which I once toted off to grade school for a day for some class project. And there was a photograph of our Grandmother Short—Katie Basset Short—a handsome woman with a fair complexion, high cheekbones, and dead straight, long black hair. *Her* mother, Great-grandmother Basset, whom my older sisters remember, was a huge woman with very dark skin, so Katie Basset's coloring, high cheekbones, and straight hair were inherited from her father—and I know nothing of him except that he also had Cherokee blood. Of all our family, Naomi is the only one who inherited Katie Basset's pale complexion and Indian looks.

In the front yard was an enormous, honey-scented mock orange bush, and Mother had planted spirea along the porch. In the backyard was a grape arbor and a vegetable garden, which was one of Mother's greatest pleasures. She grew flowers and vegetables wherever and whenever she could, and we always had good fresh vegetables on the table— tomato and cucumber salads, Kentucky Wonder string beans that she cooked up with ham or bacon; rhubarb, lettuce, spinach, radishes, and carrots, and even strawberries and raspberries.

A couple of old chickens, who laid an egg now and then, had the run of the yard. We had a gray cat named Bunny, because she'd been born on Easter Sunday, and a dog named Pal that my brother Reg had brought home as a pup. Pal, a mongrel with a dominant strain of German shepherd going for him, immediately attached himself to my mother, right to the source of all good things. He used to wait on the corner of Robinson and English for her to come home from work, watching fixedly all the way up past Lincoln Park to Logan Avenue until he saw that tiny, distant speck six or eight blocks away. Then he'd race headlong to meet her. He never chased cars like other dogs. Pal's personal quirk was uniquely his own—he chased shadows on the wall. We also had a goldfish, who'd be frozen in his bowl on those winter nights when we were without coal for the furnace. But in the morning, as soon as a fire got started in the kitchen range, the fish would thaw out, good as new, and pick up his leisurely route back and forth through his pink castle gate.

Father's visits home were times of excitement, with lots of parties with his old cronies, Mr. Tichenor, Mr. Mason, and Mr. Flye. The home brew was brought out—home brew that he'd made on his previous visit and left to age in the cellar in rows of dark green bottles with porcelain plugs. He also stored crocks of wine in the cellar—dandelion wine, cherry wine, grape wine, and applejack. The parties would get rolling, and we'd hear the men using words like damn and hell, words never heard in our house when Papa was away.

Papa was an interesting man and an attractive man, very alive, full of zest and good humor. But my little sister and I felt outside. We didn't know him very well. We had never been close to him as had our older brothers and sisters, so we played our childish tricks, saying that he had deserted us. I liked him when he charmed me, but Barbara and I felt threatened by his presence and were not of a mind to take orders from Papa when he came home. Whatever affection we had for my father came to us in a second-hand way. Naomi was the one who often reminded me that Papa used to call me his million-dollar baby, with the million-dollar smile; but though he always remembered my birthday with presents mailed from Kentucky, he remained a visitor in my life.

On the other hand, Mother's affection for all of us seemed to envelop the household like the wings of a large bird. Small, delicate, and soft-spoken, her energies in our behalf were endless. In the 1930's, the Rodgers and Hart score for *Higher and Higher*, the Broadway musical, included a song called "Every Sunday Afternoon and Thursday Night." Remembering my mother's life during those years brings that song to mind. Sunday afternoon and Thursday night, the days when domestics were free to pursue their own lives. Sometimes, with a promise to her employer to make up for time lost, Mother was able to swing an extra hour off here and there to spend more time at home, at church, or at school. In spite of her work schedule, she always managed to get to PTA meetings and was usually on hand during Parents' Day.

As the Depression deepened, everyone tried to do something to defray expenses, something respectable like taking in boarders, selling magazines, or selling door to door—toothpaste, shaving soap, pot holders, brushes, anything. Sister Mildred sold the Chicago *Defender*, which is one of the oldest Negro newspapers in America. Its editor at the time was Robert S. Abbot, one of the most influential Negroes of his day.

I was Mildred's delivery boy; she was the big sister I tagged after as a child, listening to her talk with her friends about their parties, their clubs, her French classes and typing classes at school—classes I took in high school ten years later in emulation of Mildred. And it was Mildred who got me my first library card. She was a devout churchgoer, like Mother, but she also loved jazz and dancing. Another of her little jobs, housework for Mrs. MacMillan, a milliner who lived in our neighborhood, helped pay her weekly installments on a portable, wind-up phonograph. With each payment Mildred got a free record—"Sweetheart of All My Dreams," "Momma's Gone, Goodbye," "Glad Rag Doll"—and her friends would come over on Sunday night to dance. When I was five, six, seven, I'd hang on the fringes of the party and watch them swirl around the living room. It was always foxtrots, done in the most decorous ballroom style. Mildred knew how to have a good time despite the family's hovering on the brink of an economic washout.

My brothers also began early to hustle extra money. Reg sold magazines and did odd jobs around town. Bill shined shoes, went on to learn how to press clothes, and also cut grass and did other such jobs in the neighborhood. Sometimes he'd go to a neighboring city with two or three friends to stage a "Battle Royal"—a mass free-for-all, a fist fight to the finish (all of it faked, no one ever got hurt). For this they'd earn a couple of dollars. As it has always done, the prize ring offered a glamorous escape out of poverty. In those days, very few of us thought of long-range plans for our lives, like becoming lawyers or doctors or going into any of the professions that would require college and money. Any boy who was handy with his fists went into the Golden Gloves tournaments and dreamed of becoming a champion. I remember a beau of Mildred's, Oliver Phelps, who went into the ring and billed himself as the Black Panther. As for the girls, many of them dreamed of becoming famous and glamorous dancers or singers, and they were always stitching together costumes for their dance acts or the next talent show at Lincoln Park or at school or church.

Mother, along with dozens of other parents, was able to bring home groceries from the neighborhood market with a promise to "pay on Saturday." Aunt Rosie, as the wife of a policeman, could charge at her grocery store, and sometimes Mother sent me down to Rosie's with a note asking if we could charge a few items on her account. Aunt Rosie always obliged. At the Piggly-Wiggly store, an understanding grocer named Tom Sheehan generously gave Mother credit from time to time. Arnholt's Bakery Shop sold day-old baked goods at a marked-down price, the sale carefully watched over by Mrs. Arnholt, who counted out a strict six pieces for a nickel. One of the clerks was more free-handed with the day-old baked goods, so we'd hang around outside until Mrs. A. had gone off duty, then run in with the nickel, and our friend, the free-handed clerk, would toss a dozen pieces of pastry into the sack, sometimes even including a fruit pie. There was also, for a time, an outfit called the Producers' Dairy that undercut the price of milk simply by having no bottling plant and no deliveries. You went down to the dairy with your own container and they ladled out a quart or a gallon of pasteurized milk at a substantially lower price. All milk bottles and pop bottles, of course, were precious. They could be redeemed for hard cash. But shortly after Roosevelt became President in 1933, he got down to business and set out to feed people who were going hungry. I remember twenty-four-pound bags of flour being handed out from trucks, with potatoes and other fresh produce and butter.

Meantime, there was always the chance of winning some money in "policy," although the word from every pulpit in Danville condemned gambling as a sure path to Hell. But I can't remember anyone, devout or no, who didn't dabble in the policy game. Drawings were held twice a day, and the smallest bet was a nickel. If you won, the nickel brought you five dollars. A bet of a dime, if you won, meant ten dollars, and so on. We played hunch bets and dream bets, the numbers and combinations listed in Dream Books that were always on sale around town. Some of the combinations in my day were 4–11–44 (police or car), 10–18–44 (white man), 5–11–29 (funeral), 8–24–29 (Robert), and 3–6–9 (shit). A young colored woman named Lucille Gray made the pickups from door to door, and if you hit it, you'd always give Lucille a cut of the take. Fifty cents, say, from a five-dollar win, to keep your luck running.

The songwriters, at any rate, got a lot of mileage out of the depression: "Brother, Can You Spare A Dime"; "I Found A Million-Dollar Baby In The Five And Ten Cent Store"; "Pennies From Heaven"; "If I Had A Million Dollars"; "Oh, Baby, What I Couldn't Do With Plenty Of Money And You." And one of the depression hits, "Let's Turn Out The Lights And Go To Sleep," began with the flat-out statement, "No more money in the bank. . . ."

V

Our miniscule colored colony in the North End of town was roughly three blocks long and seven blocks wide, the houses small and set close together in a most neighborly way, the streets, some still unpaved, lined with trees, elm, maple, oak, and flowering horse chestnut. A vacant field was planted with corn each spring. Another empty lot up the way had a croquet court laid out under the oak trees, where the men of the neighborhood often gathered in the evening for a game. My father used to stroll up sometimes on a summer night after dinner and play croquet with his cronies. The flavor of our little North End community was small town, almost rural. A knife sharpener made his rounds, a scrap-iron man, a horse-drawn ice wagon. We'd ride on the back step, eating slivers of ice from the floor of the wagon. An old colored man drove up and down the streets in a cart selling hot tamales, which he must have made himself. There was no Mexican community to sell them to, but nonetheless he'd moved into our midwestern town from parts unknown to peddle his wares. Some of the elderly colored ladies still wore skirts down to the floor, high-button shoes, and a shawl around their shoulders, and they carried baskets on their heads. You'd go down to Aunt Rosie's, and her mother-in-law, old Mrs. Reid, was dressed in just such fashion: old Mrs. Reid, another with a strong strain of Cherokee in her bones, looking for all the world like an ancient squaw, with her pipe or a pinch of snuff under her upper lip. An old lady named Mrs. Faisan walked through our yard every morning on her way to wherever she was going, in a long skirt and shawl.

It was always, "Good morning, Mrs. Short."

"Good morning, Mrs. Faisan. How are you today, Mrs. Faisan?"

"Tol'able well, Mrs. Short."

And when my mother was at her lowest ebb because of being poor or just being a woman with six children, she would quote Mrs. Faisan.

"Oh, yes. Mrs. Faisan warned me years ago. She always told me my children would drive me crazy."

Now in those days, if you went crazy, you were driven there by your family. It was very simple and clear-cut; there could be no other reasons. A dear friend of my mother's once went off marketing, in a moment of derangement, wearing two dresses, one dress pulled on over the other. When this story reached us, Mother instantly sympathized. "Who can blame her? Poor thing, with so many children! It's a wonder we're not all crazy. . . ."

Meanwhile, the unpaved streets in our neighborhood, rural charm or no, were usually the object of political speeches at election time. Laurel Street would be paved. Center Street would be paved. Water pipes would be laid. Every house would have electricity. New street lighting would be attended to. This was also the cry down in the East End, where unpaved streets and no water, electricity, or gas lines were the rule rather than the exception. Danville politics was all white, of course, and strongly Republican. In order to control the colored vote, they got in touch with several leaders of the Negro community; and on the strength of such promises of civic improvements, the Negro voters were organized into a Republican League. Coffee and doughnuts played a big part in local politics, and cars were always made available to get the voters to the polls. Mother used to work at the polls as a judge of registration, which meant five dollars a day; it was a coveted job, handed out by the administration. If you were one of the leaders of the Negro community, you could go to top politicians (when there was an opening within the system) and put forward names of those who needed work.

We stayed with the Republican party for a long time, because it had been Abraham Lincoln's party, and we'd been brainwashed into believing that he was the savior of our race. But there was a mass conversion to the Democratic party after it became obvious that Roosevelt had us in mind. Mrs. Roosevelt made a tremendous mark by her interest in Negro affairs, by her friendship with Mary McLeod Bethune (founder of Bethune-Cookman College), and by her championing of Marian Anderson. When Mrs. Roosevelt resigned from the D.A.R., every politically minded colored matron in Danville looked upon this as a personal vindication. As for those unpaved streets and houses without electricity or water, the political promises were eventually kept, under one city administration or another.

Beyond that, our neighborhood has shown little change since my childhood. The same houses are standing along the

familiar streets. When I was growing up, we knew everyone
in every house. On a summer morning, when I was eight or
nine, I'd wander through the neighborhood and be called
into one house after another along the way to play the piano.
Every parlor had a piano in those days. The ladies would be
outside with cloths around their heads, beating rugs, sweeping the porch and the steps, or washing windows—cleaning
house for the weekend. As a little respite from housework,
they'd ask me to play a few pieces for them. So I'd walk along
and stop to play wherever I was invited in, and I'd get back
home half sick, full of cupcakes, pie, glasses of milk, and soda
pop.

Our neighbors' names delight me, the Anglo-Saxon names
that we latched on to willy-nilly in centuries past. Bostick,
Phelps, Beecham, Young, Glover, Gilmore, Tichenor, Mar-
shall, French, McNeil, Crockett, Dulin, Mathis, McGregor.
Ironically, these are the names now adopted by second- and
third-generation Americans with non-Wasp backgrounds, who
want to sound suitably a-okay Anglo-Saxon—for business or
political reasons or merely for aesthetic reasons, I suppose.
I'm not criticizing—I wish them well. Those names weren't
ours either, six, eight, and ten generations ago.

Next door to us were the Nicholses, and when we were
very young, Mrs. Nichols gave tea parties for the children—
cream-cheese sandwiches, raisin and nut bread, and tea
served in doll sets of china. The next house belonged to the
Allen family. He was an attorney—Lawyer Allen, as everyone
called him. Another neighbor, a shoemaker, was always referred to in the same style, by my mother, as Shoemaker
Thompson.

Around the corner were the Roeys, who, like us, were usually a day behind and a dollar short. Very often there wasn't enough coal in the Roeys' house, just as at our house. Very often their electricity was cut off, just as ours was. And when their lights went out, Mrs. Roey would gather up her youngest child, Betty, who was my great friend, and come over to sit out the evening until it was time to go home to bed.

And when our electricity was cut off, we'd go to the Roeys' and sit until the last minute, my mother and Mrs. Roey always carrying on a conversation of the loftiest nature, in which the light bill or the water bill was never mentioned. One never cried poor. Never, never.

But no matter what the catastrophe of the day, my sister Mildred, Eurvabelle Roey (who changed her name to Peggy, and you can't blame her), and Marguerite Carruthers, from down the block, were always busy rehearsing. They'd formed a trio, "Bootsy, Meg, and Mid," patterned after the Boswell Sisters. Their big number was "Fit as a Fiddle and Ready for Love," which they sang at church socials, parties, and the like.

Both families also had moments of flickering solvency, when visits were purely social. Some evenings when I went over with my mother, Betty's grown-up brothers had entertained their friends for cocktails before going out. (It was always better to have your children drink at home than in some shady bar.) Mother and Mrs. Roey would settle in the dining room for one of their deep conversations. Mother would say something like, "Matty, that's such a pretty dress you're wearing." And Matty Roey would say, "Oh, Myrtle, I'm wearing my trunk," which meant she was wearing the only clothes she had—because a trunk was used for storage and that was a way of explaining that every stitch you owned

33

was on your back right at that moment. And while the conversation went on, Betty and I would sneak into the living room and smoke the cigarette butts, and if any corners of the whiskey were left from the party, we had to taste that too.

We smoked everything—cornsilk, tea, coffee. We even tried to chew tobacco. And in our backyard was a catalpa tree (or Indian bean, as it's sometimes called) that shed crisp, dark brown, cigarlike bean pods; we had to try those, naturally. They tasted terrible. Sometimes we'd save up ten cents to buy a pack of Marvels or 20 Grand, cheap cigarettes that tasted pretty terrible, too. Betty Roey was the ringleader in all this tobacco intake. And she was the one who gave Barbara the nickname "Tearless," because Barbara could put on a crying fit without shedding a single tear.

Over the way were the Masons, a large family whose children's various ages matched ours. Many evenings we'd gang up on the corner between our house and theirs to swap tales and songs and games. It was here I first learned the Thomas A. Dorsey gospel songs, because the Masons were Baptists, and these were the hymns they were singing and swinging at church. The Mason children also taught us a game that went to a funny old rhyme:

> Little Sally Saucer,
> Sitting in the corner,
> Rise, Sally, rise.
> Wipe your streaming eyes.
> Put your hand on your hip.
> Let your backbone slip.
> Shake it to the east,
> Shake it to the west,
> Shake it to the one
> That you love the best.

We used to raid the Masons' vegetable garden for green tomatoes. We'd cut them into thin slices, dip them in corn meal, fry them in bacon fat, and have a feast, no one seeming to mind in the least that we were out in the kitchen dirtying up skillets and scattering corn meal everywhere.

The Thomases lived across the street. When we moved in, and Mrs. Thomas saw Mrs. Short with six children and no husband in sight, she came right over to ask, in the kindest way, if my mother would be offended at being offered leftover food from the Thomases' larder. She always had too much food in the house, Mrs. Thomas explained. Why, her daughter, her only chick and child, ate like a sparrow, and sometimes she had so much food left over that Mrs. Thomas just had to bury it in the backyard, and it grieved her heart to waste good food. Mother accepted Mrs. Thomas' offer.

Also on our block lived the Lees. Minnie Lee headed the colored Community Center, which was so successful at drawing the young people off the streets during the Depression and into choral work, sports, and other activities. When I was in grade school, the Community Center was a great place to meet your friends and stay out of trouble. Minnie Lee's sister-in-law was Laura Lee, who founded a home for colored orphans and children who had no other place to live, boys and girls whose fathers had disappeared or whose parents had just left the scene. As far as we were concerned, no social stigma was attached to living at the Laura Lee Home, a complex of three frame buildings down in the East End, with a community dining hall and a big playground where we were always welcome to play. The children at the Home were a close part of the colored community. No bureaucratic hands-off or red tape. And they were brought to Sunday

35

School each week by an enormous, gentle colored girl named Magdalene.

As children in Danville we were very lucky. Within our ranks (we, the minority in town) were many grown-ups who took it upon themselves to be interested in our welfare. They would plan a hot-dog roast, a little party on a Saturday afternoon, a picnic in Lincoln Park, a children's play at one of the churches. There were always people who liked the idea of having twenty children at their house for the afternoon. Danville had no Boy Scouts for colored boys or Girl Scouts for colored girls, and the YMCA and YWCA were closed to us. That gap was filled by concerned colored citizens. Ezra Philpot, for example, who lived up the street, took twelve or fifteen boys out camping overnight in the woods. That was *his* contribution. And through some civic endeavor, one summer a bunch of us got a weekend at a camp, Camp Kickapoo. ("Kickapoo will shine tonight," we sang. "Kickapoo will shine, Kickapoo will shine tonight, all down the line. . . . When the sun goes down and the moon comes up, Kickapoo will shine.")

Our neighborhood hangout in grade school was the Tea Room run by Minnie Neal, an energetic and vibrant lady who even now, in her seventies, runs a boarding house for elderly gentlemen whose wives have passed on. Minnie was a great one for arranging children's pageants and mock weddings and so forth at the church.

She was the organizer of a pie-eating contest staged between me and my good friend Henry McCullough at one of our interchurch socials. Henry was Baptist, I was Methodist. Each of us was given a pie, and the object was to eat it as fast as possible with our hands behind our backs. The prize was a

36

cake Minnie had baked for the occasion. I won in a walk, and my sister Mildred was mortified. "How could you! Those Baptists will think you don't get enough to eat!" And when Mrs. McCullough remarked that Henry had gotten sick from eating so fast, my sister was further chagrined. Not only had I acted half starved, I hadn't even had the good grace to get a little queasy.

Down the block were Mr. Frank Box, the barber, whose shop was a small replica of his house and Mr. Carr, paperhanger and plasterer, whose son William was often the only other colored student in class with me at grade school. We called William "Pie-Face" Carr, because he had a pale, freckled complexion and reddish hair. He was what colored people also called a "Me-rye-nee." The word is Negro slang, and I'm spelling it phonetically because I've never seen it written down, but old-timers explain it as a derivation of "Merino," a breed of sheep with thick curly coats. Another long-gone expression that my brother Bill used to use was: "Three-quarters Kelt with molly-gloss hair," which meant a colored person with fair skin and straight hair. (Me-rye-nees had fair skin and *curly* hair.) "Kelt" was Negro slang for a white person, and the "Molly" in molly-gloss has some sort of Scotch-Irish connotation. But that was Bill's phrase for a mulatto or quadroon with straight hair. "Three-quarters Kelt, with molly-gloss. . . ."

A couple of blocks away, across from the Garfield school, was the Pamplin house. The Pamplin sisters, one tall and one short, like Mutt and Jeff, ran a high-class catering service and were called on by all the grand folk in Danville to do parties. But it was their brother who delighted the school children—Pamplin the Devil, a professional juggler, who was usually out of town in show business. But on occasional afternoons when we'd come from classes, Pamplin the Devil would be on his front lawn, practicing his juggling act—everything flying.

Jessie Robinson, who is one of Mother's closest friends, lived in a little red-brick house with white trim. A few years ago Jessie told me that every now and then when she telephones, she says she's Lady Bird and my mother says she's Jackie, and they have great conversations.

There were Helen and Clem Barker. Mrs. Barker was another lady devoted to the welfare of the neighborhood children, and she considered my mother almost a sister. Our house was Helen Barker's refuge when Clem ordered her out, which was his style after a long, hard party on a Saturday night. An upstairs bedroom at the Barkers' was let out to Stella McGill, who worked as an elevator operator in a downtown office building and who chose me as her pet when I was little. Stella would look after me whenever she was off work —I remember lots of nice presents and lots of attention.

There were the Jacksons, who had a grand piano; the Gaddys, who whitewashed the trunks of their trees and gave lawn parties in their garden; the Hosbys, who had a player piano with "The Sheik of Araby" and rags and lots of good, hot music, and who sometimes gave Saturday-night drinking parties that ran on into Sunday morning; Ruth and Bill Shields, who had no children, so Bill would take me to Father-and-Son banquets at the church. Next, the Mortons, whose granddaughter Dessie was the only girl I truly cared about in grade school, the only girl I thought of as my girl; the Colleys—old Mr. Colley had been a printer and ran his own shop; his grandson, Bobby Colley, sang in a quartet inspired by the Mills Brothers. He and Raymond Best, who was also in the quartet, pursued their singing careers for a while in New York. Then the Turners. Robert Turner had a steady job with the Chicago and Eastern Illinois. He was a well-read man with an extensive library and a deep interest in music, who once trained four of us in quartet singing. His son, Concord, an only child with the best of everything (he always wore a necktie to school), was a good friend. I'd go over to play the Turners' piano and read Concord's books, and we'd talk thoughtfully about the world.

Up the street was Mr. A. D. Hayes's grocery store with its big front porch, where many of the men in our neighborhood sat out the Depression, chewing tobacco, smoking their cigarettes or pipes, and watching the days go by. Mr. and Mrs. Hayes owned one of the few cars on the block. It was a dark green sedan with wooden-spoke wheels, a tall automobile in which the Hayeses rode like royalty at all of ten miles an hour, back and forth to church every Sunday, seven blocks each way, and never gave any of us a lift. Mr. A. D. Hayes was the superintendent of our Sunday School, and if there were ever one moment's inattention, one moment of giggling or whispering, he called us to fearful order. And if any of *our* family were the ones to misbehave, Mr. Hayes had only to say, "These children have had no raising," and it would be a knife in my mother's side.

Those were the days when staring out the window or leaving homework unfinished was equal, in today's terms, to a sit-in or a riot in the study hall. When you were told to be home from the park at eight o'clock, you were home at eight o'clock—until you were thirteen or fourteen and decided it was time to show your independence, so you swaggered in at eight-thirty.

"You watch out, you'll get knocked in the head, staying out so late," Mother used to tell us. We'd never heard of such a thing happening to anybody, anywhere in town, but that was Mother's cry: "You'll get knocked in the head . . . knocked in the head." And if you really got too smart and independent you were threatened with St. Charles, the boys' reformatory. "Just watch your step. You'll wind up one of these days in St. Charles."

The Rouses lived in our neighborhood, Mr. and Mrs. Rouse and their only child, Leona, who was raised in the old-fashioned southern way to address her parents as "Sir" and "Ma'am"; Leona, whom we nicknamed "Prissy," because of her ladylike ways. When I graduated from high school, she took my yearbook home overnight to write a real inscription, not just "Good luck" or "Here's best wishes."

Leona, still one of my dearest friends, wrote:

Dear Bobby, Remember our little theaters we used to have, that were located just around the corner from Times Square, and our own original song about Little Red Riding Hood? If we ever learn to write music, the five of us might get a copyright. After all, it's pretty good. Do you remember getting some of our cherry cobbler, after Reginald and I had slaved to get the cherries. . . . Weren't we just too, too much when we got our bicycles? Where's yours? You wouldn't be using it for work, would you? Don't forget those solid picnics we used to have, especially the one when Barbara and I got lost on our way to the Harrison Park woods. You cat (smile). So much for remembrances . . . Bobby, keep up your music, and when you hit the top, remember me as a friend . . . My pen's running out of ink . . . Always and always, Leona.

VI

Our little theaters that Leona remembered in her inscription. She and I, Betty Roey, Viola Haskins, and my good friend Junior Napier were the producers, composers, directors, and cast. My sister Barbara was too little to take much of a part, but we let her tag along. Admission was a penny, but sometimes we had no audience at all. Most of the grown-ups were away working during the day, but that didn't bother us a bit; the performance went on as scheduled. One neighbor, however, often came to see our shows—a sweet man named Bud Williams, who must have weighed close to four hundred pounds. When Bud died they had to lower him out a window and take him away in a truck. But Bud enjoyed our revues, because he too sang and often appeared in shows around town.

Most of the singing numbers and the dialogue in our shows were inspired by the movies. Betty Roey would be Lupe Velez, and I would be Hoot Gibson, on my knees, proposing.

"Lupe, will you marry me?"

And she would say: "Oh, Hoot, I can't think now. . . . Come

back at six o'clock, Hoot, and I'll give you my answer. . . ."

And then I would sing to Betty "Moon Song," which was very popular at the time. Kate Smith had sung it in a movie, big Kate Smith framed in a window in the moonlight singing her heart out because she had at last realized what the audience knew all along—that the man she loved loved somebody else.

The story of Little Red Riding Hood was one of our more ambitious and original efforts, with every line set to music. The lines, written in verse, and the music, a waltz, were entirely of our own composition:

Red Riding Hood: Oh dearie, oh dearie, my grandma is sick.
These beautiful flowers for her I will pick.
I tramp through the woods and I fall fast asleep.

The Wolf: And I, the big wolf, behind silently creep.
I almost devour her when up she awakes.
Pray, where are you going and what do you take?

Red Riding Hood: I'm going to my grandma's, and I have a cake.

The Wolf: So, let's have a race, let's have a race.
You take the short way, and I'll take the long
To see who gets first to grandmother's place.

I played the wolf, and Betty, as I recall, played Red Riding Hood.

Betty Roey was a talented and imaginative leading lady, and she sang very well, but like many prima donnas, she was temperamental. Betty would learn a part completely, go through all the rehearsals, and at the last minute say she didn't think she wanted to be in the play after all. Then we

42

had to call on Viola Haskins, who served as Betty's stand-in. Viola was never sure if she should take the part or not, but we'd finally persuade her, and Viola would start learning her lines. Meantime, she was being threatened by Betty Roey. "If you go near that play, Viola Haskins, I'll beat you up!" So we'd have to walk over to Viola's and protect her all the way to the house where the show was going to be put on, because Betty Roey would jump out from behind bushes and pull Viola's hair and pinch her and slap her, and Viola would cry.

Up the way from our house lived the Woodards, a handsome family with nine children. Billy and Jimmy Woodard, my particular buddies, were the desperadoes of the neighborhood, and Billy Woodard had been known to step out on his front porch and fire at me with his BB gun, as I walked past on my way to Sunday School. *He* wasn't going to Sunday School.

Now, I'd always been taught to stay close to home, but the Woodards were adventurers. They roamed all over town, and they were the ones who introduced me to the Harrison Park woods, way out of my territory. We'd spend the day there, swinging on vines, dragging our feet in the creek, hiking and hiding out and playing Tarzan, and if we got hungry we'd eat pawpaws and red haws. We knew those woods like the inside of our hats, every trail, every vine, every brook, every mark and sign. Two white boys sometimes joined us on our expeditions—John Murana, whose father had a grocery store, and Jerome Filicsky, who lived behind the Muranas—and we didn't know if we were white or colored. We were in and out of each other's houses and in the backyards, then off to the fields and into the woods. In wintertime, when we'd been

sledding, we'd stop off in each other's kitchens to get warm
and have a cup of cocoa. In the summer we made lightning
raids through people's gardens, shaking down cherry trees,
stealing raspberries or strawberries or whatever was in season. We stole apples, green apples, which we ate with salt,
and then got bellyaches, just as we'd been warned. The next
day we'd be out stealing more green apples from someone
else's trees.

Every now and then we'd go up to the rich section, the
white section of the North End, to show our muscle and give
the rich boys the special treat of our company. There was
never any meanness, just a little shoving around, touch football or shooting baskets or whatever. We were all on friendly
terms. Usually they had been in school with us or with our
brothers. Of course, a rich boy's bike, left on its side unat-
tended, was an open invitation to borrow it for half an hour
or so, and once in a while we might shang a football that
didn't seem to belong to anyone.

That neighborhood was my first introduction to finery of
any kind. The houses of the well-to-do, out there in the North
End beyond Harrison Park, were spacious and elegant—lots
of English Tudor and variations of the Frank Lloyd Wright
theme, always with lots of space in between, deep lawns and
graceful trees. The Depression never seemed to cross their
garden walls.

Back in our neighborhood everyone felt the bite. Everyone
was in it together, and poverty and hard times brought us
all close. The white families sprinkled within the unmarked
colored boundaries of the North End weren't antagonistic
about our presence, nor did they sell their property and move
on. They were friendly, church-going people, insurance col-

lectors, butchers, truck drivers, who were in straits as precarious as our own—though of course if a job were available, the white worker got it first.

It may have been the Depression that kept our white neighbors in residence, but whatever their reasons for staying put, we all got along together just fine. In recent years, it hasn't been so pleasant. As Danville's colored community has grown and expanded into hitherto all-white neighborhoods, ugly situations have cropped up—anonymous phone calls and anonymous letters, the usual threats and frenzies, and police protection has had to be provided. In a perverse way, we can look back on the bad days of the Depression as the good days. Poverty was a great leveler.

To our colored brethren down in the East End, on the other hand, we were the "North Enders," and we were accused sometimes of being the uppity-ups, removed and out of touch with Danville's real colored world. The only trouble we ever had in Lincoln Park was between the East End kids and the North End kids. It wasn't at all a constant battle, just occasional flare-ups—usually between the girls. The boys stayed cool in their rivalries, but a colored girl from the East End would get mad at a girl from the North End, and it was always you-think-you're-better-than-I-am.

One gang of girls, Tink's Gang, used to come up from the East End to Lincoln Park every Sunday, and it was Tink's Gang who once drove Leona Rouse, Viola Haskins, and Betty Roey out of the park because of some insult, real or imagined, and chased them home, ten or twelve blocks, all running as fast as they could run. Spot, the Rouses' dog, saved the day. He was a rough, tough old bird, and when Leona screamed to him for help, Spot charged out of the Rouses' yard and cleared the streets.

My brother Reg spent a lot of time in the East End. At an early age he found his way back and fell in with the old families who'd known my parents years before. Particularly Mother's brother and sister, Uncle Bill and Aunt Rosie; he made their homes his second home. Often he called to say that he was staying down there for the night, and of course he got a square meal because they always had a pot of something good cooking on the back of the stove. Reg was a good-looking boy, a likable boy, a fine dancer, and extremely popular with the girls—with everybody. He was also a natural athlete, strong and quick, who established himself as a good fist fighter. People often set up matches between Reg and other boys because they wanted to see a good fight. One great day he took on a roughneck from the Soldier's Home area, a boy who was said to be the toughest and meanest in town, and Reg licked him. Both my brothers played ball of all kinds and were always in sports at school. Sports were never a big part of my life—I couldn't even handle a yo-yo with any expertise. My brothers excelled with yo-yos, all the tricks.

Bill, like Reg, was also a much-sought-after young man, good looking and a whiz with the girls. All Bill's teachers liked him; he was a good student and had a marvelous sense of humor, with a gift for mimicry. I didn't spend much time with Reg and Bill. They were too busy with their own friends and their own lives to tote me around. And I suppose there's nothing worse than a kid brother to cramp your style.

On one early excursion, when Bill was in charge of me for an afternoon, he took me along to a creek that was a hangout for his pals. Everyone was swimming or fooling around on the bank. Since I was there, I might as well be taught how to swim—and the swimming lesson began with "Stand right there, just stand right there." Well, I was too small, and the current was too strong. I lost my footing and was twenty feet downstream, thrashing and sputtering, and going under for the fourth and fifth times, while brother Bill was back on the shore, roughhousing with his friends, saying, "Save that boy! Save that boy!" So someone waded in and pulled me out. Bill never took me swimming again.

VII

My mother was not geared to cope with hard times. A vain and impractical woman in many ways, she didn't know how to cut corners. We were one of the first families in the neighborhood to have a telephone, because she insisted on having it, even though it was often cut off for non-payment of bills. And she insisted on having a new table, with little drawers in it, on which the telephone sat, dead or alive. She insisted on all kinds of things—new runners for the dining room table, new curtains when they caught her fancy, a new chair for a corner of the living room. She had no compunction about going downtown and buying these things without a nickel in the bank, and both Mother and Aunt Rosie were great ones for buying from door-to-door peddlers.

Given a dollar to feed us, Mother didn't know how to spend that dollar in the best way. She never learned to eat margarine; it had to be butter or nothing at all. And she didn't know the trick of stretching a meal with rice and gravy, for example. Or if our little sister Barbara didn't like what was being served for dinner, Mother would give her some money to run down to the grocery store and buy whatever she did want. Usually it was weenies. Barbara liked weenies for dinner. The rest of us could eat what had been put before us, and it was just fine. But we understood that Mother was trying to make it up to Barbara, because she was the baby of the family, with no father in residence; if Barbara craved weenies for dinner or a new dress for a birthday party or whatever, these were compensations, and Mother would scratch together the money somehow.

Mother was also vain about her appearance. She loved getting all dressed up, with the hat and the gloves and the little gold earrings in her pierced ears, and her hair marcelled by a lady who came to the house. She wore her hair long with a knot at the back of the neck, even though bobbed hair was the style. Any time she talked about cutting it, my father, who had grown a heavy moustache when he was a young man and wore it for the rest of his life, would say, "You can cut your hair the day I shave off my mustache."

Mother was a gregarious and social-minded lady, deeply involved in church activities as well as in club and community organizations. The list is awesome: the Priscilla Arts Club (a sewing circle), the Helping Hand Club, the Trustee Helpers, the Missionary Society, the Board of Stewardesses, the church choir, teaching in Sunday School, the Colored Women's Charity Club, several whist clubs, the Household of Ruth (women's auxiliary of the IOOF), the Eastern Star Lodge (women's auxiliary of the Masons). A distinct separation was made between colored and white in all the great do-gooding lodges, as it was in American Legion posts. Colored fraternal organizations were entirely independent of the white fraternal organizations. The colored Masons, for one, had founded their own lodge in the 1780's. They called themselves Prince Hall Masons, in honor of Prince Hall, a free Negro who had fought in the Revolution and had submitted a petition to the Massachusetts legislature protesting the kidnapping and sale of free Negroes. In his petition, Prince Hall specifically asked for the return of three Negro sailors, citizens of Boston, who had been lured aboard a ship with a promise of work, then shanghaied to Martinique and sold into slavery. Governor John Hancock protested to the Governor of Martinique, and the three Negro seamen were returned to Boston amid hosannas and celebrations in the streets. My father was very active with the Prince Hall Grand Lodge in Danville and became a thirty-second-degree Mason.

Sister Mildred was also a clubwoman. She and her friends formed a so-called sorority, Eata Bita Pie, or the EBP, and they had a sorority song that included the names of all the members. She belonged to the Live Wires, a club for high-school girls, begun by Mrs. Ella Primer, whose only daughter had died. The Live Wires met once a week for refreshments and chitchat. They may have had some aim along the way, but I don't know what it was.

Mrs. Primer lived with her dog Pee Gee, an evil-tempered, black brute who was kept tied most of the time, but he occasionally got loose and terrorized us all. The house was a tiny cottage packed wall to wall with furniture, scores of pictures, a piano draped with a Spanish shawl. Ella never threw anything away. Her favorite dress was yellow with lace trim, a model her lodge sisters had once selected as their group costume for some festivity. Ella hadn't been able to afford it, so the lodge sisters took up a collection and bought the dress for her. Ella always said she wanted to be buried in the yellow lace-trimmed dress, and I'm sure she was.

The toniest of Mildred's clubs, the snappiest and most high-hat, was the Social Aristocrats, which she joined after graduating from high school in 1932. The Social Aristocrats had been started by Dorothy Taylor, a fashionable and mannered colored lady, whose husband was a plumber. Dorothy Taylor came from Chicago where she'd been a member of Chicago's colored elite, and she decided it was time to polish up the young ladies of Danville in the social graces. She read a chapter from Emily Post at each meeting and gave lessons in what to do, where to do it, and how. Mrs. Taylor personally selected her buds, membership was by invitation only, and the Social Aristocrats wound up the season with a formal dance at the Harrison Park pavilion, with music supplied by a white orchestra.

Dances were a prime social occasion, although ministers, in those days, had a great deal to say about the temptation and sin that were part and parcel of dancing. These sermons usually began with a quotation from St. Paul, who was good for any number of texts. From there, the minister took off against dances, dance halls, dance-hall owners, the dancers themselves, and that sinful, devil-made music called JAZZ. But while the congregation listened respectfully, mothers still sent their daughters to dances, carefully chaperoned to be sure—but their daughters had to be in the social swim.

In Mildred's day, many semiformal dances were held at the Lincoln Park pavilion, where chaperoning parents could sit outside on the benches and watch what was going on. A dance announced as semiformal meant that boys wore dark suits, the girls wore evening gowns, and dance cards were to be filled out, the mothers taking careful note, not only of which young men danced with their daughters, but how they

51

behaved. Where were the boy's hands while they danced? Were they dancing too close? Were they dancing with a bit too much flash? It wasn't uncommon for a mother to step out on the floor and call her daughter and beau to order. ("Oh, Mama! *Please!*") Some girls weren't allowed on the dance floor at all, like the two sisters in our neighborhood, who were taken to parties by their father. All dressed up, just like everyone else, they had to sit out the evening on the sidelines, under their father's eagle eye. They could talk with the young men, but they could not accept an invitation to dance. Look, but don't touch, was their father's motto.

My sisters, too, were brought up with a certain fear of the devil about men. My mother, while she was secretly pleased when my sisters had admirers from other places, admirers who wrote nice letters and took trips to see them, really preferred the hometown boys. Someone whose background she knew, someone whose parents were friends. Everybody knew what happened to a girl who slipped from the straight and narrow with a smooth-talking stranger. That was The Downfall. He introduces her to a lovely lady in silks and satins, and the next thing she knows she's sitting in a parlor with other broken blossoms. In no time at all, it's drink and dope and her hair falling out, and she dies of disease. The end.

The Danville colored community had very little of the Blue-Blood-Society syndrome found in big cities; the Blue Blood Societies, as the colored elite called themselves, determined their membership by texture of hair and color of skin. The straighter the hair and the paler the complexion, the higher one stood on the social ladder. They did this, I guess, to protect themselves. By being as white as possible, they thought they had a chance of becoming first-class citizens.

But not until a few years ago could a really dark colored woman with kinky hair dare think of herself as being beautiful. Oh yes, some exceptional women with dark satin coloring, marvelous features, and long straight hair were considered pretty, but they were a rarity. And they had a rough time of it within their own race even so. Dark skin was not much of a calamitous social stigma for men, but dark women were given a difficult road to go. One terrible old rhyme went:

> If you're white, you're right.
> If you're yellow, you're mellow.
> If you're brown, stick around.
> If you're black, get back.

The rhyme was recited jokingly, but it was joking on the level. Pale skin and straight hair were prized and admired. I can remember evil, catty comments the high-school girls made about each other. A pale-skinned classmate would be jealously dismissed as "wasted yellow," a dark-skinned classmate put down as a "black ink-spitter." And I also remember a remark by a fair-complexioned cousin, whose husband was a deep brown. "Of course," she said silkily, "it takes a really dark colored man to fully appreciate a light-skinned woman."

There were often vast differences in shading, texture of hair, and eye color within the same family, between brothers and sisters. My mother, for example, was medium brown, her brother Bill was quite dark, and her sister Rose was lemon-colored, from who-will-ever-know-what ancestral chromosomes. And there were several examples in Danville of the ultimate in "whiteness"—one, a little girl who moved to town when I was in the sixth grade. June had long fair hair, blue eyes, and white skin, but the cousins with whom she lived were darker than I am. Our teacher was undone by this "colored" child, who was as white as she. Colored children had always been colored children, and here, for the first time, was a colored child who wasn't colored. Little June had knocked the natural order of the universe into a cocked hat.

Among the old-timers in Danville was another white Negro, an elderly gentleman with pale skin and pale eyes, who long ago had been a neighbor of my parents down in the East End. Mother once met him on the street, and not having seen him in such a long time, didn't recognize him in passing.

He called out to her, "Hello, Mrs. Short." Mother walked straight on.

"Hey, Mrs. Short. Hello, there. How are you?" Still Mother ignored this man, but he followed her.

"Mrs. Short!"

Then, at last, she saw who it was and apologized for not having stopped to say hello. He laughed and laughed over this.

"I bet you thought I was some old white man yelling at you on the street."

But it's because of all these variations within our race in hair and skin and eyes that I prefer to use the term "colored," rather than "black." If you're three-eighths Indian or one-half white, or any such assortment and mixture, which most American Negroes are, you're not black; you're colored. Furthermore, I was brought up to say "colored." Black was always part of an insult. Shut your black mouth. You black son-of-a-bitch. Get your black ass out of here. And so on.

Very well, Danville colored society drew no color line, even though light complexions were admired. We had no

Blue Blood Societies, per se. The list for dances, banquets, and excursions was based on who you were, who your family had been, and your standing in the community. Several dark, dark women belonged to the circle of the local elite, women who would not have been acceptable to Washington, D.C., New Orleans, or Chicago society. But in Danville they were included, and they were at the parties. The Laissez-Faire Club was a case in point. Everyone in town who was anyone was on the list for the Laissez-Faire, no matter what their color, light or dark, ginger or jet. It was one of the top-drawer clubs in town, founded in the 1920's as an auxiliary of the Second Baptist Church and largely made up of married couples, with a few widowed ladies and gentlemen. They had at least one big dance a year and lots of banquets and outings. To their credit, the Laissez-Faire has become less and less caught up with socializing over the years, and more and more concerned with vital issues of the day.

Another splashy social event was the annual minstrel show and ball given by one of my mother's clubs, the Danville Colored Women's Charity Club, with the proceeds used for baskets of groceries to be given to the poor at Christmas time. (Bless their hearts, many of the members themselves were only a whistle away from poverty row.) These minstrel shows were really revues; they had no minstrel circle, no interlocutor, no Mr. Bones, no end men. None of that. They were called "minstrel shows" for lack of a better term. The entertainment was chiefly home talent, except for a star performer imported as the headliner and an orchestra brought in for the ball.

I was about eight when I was finally allowed to go, and I'd been begging for years to see the minstrel show. I remember being dressed up in a green suit with short pants, white stockings, and my Sunday shoes. All the ladies were turned out, à la mode, in the slinky, bias-cut evening gowns of the era, usually satin in such pale colors as beige, ivory, and gray, with an occasional black or red satin flashing in the crowd. I recall those dresses well, because during the dancing I walked through what was to me, as a small boy, a sea of satin behinds. The gentlemen, of course, were in their best. Those who had tuxedos wore them, the others wore dark suits.

Bud Williams always sang in the show—"Love Letters In The Sand" or "My Blue Heaven." That year my sister's trio, Bootsy, Meg, and Mid, did their specialty, "Fit As A Fiddle And Ready For Love," and Lucille Kenner sang "Give Me Liberty Or Give Me Love." For the finale, the entire ensemble sang "For All We Know We May Never Meet Again."

But the star of the evening was Hazel Myers. Hazel Myers was a colored woman, originally from Danville, who had gone into show business early in the 1920's and achieved a certain success as a blues singer. She made a lot of records and was often mentioned in jazz journals of the day. One of her songs that evening was called "Stop The Trains." I'll never forget it. Hazel Myers was the first blues singer I had ever seen and heard in the flesh. She was a short woman, dressed in black, her hair glossed straight back, like Bessie Smith's. Her voice was enormous, a powerful and dramatic voice that filled the hall without any mikes. "Stop the trains . . . stop the boats . . . stop the pain in my soul . . . my man's gone." I couldn't think about anything else for days. The music, the song, Hazel Myers, and the way she sang! "Stop the trains . . . stop the boats. . . ."

About ten years later, Hazel Myers gave up her professional career, put all the blues songs and the jazz behind her, and came home to Danville; she settled down with her relatives, joined the church, and sang in the choir.

VIII

When I was in high school, feeling my oats and making sophisticated cracks about the number of children in our family and the trouble it took to raise so many of us, Mother's answer was always the same. The Good Lord has seen us through. The Good Lord has never failed us. For at the center of our lives, in good times and bad times, stood the church.

We always said grace at table and prayers before bed, and at Sunday dinner each of us recited a verse from the Bible. During the week Bible study classes were held at church for both grownups and children, and there were Christian Endeavor meetings for the young people, church socials of one kind or another, and on Sunday, Sunday school, followed by morning service and often an afternoon or evening service. Sermons were long-winded in those days, and church could last for two hours if the minister were of a mind.

We were Methodists—the African Methodist Episcopal Church, or Allen Chapel, as the A.M.E. is often called. It was founded by Richard Allen, the colored minister who held the first A.M.E. services in a converted blacksmith shop in Philadelphia in 1787. Allen Chapel was highly formalized in its rituals, all in the tradition of the Methodist Episcopal litany. The choir marched in to "Holy, Holy, Holy," the scripture lessons were read and responses spoken, the Apostle's Creed was recited, the Doxology was sung, and the benediction was formally pronounced at the close of the service. Children were baptized with a few drops of water on their heads, unlike the Baptist Church. When the Baptists baptized you, you were really baptized. Their church had a special baptismal chamber with a tank, and that tank was filled up and you were dunked in in your white baptismal robes. We'd peek in the chamber and giggle just at the thought of such goings-on. We'd seen riverside baptisms in the newsreels. These were always good for a few frames, with the crowd on the bank, and the minister in mid-stream with a parishioner in his arms.

The old building that had once housed Papa's ice-cream parlor was now a sanctified church, and this too fascinated us children—the abandon of the "saints," the hand-clapping, the dancing and shouting and speaking in tongues. The evening services, held by Reverend Bell, a reverend by self-ordainment, often went on until eleven or even later. To me, the music was the big attraction. This was soul music, often with only a piano accompaniment, but sometimes with tympani, and it verged on pure jazz—perhaps it was pure jazz. All of it was as far removed from our church services as night from day, which made it only the more appealing. Many nights, when the sanctified church couldn't find another pianist, I'd slip onto the piano bench, aged eight or nine, and accompany the singing. For this, I'd usually receive twenty-five, maybe fifty cents.

Revivals were held in town at least once a year and generally lasted for a week, with a different minister preaching each night. All the colored churches took part, and the goal of this week-long bout was to bring in the poor sinners, hit them where it hurt, drive them to repentance, and sign them up with one of the churches. As the preaching and singing and praying boiled to a climax, weeping, trembling sinners sprang up from the crowd and ran to the altar to kneel and repent. Mother dragged us along to the revivals, and I would sit there, half embarrassed and half fascinated; all those young ladies wriggling and writhing and churned to fever pitch, then running to be saved. And in six or eight months they'd be right back to their old habits, dating and wearing tight dresses, having a little drink, and staying out too late with the wrong men.

But it was the revival meetings that preserved the old spirituals. We didn't sing them at Allen Chapel as part of our formal service, although spirituals are inherent to Negro church. They were heard only in concerts or at Sunday-night musicales or occasionally at a lay service, if for some reason the minister was unable to be at church on Sunday morning. One of the old people would quietly start to sing "Steal Away," or "Nobody Knows the Trouble I've Seen," or "Down by the Riverside."

Around 1930 a colored composer in Chicago, Thomas A. Dorsey, began to write what I think of as modern spirituals. These were the gospel songs that borrowed both from the early spirituals and from the blues; they had a built-in syncopation and a rhythm of their own that you could lean right into, clap your hands, and sing out. Dorsey began composing these hymns after he'd found salvation in the Baptist church and renounced his past as Georgia Tom the blues pianist and composer. He'd traveled with Ma Rainey in the old days on her tent-show tours and had composed her theme song, "Stormy Sea Blues." Dorsey's gospel hymns caught on like wildfire in the Baptist churches, then little by little made their way into the services of all the Negro churches. By the 1940's they had jumped the color line and were being sung by white congregations, particularly the fundamentalist faiths, with an organ or piano beating out that gospel syncopation. These hymns have now become a new American folk music, songs like "Hide Me In Thy Bosom," "A Little Talk with Jesus," and "Singing in My Soul" and "Precious Lord, Take My Hand." All pure Americana, just like the spirituals from the old South, or cowboy songs from the old West.

At Christmas time we had a pageant with all the beautiful carols, which I loved and which could only be sung at one season of the year. The nativity in the Christmas pageant was a tableau vivant with a brown-skinned Holy Family, with brown shepherds, brown Magi, and brown angels, and it was bliss. I sometimes played a small part, but best of all was my mother in the church choir, dressed as an angel, in white robe and wings, her hair unbound and hanging around her shoulders. At Easter, the church usually presented a cantata with solos, trios, exultant choral movements, and often a pageant with scenes involving children.

Musicales were held at the church on Sunday nights once a month and included all the local talent from the neighborhood colored churches. On these occasions spirituals were sometimes sung, but as a rule the musicales leaned heavily toward "Indian Love Call" or "Roses Are Smiling in Picardy." In Sunday school, the younger children took part in "toy symphonies." A recording such as Delibes' *Pizzicato* or *Cinquantaine* (the "Golden Wedding") was played on a victrola and we kept time with triangles, bells, tambourines, woodblocks, and cymbals. And at the party evenings known as Christian Cabarets, everyone sat at little tables drinking soda pop and lemonade and eating ice cream, and a cabaret show was put on. Mock weddings were staged, with flocks of little children in grown-up clothes, a miniature bride and groom and a miniature minister. Mock weddings were also staged by the men of the congregation— the oldest gag in the world, men dressed up as women, as the bride, the bridesmaids, and the mother of the bride.

An interchurch pageant, in observance of National Negro Health Week, was organized by Mrs. Dixon, the wife of the Reverend Dixon of Shiloh Baptist. Mrs. Dixon was also our accompanist, an attractive, sexy lady who played a mean, dirty piano, which to me was the best part of the whole show. I was in a skit with the Dixons' son and daughter; we appeared as the Gold Dust Twins and Old Dutch Cleanser, the leitmotif of the revue being cleanliness and good health— brush your teeth, take lots of baths, and eat your green vegetables. Nowadays, of course, it would be considered the height of bad taste to dress up two little boys as the Gold Dust Twins, but there we were, looking like a pair of Zulu pickaninnies.

We had church picnics, the matrons outdoing each other in the good, good food that was spread out on the serving tables, and then we'd have sack races, three-legged races, the fat ladies' race, and the fat men's race. And everyone sang "K-K-K-Katie" and "Long, Long Trail A-Winding" and

"Smiles." But at none of these church parties could we ever play anything as jazzy as Nathaniel Dett's "Juba Dance," which like the spirituals has now become an American classic. A song, however, that we all learned at church and often sang, was the Negro anthem, "Lift Every Voice and Sing," composed in 1900 by J. Rosamond Johnson. The words were written by his brother, James Weldon Johnson. It was an impressive song, but one doesn't often hear it anymore:

> Lift every voice and sing, till earth and heaven ring,
> Ring with the harmony of liberty.
> Let our rejoicing rise, high in the listening skies,
> Let it resound loud as the roaring seas.
> Sing a song of faith, that the dark past has taught us,
> Sing a song full of hope that the future has brought us,
> Facing the rising sun of our new day begun.
> Let us march on, till Victory is won.

Now, a majority of the parties and banquets and entertainments were devised to raise money for the church. There was always a mortgage to pay off, or improvements to the property, or simply day-to-day maintenance. Allen Chapel had its own particular financial headaches because the original church, a brick building with stained-glass windows, the interior done in the Gothic patterns so beloved by church architects in the old days, had burned in 1935. The congregation moved from place to place until Allen Chapel finally came to roost on Jackson Street, down in the East End.

We had a succession of ministers. The A.M.E. church was a highly political organization, and a minister could rise to the upper church hierarchy if he were forceful, politically hep, and a successful fund raiser. So there was a lot of shifting about from parish to parish as various ministers proved themselves, then rose in rank and title, leaving empty pulpits behind them. Over the years we had the Reverend Stone, who was possibly given to drink, a half pint here and there. The Reverend King, very social and energetic. The Reverend I .M. D. Washington, a fine minister in every way. The Reverend Wright, who was most unpopular and was actually attacked, physically, by one of the church trustees during a vestry meeting; his grandson was my archenemy. The Reverend Searcy, a lovely man, on the edge of retirement. But although ministers came and went, the pattern of church benefits rolled on.

Teas were popular among the ladies, with a silver collection taken after refreshments were served. It was always important that the home where the tea was to be held should have a proper dining room with nice curtains, candles on the table, and the best china. One of the high points on this circuit was a Colonial Tea, or a Martha Washington Tea, at which the colored matrons would arrive dressed as colonial dames, with their hair powdered white. . . .

Fashion shows were a regular feature on the calendar of interchurch activities, the ladies parading for each other in their finest of finery. The two swankiest matrons in colored society (the swankiest in my young eyes) were Mrs. Chavis, the wife of Ray Chavis, who had a moving and storage company, and Mrs. Frazier, the wife of Dr. Frazier, the dentist. Both gentlemen were well heeled, and their wives were always turned out in the latest vogue—so up-to-the-minute and so chic, in fact, that during church fashion shows Ruth Chavis and Anne Frazier were usually seated up on the platform so that their clothes could be seen and admired by everyone throughout the program.

One year, the big money raiser was a gala pageant called *Heaven's and Hell's Highway*, promoted and staged by a traveling producer and director, a lady who came through town and made a deal with three of the colored churches. She would put on the show, and in return the gate receipts would be divided between her and the participating churches. She auditioned and auditioned and rehearsed and rehearsed her stars, all of them nonprofessionals from the various congregations. I was too young to be in it, but sat in the front row, jubilant and goggle-eyed as the spectacle unfolded. Mr. Barney Jackson, a friend of my parents, was formidable in the role of the Devil, dressed in a red suit with a long tail, a large pitchfork in hand. A roster of angels surrounded the Pearly Gates at one side of the stage, while Mr. Jackson operated more or less downstage, doing his best to tempt weary wanderers into Hell before they could cross the stage and into the shining portals of Heaven. There was lots of singing throughout, with such old spirituals as "Trampin', Trampin', Tryin' To Make Heaven My Home." My mother's injunctions against bad language were so severe that we were barely allowed to utter the name of the show at home, and if we did say it, right out, "Heaven's and Hell's Highway," the sound of the word "hell" seemed to hang, shockingly, in the air. Even in much later years, the great Marian Anderson, when singing certain spirituals in which "hell" was in the traditional lyrics, would coyly and purposefully leave the word out.

It was at church parties that I first heard the poems of Paul Lawrence Dunbar, the nineteenth-century Negro poet, who wrote lyric verse in the literary style of his time as well as in dialect. Halley Thompson, who was in Sunday school with us, was very good at recitation and had memorized a lot of Dunbar. Among her best pieces were his dialect poems —"In De Mornin' " and "When Malindy Sings."

We also were aware of Phyllis Wheatley, once a slave girl, who was writing poetry before the Revolutionary War. She'd been brought from Senegal as a child and sold off the docks to a Boston man named John Wheatley, who gave her his family name. Mrs. Wheatley taught her to read and write, and by the age of twenty Phyllis Wheatley was renowned for her verse. George Washington sent her a fan letter, and she went to England to be feted and to read her poems to the nobility. Indeed we knew about Phyllis Wheatley—the club for colored girls at Danville High School was named for her.

We were surrounded by the lore of our heritage: Frederick Douglass, Booker T. Washington, Dr. George Washington Carver; Franklin Roosevelt's "Black Cabinet" and William Hastie, the first Negro Federal Judge. Jesse Owens was a hero, as was Colonel Hubert Julian, a great aviator and daredevil. But Joe Louis was our greatest hero of all. (After he married Marva Trotter, she brushed off some of his stardom, with rafts of little colored girls being named after her. There are lots of Marvas around today.)

All of us in Danville were caught up with Joe Louis' rise to the championship. He was our special hope and pride, and when he lost his first match with Max Schmeling in 1936—a knockout by Schmeling in the twelfth round—we felt a tremendous dismay and despair, even my mother's friends did. The ladies had rushed out of choir practice that night, jumped into a taxicab, and sped home to be at the radio. After the fight, they all made conjectures as to how and why

Joe had lost. One of the ladies was Mattie Reeves, tiny and dark-skinned, who worked as a maid at Deutsch Uptown, the fanciest women's ready-to-wear emporium in town.

"Joe was doped," said Mattie. "In his orange juice or in a glass of milk. Or they could have put something in his oatmeal at breakfast this morning. Why, just before the fight, they could have offered him a dish of cream with dope in it." (Mattie never said ice cream. She was southern, and she used the southern expression. So "dish of cream" became a household joke, and Barbara and I loved to say this, making fun of Mrs. Reeves, who taught the beginners' class at Sunday School, who adored children, who loved all of us more than life and was always good for a nickel on a Sunday afternoon.)

Paul Robeson had emerged as a star on the concert stage, in the theater, and in the movies. Marian Anderson was rising to the peak of her fame. I remember my mother's pride in Marian Anderson, but when she finally heard Miss Anderson sing on the radio, Mother didn't understand what the ruckus was about. The broadcast was opera, and Mother's taste in music did not include opera. To her, it was odd music and an odd way of singing. Mother stayed with the semi-classics, Victor Herbert, "The Rosary," and "The Holy City."

We gave speeches on our heroes at school. Louis Armstrong was another, and his biography, *Swing That Music* (to be found in the public library, *not* in the school library) was a favorite with colored boys and girls, who used it for book reviews and reports over and over again. My special hero was Duke Ellington, and I'd get up in class to talk about him any time I was given the chance. We didn't talk about Jack Johnson at school because he'd been in so much trouble with all those white women trailing after him—victimized by his color and by the fight game. When I was in high school, if anyone mentioned the slightest conversation with a white girl, Mother would warn me to watch out: "Remember what happened to Jack Johnson."

Marcus Garvey, with his Back to Africa movement and Black Star Shipping Line, was another lost Negro figure. He had fancied himself a great statesman, dressed himself in feathered hats and light-opera uniforms, and wound up in jail for fraud. For years we heard the saying, "Don't be a Marcus Garvey," which meant don't be a damned fool.

Countee Cullen and Langston Hughes, leaders in the Negro Renaissance that began in New York in the 1920's, were writing at the time, but we didn't know about them in Danville. I remember seeing a copy of *Nigger Heaven* by Carl Van Vechten at a neighbor's house. The title caught my eye, but I was too young to be interested in reading it. I did read books by Octavus Roy Cohen and Julia Peterkin, both of whom were white but wrote in Negro dialect. I found these books enormously interesting, because they were about Negroes in the deep South, a world that was utterly foreign to me; I learned how the impoverished southern Negroes lived, how they spoke, the things they ate (hearts of palm, possum, catfish), their habits and customs. All of this was as exotic and unreal to me as was Harlem, at the other end of the scale.

During our high-school years we became aware of Richard Wright when *Native Son*, his first major work, was published in 1940. Reading that book was a horrifying experience, but it made all of us, suddenly, much more socially conscious, much more concerned with the Negro world we had never known. It was possible to live in Danville without thinking about such things too much. To this day, a certain area of my brain refuses to read truths about cruelty. I can recall the headlines about the Scottsboro boys in the Chicago *Defender*, but I couldn't read the news reports through. I could barely finish *Native Son*. And *Black Boy*, Wright's next big novel, I never finished at all, knowing full well what it was all about.

Negro writers, past or present, were never mentioned in our school curriculum, and scant attention was given to Negro figures in American history. Once, when I made a report on Booker T. Washington, I had to go to the public library to get information because there was almost none to be had in the school library. All our textbooks were geared to the white Protestant view. In a high-school economics course, for example, a textbook flatly informed us that Italians and Chinese were undesirable as citizens of this country, the Italians because they contributed to the gangster element, and the Chinese because they dealt in dope and "trafficked in women." (This last, ominous phrase in pale language didn't tell us what we wanted to know at all; we wanted details!)

IX

I liked school from the start. Kindergarten was a breeze, with lots of time given to self-expression, naps, drawing with crayons, toy symphonies—just like Sunday school—and story-telling by our teacher, plump Miss Hamilton. The first day Mother took me down on the Gilbert Street bus. Fare, one nickel. After that, I rode back and forth by myself with the other children. Anne Kenner and I were the only colored babies in the class, and I don't remember any difference ever being made between us and the rest of the children. And thus it went through the early years of grade school. On Valentine's Day, always a sweet kind of day at school, I got my share of cards, even though I was usually the only colored child in class. The innocence of children is astonishing. All the kids had their romantic attachments, their girl friends and boy friends, and I remember once a pretty little girl named Betty Orr, who was blonde with a Dutch bob, writing me a note that said, "Dear Bobby, I love you with hundreds of love and kisses. P.S. Give this to Paul." So I passed the note to Paul because it was meant for him, too. I was caught passing the note and brought before the class. I was lectured, she was lectured, he was lectured. We were all lectured for writing notes and passing them around. But no racial overtone was implied. None of that.

And in the fourth grade we gave a play, *The Constant Tin Soldier,* from a Hans Christian Andersen story. The heroine was played by Patty Lemmon, another little girl with blonde hair and a Dutch bob, and I was her lead, the constant tin soldier. There was a total absence of any kind of overt prejudice in those years, and it was kept that way by our teachers—which I was not aware of then. I never expected to be treated differently than my classmates. I didn't know that colored children anywhere could be given a bad time at school.

Lots of attention was given to music, with a piano in almost every classroom and a teacher who could play it. Everyone at that time played the piano at least a little, just as today an entire generation plays the guitar. One of the biggest departments in the Five-and-Ten, for example, used to be sheet music, and many Five-and-Tens had a piano and a clerk who could run through the latest hits for the customers. And so, for our daily singing class, our teacher could sit down at the piano, put the music book on the rack, and we were off. Many of the songs we sang were set to melodies from the classics. We sang "Let's be Fairies in a Ring," to the gavotte from *Mignon* and "Forth to the meadows, ye fair merry maidens," from Mendelssohn. We sang a musical version of Wordsworth's "Daffodils": "I wandered lonely as a cloud that floats on high o'er vales and hills. And all at once, I saw a crowd, a host of golden daffodils. . . ." One charming and surrealistic song went:

Tasty dish of caraway and cottage cheese,
And a spicy yellow pippin if you please.
That's a dinner, you will like it so,
That you linger longer when it's time to go.

Which was matched only by the surrealism of another charming song, whose words went this way:

Tiny pocket so small,
Far too small for this roll.
If I nibble one bite,
It will still be too tight.
Why not swallow it whole?

The second chorus was equally obscure:

Cross is Bobby with me,
Will no longer tease me.
Gracious, I am so sad.
Bobby, do not stay mad.
Come now, Bobby, tease me.

The "Bobby" in that song, by the way, had nothing to do with me. The name didn't change with each singing class. That's the way it was written, and that's the way we sang it.

We learned "Trees" in the first grade, the most famous of Joyce Kilmer's poems, a song that no one seems to sing anymore. In those days "Trees" was second only to the national anthem; every schoolchild in America knew "Trees." One day when we stood up to sing, with our teacher Gertrude Swain at the classroom piano, I was plucked out of the crowd and chosen to give a solo of "Trees" at the Arbor Day celebration.

I think that I shall never see
A poem lovely as a tree.
A tree whose hungry mouth is pressed

Against the earth's sweet flowing breast;
A tree that looks at God all day,
And lifts her leafy arms to pray;

A tree that may in summer wear
A nest of robins in her hair;
Upon whose bosom snow has lain;
Who intimately lives with rain.
Poems are made by fools like me,
But only God can make a tree.

Poor old "Trees." * That poem lent itself to unending parody and a lot of crude jokes. In 1937 in New York, I heard Joe E. Lewis do a turn on "Trees" at the Frolics Cafe, stopping after each phrase to throw out such lines to the audience as, "I'd like to know if there's anyone here upon whose bosom snow has lain . . . ?" Or, "Has anyone here ever lived *intimately* with rain?" And so on. I, however, was a first grader, it was Arbor Day, and a tree was going to be planted—all those words about hungry mouths, flowing breasts, lifted leafy arms, and the rest of it were deemed highly poetic and inspirational. My accompanist was Ruth Allen, one of Lawyer Allen's daughters, who was in the seventh grade and played the piano very nicely. She and I rehearsed, and I sang my solo for the Arbor Day assemblage.

After that I was invited to sing "Shanty in Old Shanty Town" at a jitney supper at school. Then the Phyllis Wheatley Club put on a high-school assembly, and I sang in their show. That particular assembly was a landmark, because it was the first time the colored girls in high school, all ten or fifteen of them out of about fourteen hundred students, had stepped forward to indicate that they too existed. Their show

* Doubleday Doran Copyright © 1918.

73

was a very subtle and ladylike way of saying, "We're going to do what you're doing in high school, and we're going to do it as well, if not better."

Our grade school had a music cycle for the Christmas season, with each grade given a set of carols to learn. When you were in the first grade and heard the eighth grade singing their Christmas songs, you knew that in seven years it would be your turn to sing those songs. When I left Danville to go on the road, I missed out on some carols I'd looked forward to: "Lo, How A Rose Ere Blooming" and "I Heard the Bells on Christmas Day." I haven't caught up with them yet.

Meantime, we were drilled in sight reading and in theory, with all the memory gimmicks that music teachers love so well. Every Good Boy Does Fine gave us E, G, B, D, and F, the lines of the treble clef. F-A-C-E gave us the spaces in the treble. Go Dick And Eat Beans, or G, D, A, E, B, were the lines in the bass clef. And B-E-A-D signified the keys that could be flatted. (We had the same sort of mnemonic gimmicks in Sunday school; one of the elders taught us I Just Live Every Day to help us remember the four major prophets of the Old Testament; I for Isaiah, J for Jeremiah, L for Lamentations, written by Jeremiah, E for Ezekiel, and D for Daniel.)

For me, one of the best years of all at the Garfield School was the third grade. I'd been looking forward to third grade, and I got there six months early because I was jumped ahead in the middle of the second grade. Miss Lucille Abbott was the third-grade teacher, and Lucille Abbott played the piano like a pro, in that marvelous, hot, early thirties, ragtime beat. She always started out in a conventional tempo, but by the end of the first stanza she was carried away; "Shine, Blessed

Star From Heaven," or "The Pilgrim Maiden's Song"—Miss Abbott turned them into jazz, raw razz. I couldn't wait for school in the morning and those ragtime songs. After classes were over, she and I would play for each other on the piano in the gym. One of her best was "My Extraordinary Gal," and then I'd play and sing, "That's the breeze that's filling the sails that's moving the ship that's sailing the sea that's bringing my lover back to me. . . ."

In the fourth grade I fancied a teacher named Marion Campbell, who was my first and absolute love in grade school. She and I would sing the popular songs of the day for each other, all the Dick Powell and Bing Crosby ballads. I adored her, because she always asked me to play the piano, and when she announced to the class that she was going to be married, I was very upset and very angry. Miss Campbell was leaving. *My* Miss Campbell was leaving.

By the time we were in fifth grade, our innocence was lost. I no longer liked to sing those Stephen Foster melodies about Old Black Joe and Swanee River: "Oh, darkies, how my heart grows weary. . . ." And I didn't like to sing "Carry Me Back to Old Virginny," even though it had been written by James A. Bland, a Negro composer: ". . . That's where this ole darky's heart am long to go. . . ." No, thank you. When those songs were sung in our classroom, I stood there with my mouth closed. It was bad enough to have to hear all those darky lyrics, but our teacher was also reading Mark Twain aloud to us, and Twain is full of "niggers" and "half-breeds." Being the only colored child in our classroom, each time these words were read aloud, everyone would turn around and look at Bobby Short, because he was that person. I finally stood up one day and asked if there weren't something better for us to hear than Mark Twain, with all his tales about niggers and half-breeds. It was explained to me that Mark Twain was a foremost figure in American literature, that I was being oversensitive, that the other children were entitled to hear Mark Twain . . . and the readings went on. Later, I came to appreciate the sophistication and social commentary that Samuel Clemens masked as the folksy, yarn-spinning Mark Twain, but we couldn't handle that kind of sophistication in the fifth grade in Danville, Illinois.

Our teachers were usually hometown girls, and we liked that. We favored the hometown girls and gave showers for our teachers, just as various churches gave showers for their ministers, a custom that probably stemmed from the old days when teachers and preachers received little, if any, salary and were largely paid with board and room. A shower was always planned as a surprise. One day the teacher would arrive in the classroom after lunch, and a big box would be on her desk with all kinds of canned goods and groceries. Poor children often couldn't bring food but gave some other little gift. Once, in the sixth grade, I gave a string of blue beads, because our cupboard was bare that day. Otherwise, Mother usually sent me off with a gift of canned corn or canned peas.

Meantime, I was picking up any and every song that caught my fancy, but no one seemed particularly excited by any of this. They thought it was very nice, oh yes. They were delighted that I had a knack for playing the piano and could give them a song at church entertainments or at school. But beyond that, what could they say? They could only hope that when I grew up I would hold down a steady and responsible job, in the civil service perhaps, like Uncle Arthur on the police force, or Anne Kenner's father and Billy Fletcher's father, who were firemen, or that I'd work as a mail carrier, as my father had done for a while.

Eventually, however, Mother arranged for me to have piano lessons with Helene Edmunds Smith. Mrs. Smith was one of the first Danville colored women to have a teaching degree, but colored teachers had no place in the local school system except at the Jackson School, where the children were predominantly Negro. Jackson went only to the seventh grade, so there were simply not enough positions on the faculty for the number of qualified colored teachers in town. And yet teaching was considered a worthwhile profession. More and more colored students got their degrees in education and came home from college only to face a school system that could not and would not employ them. Mrs. Smith, like so many others, was reduced to substitute work at Jackson, and she also gave music lessons—at twenty-five cents a lesson. She drilled me in the rudiments and introduced me to the Czerny exercises. But the lessons were a losing battle from the start. I could not concentrate on learning to read music, I could not focus on those myriad notes on the printed page. It was so easy to play by ear. Most of the time, I went through my exercises and harmonic drills by imitation. Whatever Mrs. Smith played for me, I would play back more or less accurately. I quickly mastered a piece called "Firefly Waltz," by God-knows-who, and performed in a recital at the Second Baptist Church, stage-managed by Mrs. Smith. Step by step, she taught me how to walk onto the stage, bow, address the audience ("I will now play for you the 'Firefly Waltz'"), move slowly backward to the piano, place the music on the rack, and play; then rise, take a low bow, and exit. I did exactly as Mrs. Smith had taught me, except for one small point. Having put my copy of "Firefly Waltz" on the music rack, I never looked at it again, but turned and stared straight at the audience, from first note to last. That was my one and only appearance as a serious music student.

X

About a year later I was playing the piano in the local saloons.

Illinois has always been pretty much a wide-open state. To the south were river cities such as East Saint Louis, where the night life was unimaginably bright, and up near Chicago in towns like Calumet City, block after block was devoted to cocktail lounges and nightclubs, live entertainment, girls and gambling, the works. In its way Danville served as "sin city" for the surrounding area. It never got out of hand, but on the outskirts of town were bars where you could drink all night; girls were available, if you knew where to look, and gambling was legalized at one point. There was a game called "26" that could be played in any corner bar. The "26" girls, who worked the bars and got a cut of the winnings, rolled the dice with you. It usually cost twenty-five cents to play, and you won chips that could be cashed in for drinks. Danville was a boon for the male students at the University of Illinois. They could drive their rickety cars over in thirty-five or forty minutes and at least get a drink, which they couldn't get back in Urbana.

My introduction to Danville's dine-and-dance scene began simply enough through a young saxophonist named John Dyer, a family friend and a good musician, who was nicknamed "Hooks" because of his bandy bowlegs. John came to the house one day and asked Mother if I could appear with his group, which was playing at a roadhouse called the Edgewater. I was beside myself with excitement, crazy to go out to the Edgewater and work. Please, I begged. Let me go with John Dyer.

Mother was always of the opinion that if you knew someone's relatives and they were respectable, church-going people, there could be no question. If I, at the age of nine, were to play the piano in a roadhouse, it would be perfectly all right because I would be in the care of John Dyer, whose aunt was a church friend of Mother's. It didn't matter that my mother had never set foot in a roadhouse.

The Edgewater was about thirty minutes from town, out on the Perrysville Road, then a turn downhill on a dirt track that led to the wooded edge of a creek. Hence the name. The owners were two easygoing characters named Jake and Gotch. The bad old days of Prohibition were finally over, the lid was off, and the Edgewater boomed on Saturday nights. The clientele was white, the entertainment colored. The star of the evening was usually Ellyn Treadwell, a local pianist and the party girl of all time. She was accompanied by a saxophone, drums (bass fiddlers were hard to come by), and an occasional trumpet on big nights, while the crowd danced their heads off and whirled and hugged and drank and whooped it up. I loved it. What child wouldn't? Watching all those grown-ups dancing and carrying on like no tomorrow. "Mood Indigo," "Dinah," and "Nobody's Sweetheart Now" were the staples, with all the popular songs of the day as they came along. Ellyn Treadwell also sang, and she had a husky voice that wrung the last drop of heartbreak out of such tearjerkers as "My Man" and "The Man I Love." There were always requests for risqué songs ("sophisticated songs" as they were often called), and Ellyn and her boys always came through with a sly little number titled "Yas, Yas, Yas," while the crowd screamed and clapped. More! More!

Another star on the tavern circuit was Bernice Hassell, or "Hassell," as she was always called, a colored woman who played a natural jazz piano and, like Ellyn Treadwell, could turn on a roomful of people. There was Ruth Barnett, also colored and famous around town for her torchy versions of such standards as Johnny Mercer's "When A Woman Loves A Man." And there were the Three Shades of Brown—Maudie Morton, Isabelle Stone, and Bertha Burnett—who'd flash out to "Bugle Call Rag" and dance up a storm.

On the evenings when I appeared with John Dyer's group at the Edgewater my salary was often the staggering sum of one dollar, but this was supplemented, as a rule, by whatever had been collected in the kitty. The kitty was anything that could hold cash, from a cigar box with a slit in the top, to a fancy container shaped like a cat with "Feed the Kitty" written across it. When the action wasn't fast enough, they sent me out to pass the kitty through the crowd and collect the quarters and halves and the hoped-for but rarely seen dollar bills. At evening's end the take was divided equally among the musicians, sometimes it came to as much as three dollars apiece, and I was driven home, usually to find my mother sitting up by the front window waiting for her baby son.

After my start at the Edgewater, I branched out to other roadhouses of the same ilk. The Pullman Club, Burke's Tavern, and the Hottentot were on my list of gigs, each with their own drummers, horn players, and fast talkers. One big colored bar was called Jimmy Harold's, and a colored man named Day had a place called the Panama Tea Garden. I worked for a while at Louis Knake's Cafe. He was a very kind man (white), whose daughter, Lila Mae, played the xylophone at school assemblies and in local talent shows.

On a weekend night, if I didn't have a set engagement at a roadhouse, I was taken off on barhopping tours. Someone was always showing up at the front door, someone whose mother was an old friend of Mother's or whose father was an old friend of someone else in the family, and they'd shepherd me from tavern to tavern, most of them nothing more than a scruffy hole in the wall with a bar, booze, some tables, and a dance floor, where I'd play and sing and they'd pass the hat. There were also taprooms at the Hotel Plaza and the Hotel Savoy where I could stop and do my number, but the Hotel Wolford was a little too grand for that sort of soliciting.

A good night's barhopping usually brought me a couple of dollars to take home. But times were tough and bars were not always full, even on weekends. Sometimes on a weekend night at a roadhouse on the outskirts of town, I'd go to sleep at the piano during a lull, my head on my arms. When the lights of approaching cars were seen around the bend, they'd wake me, and before the customers got to the door, I'd be sitting up and playing "Nobody's Sweetheart Now," full tilt. Or "Nagasaki," or "Tiger Rag."

One day I went off with the Woodard boys to play in Harrison Park, which we'd come to look upon as our private preserve. We wandered out of the woods on a footpath that led to the back lots of Maywood Drive where the rich folks lived, and strolled along Logan Avenue, just looking around the neighborhood to see who we'd run into and maybe get up some touch football. On this particular junket we met several of the Gibson boys, whom we knew through school.

The Gibsons were a warm, friendly family. Berlin J. Gibson was a grain broken with headquarters in Indianapolis. Mrs. Gibson had been Evelyn Olson before her marriage, and the Olson house on Hazel Street was surpassed only by Joe Cannon's mansion down on Vermilion. The Gibsons' household was run by their maid, Hazel Chinn, who'd lived next door to Aunt Rosie for many years and was an old friend of Mother's. So we played for a while in the Gibson backyard, and Hazel brought us a plate of cookies.

Did the Gibsons have a piano? I asked Hazel. Indeed the Gibsons did have a piano. She led me through the pantry, the kitchen, the breakfast room, the dining room, and across the living room into a smaller room, where there stood the biggest grand piano I'd ever seen. It was a Knabe; I'd never played on such a fine piano. It was like finding gold. I've forgotten what my selections were that first day at the Gibsons', but I remember the family coming in to listen, and their astonishment and pleasure. Dear Hazel stood there with a big grin, but my cohorts, Billy and Jimmy Woodard, were bored and disgusted with it all. "Cut it out, Short. We didn't come over here to listen to you play the piano."

That was my entrée into a brand new world. I'd seen the low life of Danville, but the Gibsons introduced me to the high life. I became their special project; they showered me

83

with kindness and enthusiasm and encouragement. I was in and out of their house like one of their own children. And any afternoon after school I could play their piano for an hour or so before going home to supper. The Knabe had an electric Ampico attachment fitted under the keyboard; you pulled out a shelf, put in the piano roll, closed it, and the piano played away by itself. I picked up a number of new songs from the Gibsons' piano rolls, including a splendid arrangement of "The Shadow Waltz," and another of "Love Lies." Within a few weeks I'd been presented to the Gibsons' circle as their built-in entertainment, playing and singing at parties. From there I was invited to perform at entertainments all over town—at the country club, the Kiwanis Club, luncheons, teas, the Elks Club and YMCA functions, dressed for my performances in a gleaming white tuxedo. Mr. Gibson had decided I should have a special suit for these upper-crust appearances, and he'd had the tuxedo made for me by Mrs. Larsen, a local seamstress. I'd worn tuxedos before, even tails, in mock weddings at church socials. But a white suit of my own! Oh, I wore that white tuxedo with such pride.

I was still in the fifth grade when Mr. Gibson took me to Indianapolis to play for a convention of grain brokers. During the afternoon, I went out on my own, to look around the city. I wanted to see Cab Calloway, who was playing at the Circle Theater in the center of town. But Indianapolis was segregated to the teeth, and they wouldn't sell me a ticket.

Back at the hotel, I expressed my disappointment, and that evening Mr. Gibson sent me to the theater with his butler, Raymond. We didn't go near the box office, but instead went around to the stage door. I don't know what strings Mr. Gibson had pulled, but Raymond and I were shown a spot to

Young photographs
of Mama and Papa

Grandmother Katie Basset Short

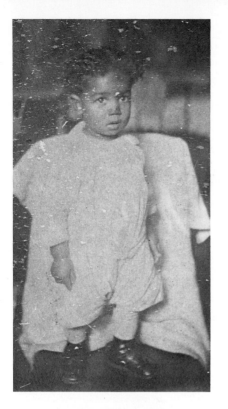

Uncle Bill Render
with Aunt Rosie
(left) and Mother

Left: Uncle Arthur Reid

Far left: The contest winning picture

Right: Barbara and I at 1135 North Robinson Street

The Golden Rod Chapter of the Eastern Star Lodge. Mother is in the third row, two in from the right. In the top row, third in from the left, is Ellyn Treadwell.

Courtesy of Mrs. Nannie Wright

Bill   Barbara

The Social Aristocrats with their founder, Mrs. Taylor. Mildred is second from the left, Eurva Belle Roey fourth from the right.

Our graduating class at St. Joseph's in 1937 with a picture of Father Garvey, the school priest. I'm in the last row, at the right.

Naomi

Reg

One of the New York photographs, 1937

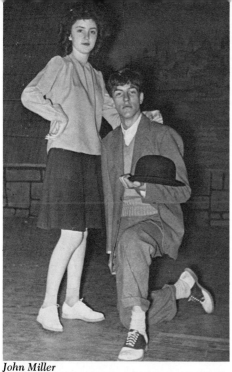

Dick Van Dyke rehearsing with Billie Carter for the 1941 Moments Musical at Danville High School.

John Miller

The Club Caliente, 1940

High school yearbook photo, 1942

Hazel Meyers

My cousin, Carl "King Tut"
Reid, and his Jug band

Ivie Anderson

Fletcher Henderson

Fredi Washington

Carl Van Vechten

Faith Bacon

The Peters Sisters

Timmie Rogers

Bunny Berigan

Culver Pictures

Acme

Joe Louis

The Three Stooges

Cab Calloway conducting. Benny Paine at the piano.

Opposite: Bill "Bojangles" Robinson

UPI

Thomas "Fats" Waller

Wide World

Ethel Waters

UPI

Art Tatum with Mildred Bailey. Sidney
Catlett at the drums.

stand in the wings where I could see the show, and when Cab Calloway came down from his dressing room, he came right over and spoke to me.

"Who are you?" he asked. I told him who I was.

"And what do you do?"

I told him I played the piano and sang. He didn't say another word, but went out and did his show. Just before the finale Calloway announced to the audience that there was a young man backstage who said he played the piano and sang.

"Shall we get him out here and see what he can do?" The audience clapped, and there I was—out on stage with Calloway and his entire orchestra, frightened to death. Benny Paine gave me his seat at the piano. My mind went blank except for one song—all I could remember was "Hot Lips," the theme song of Henry Busse, the great trumpet player. I got through it all right, wobbled off the stage, and was given a big hand by the audience. Back in school on Monday morning, nobody believed my story. People like Cab Calloway were completely beyond our reach. You just didn't go to Indianapolis and meet a big star like Calloway. It was preposterous. Billy Woodard said, "Oh, come on, Short! That didn't happen to you."

I have no way of estimating what effect my relationship with the Gibsons had on my later life, but it was an exciting time and a pleasant time. I loved the attention, I loved my appearances in my white tuxedo, I liked all the new adventures. I felt that I had a gift, and I enjoyed performing. I didn't know then and I don't know now how well or how badly I sing and play the piano, but I knew that I was a good performer. What's more, the money I earned (two or three dollars, usually, for entertaining at society parties) always

85

helped toward our household expenses. And I was in demand on every side, not just in Danville, but throughout the area, both in Illinois and Indiana. On many afternoons or evenings, the phone would ring with an immediate invitation to come over and entertain visiting friends and relatives. If the phone was disconnected, they'd stop at the house to ask if I were free for an engagement.

There were a couple of sour moments, few and far between, but well remembered. On a Sunday afternoon, for example, when I was invited to someone's house to play for their out-of-town guests (a white family, white guests), they asked if there were anyone else who could also come over to entertain. I suggested Flossie and Frances Alexander, two little colored girls I'd known for a long time. Flossie sang with great style, and her sister danced with lots of pep and verve. We put on a show for them and then were driven home. One of the guests insisted on coming along with his young son, who sat in the back seat with me and the Alexander girls. After dropping off Flossie and Frances at their door, the guest made the damnedest remark I'd ever heard. He turned and glanced at his son and me and with a great guffaw said, "Imagine! The two boys sitting back there with all that coal!"

Another bad moment occurred when I was about nine or ten, at an Elks Club dinner, one of those small-town smokers where the girls come on later and strip. The M.C. was a stranger, a real show-business smart.

"And now our next performer, who will play and sing for us. . . . Here he is, gentlemen, Danville's own—Bobby Black."

I just stood there in the wings. Go on, go on, they told me. "But that's not my name," I said. When I finally got out on stage, the M.C. asked what was wrong. I explained, "My name is not Bobby Black. It's Bobby Short."

"Oh, really?" said the M.C., and then announced to the audience with a big grin, "The young man says he's not black. He's short. I'm *so* sorry. . . ."

One lesson I also learned from all this: there were always people trying to be big shots, people who made flashy, noisy promises as they clapped you on the shoulder. "Why, listen here, young man, you should have a week at the Fischer. I know exactly who to call. I'll call him in the morning. Say, we're just going to get you a fat contract!" So I learned when I was ten years old not to expect anything until it happened. A child catches on quickly to the fakers and the show-offs. You learn to recognize who's on the level; you know who's kind and who isn't kind.

Mother was always intrigued with where I went and what happened. She didn't care about the roadhouse engagements; I was guarded in my talk about all that, or it would have been curtains. But after a private party at one of the grand houses, I would be bombarded with questions. It might be twelve o'clock at night, but Mama would still be saying: "What did they have to eat? What did *you* have to eat? Were they nice to you? And who else was there? Oh, I know her. A very tall lady? And her husband is a nice little fat man? No? Then it was somebody else. Why, it must have been her sister who lives over in Champaign. Yes, that's who it was. . . ." And always, "I'll bet so-and-so was surprised to see you up there, wasn't she!" That would be the maid.

Mother, like so many people who are servants, had a tremendous concern in her employers' doings, their friends and acquaintances—every angle, in fact, of their private lives.

One family had a son who was about to get married, and when Mother heard who the young lady was, she was utterly scornful. "That poor rake!" (one of Mother's favorite expressions for someone who wasn't up to snuff). "I've known her family for years. Why, she's just a poor rake."

Mother had firm ideas on every score as to what was suitable and what was not. Once in grade school, the principal came to me and said that the missionary society of her church was putting on a pageant, and she wondered if my mother and I and one or two of my brothers and sisters would take part. They needed colored players for scenes demonstrating missionary activities among the natives of Africa.

"Africa?"

"Yes, Africa. It would be so nice if your family would take part in our pageant. Would you ask your mother when you get home from school?"

Yes, I'd deliver the message. But I thought to myself, Mama is not going to go for this. I was right. Mama's answer was short and sweet: "Indeed not!"

Another time, when I was still in grade school, Mother put her foot down on a point of propriety at the Danville country club, where she worked as a waitress now and then. She always had a freshly laundered black uniform and white apron hanging in her closet in anticipation of such jobs, and her hair would be marcelled for the occasion. The country club was a good gig, especially on Saturday night: five dollars plus tips. One Saturday night, the swells at the club were being entertained by Jack Swift, a singer from Chicago, who sang with Joe Saunders' orchestra at the Black Hawk restaurant there. He often came down to Danville, a handsome man who set all the eligible ladies a-flutter, and the country club was his bailiwick. One of his songs that evening was "Goin' To Heaven On A Mule." A pseudo-darky song—folksy-darky, like "Shortnin' Bread" and "Old Man River," without which no baritone, in the 1930's, could get through a concert. "Goin' To Heaven On A Mule" was a grand showpiece. At the end you could really swell up and finish off full fortissimo with lots of pathos and heart.

Before he went on that night, Jack Swift mentioned he'd like to sing that song with a small colored boy, as part of his staging, I suppose. Several people suggested me, and someone asked Mother if they could call the house and pick me up. The answer was again brief. Indeed not. No child of hers was going to sing about getting into heaven on muleback. It wasn't fitting, it wasn't proper. Nothing could dissuade her. Mama said no and went back to work.

Mother also said no to bubble gum, to such victrola records as "Shake That Thing" and "Tight Like That," to wise answers from small children, like "What's your name?" "Pudding and Tame. Ask me again and I'll tell you the same." To making fun, when it was your turn to say grace, with "Good food, good meat, good Lord, let's eat." To any kind of bad talk, like calling a young girl a heifer, which was old-time slang that Reg sometimes used. Another expression he brought home was "I'll climb your frame." This was immediately declared out of order. "Where'd you learn to talk like that? I'll bet you picked that up down at Rosie's."

And Mother did not approve of hard liquor, beyond a sip of wine now and then, on a cold winter night, perhaps; a small glass from the crocks in the cellar, just before going to bed. That would be the festivity of the evening. One time, though, when she had a bad cough and sore throat, someone recommended a hot toddy of bourbon, cherry bark, and rock candy. A beau of Mildred's was sent to buy the bourbon, and Mother admitted that it was one of the best cough remedies she'd ever tried. (Coughs and colds in our family were usually cured by Father John's Emulsion, and everything else by Mother Gray's Tablets.) Much as Mama adored her sister Rosie and her brother Bill, she could never reconcile herself to their drinking. Both Rosie and Bill enjoyed their liquor. At family get-togethers, Mother would sit by, silent and stonily disapproving, as Bill and his wife Roberta and Rosie knocked back their white lightning. Uncle Arthur Reid did not approve of spirits, either, and there were unhappy times when he came home from his job on the police force to find that Aunt Rosie had been celebrating, and no dinner was on the table. A terrible row would follow, which upset Mother deeply, because she loved Rosie and didn't want her to be hurt. I remember Mother saying that when she had married my father, Grandfather Render told Papa: "If you ever get tired of my daughter, don't knock her around. You bring her home to me."

XI

By the time I was nine, I was living in several different worlds. My home world centered around the family, church, school, and our neighborhood. Here I had two sets of friends; one set was bound to reading, studying, being well-behaved, with our little theatricals or playing school on the porch. The other group was bound to being bad, playing rough games, skipping school, hiding out in the woods, peeping in windows at night. And then this new life came along, of working in saloons, and then yet another world, of performing for the Gibsons or at luncheon parties and teas. But the diversity of all this never occurred to me at the time. I slipped from one level to the next without a second thought. And I liked it. I liked the variety, all the new adventures.

Now before this adventuring began, when I was still reciting pieces at Sunday school or singing "Trees" on Arbor Day or playing "Shanty Town" at a school party, I went through a phase of dedicated purity. Possibly it was because of all the church-going. Possibly because of the loving attention I got from my mother's friends—Stella McGill, Mary Harris, Ruth Shields, and Birdie Philpot. (Birdie, who had once entered a picture of me in a baby contest—and the picture won first prize.) I loved being their little darling, and I worked at it. I was polishing myself for the golden books of Heaven. I even had a checklist of good deeds. Was my homework finished? Had I smiled at my teachers? Had I been polite and helpful to old Mrs. So-and-So? Had I cleaned my teeth and said my prayers? Was there any way that I had failed to be the perfect little boy? I had a personal vision of God who, like Santa Claus, was making a list and checking it twice. I must have been insufferable.

However, after I began my tours of the bars and taverns of Danville, and the parties given by the Gibsons, the Heglers, and their friends, I became a professional child overnight. I discovered that it was possible to look good but be bad. I was the stage brat whose manners were often calculated to please the grownups, just as if I were stepping into the spotlight every minute of the day, smiling and bowing charmingly, always with face and eyes lifted to the first row of the balcony, because it's more becoming to take your bow toward the balcony than to duck your head and bow to the first few rows of the orchestra.

A lot of adulation and rich praise was now coming in, both from the evenings when I put on my white tuxedo and went off to grand Danville parties and from the evenings when I beat out "Nobody's Sweetheart Now" to the buzzed customers at the Edgewater. God's golden book in Heaven was of no further interest to me. I only had to *play* the part of the perfect little boy. I discovered I could manipulate grownups. I knew which teachers could be wrapped around my finger; I knew who was good for a nickel if I craved a Baby Ruth or a Milky Way or a pocketful of jawbreakers and licorice whips (the red ones, not the black). I became so blasé and jaded, as a professional child, that I once made a bored remark at the family dinner table to the effect that every day I was getting cuter and cuter. With this I was given a smart slap from across the table.

At the same time I became a little bit evil, a little bit mean to my contemporaries, who couldn't fight back in terms of sophistication. I became too smart, and I also became suspect to several neighborhood mothers with a quick eye for the wise child who has been around. I had been working in the pits, down there with the nitty-gritty on weekend nights. I knew more than I should have known, and I was imbued with some vague power—I was too big for my britches.

Some grownups recognized this, but others still looked upon me as a paragon. (He's getting cuter and cuter every day.) I remember once in Lincoln Park, I was aiming a broadside kick at the backside of another child, when Minnie Lee caught me. I wouldn't have taken that swing had I known she was around; I was very smooth at maintaining my image. Minnie Lee literally shook me by the collar. "You, of all children, to behave like that! It's unforgivable."

So I played up to the picture of what a flawless child should be, and the expectation of flawless behavior went on, even at home when I came back from my tour in show business. "You, who have eaten in the finest hotels! What's happened to your table manners. . . ." Or whatever.

Added to this was Our Race. To step out into the world as a representative of the Negro people and to move so freely among whites as an entertainer was a double albatross around my neck. Everyone demanded that I be immaculate in thought, word, and deed, because I had a chance that other colored children did not have. I was the emissary sent into the white camp. One Sunday, when I was about fifteen, I had a head-on encounter with Mrs. Whitted, a senior member of Allen Chapel, who met me as she was going into church for the morning service. I was leaving a Sunday School session, where I played the piano, to go home for a nap. I'd worked until three the night before and had another job lined up for that afternoon in some neighborhood honkytonk. But Mrs. Whitted would hear none of this. If I missed church, I would be letting everyone down. Bobby Short should be in there at the morning service, singing his hymns, saying his prayers, on deck when it counted, the model boy of the colored community.

"But I'm sorry, Mrs. Whitted. I've got to go home and get some sleep before I go to work this afternoon."

"You watch your step, young man." She spoke in the voice of doom. "God gave you that talent, and he can snatch it away, just like that. Snatch it away! Snatch it away!"

The town had a lot of child talent, either appearing in shows at school or really out in the local big time, performing, as I did, at the Kiwanis Club, the Elks, and so on. There were accordion players with their big satin sleeves, young singers, and lots of child dance acts, their numbers always based on routines from the movies—a big Warner Brothers musical number reduced to two people. "Shuffle Off To Buffalo" was a standard, the kids coming on dressed in bride and groom outfits to sing and do their little tap dance. And there were lots of Spanish dances, Uncle Sam dances, and top hat, black satin pants, and cane dances.

The routine was as sophisticated as the teacher. Bozo Lete and Lois Jean Connor were a team with a very smart routine.

They were devils on stage. Lots of energy and lots of style, and they were really out there doing it. An ex-hoofer named James Marlatt, who had a dance studio in town, was their teacher. If I went some place to perform, a school show, a talent show, anywhere, and Bozo and Lois were on the bill, I sharpened my edges. I couldn't afford to let down. Bozo was a good-looking, tough little blond boy, whose real name was Achille Szilagyi. Lois Jean Connor was a cousin of Donald O'Connor (the family name was originally Connor) and a cousin of Patsy O'Connor, the first child star from Danville. I don't know what happened to Patsy O'Connor. She was in a movie, it came to town, we all went to see her, and that was the end of that. Donald O'Connor appeared out of the blue. Patsy and Donald must have had a career going in the outer reaches; we didn't know them at school, because they lived in South Danville. Another good dancer in our crowd was Barbara Jean Neal, whose mother was the organist and music director at Allen Chapel.

When I was in the sixth grade, the Danville *Commercial News* sponsored an amateur contest for the entire township. Everybody entered; all of us who'd been performing in the area for years, and a few ringers, whom we viewed, of course, with disdain. Like the middle-aged white lady dressed in her Sunday best, a band around her forehead, one feather sticking up at the back of her head, and she sang "Take Me Back To The Reservation."

The paper was full of write-ups and photographs over the weeks as the contest went on and the field narrowed down. I passed from the preliminaries into the next round, and then to the next and the next, and finally we came to the run-off. I was in a special category called Advanced Talent, that in-

cluded Anne Kenner's brother Gilbert, who sang, and Lois
Jean and Bozo, who did one of their demon dance numbers.
I wound up that night with fourth prize. Mother was so out-
raged she wouldn't even let me stay to be photographed.
"Let's get out of here!" she snapped, and whisked me away.
The fourth prize was four dollars, I believe. The grand prize
was fifteen dollars, won by a girl singer and her rendition of
"Goody Goody." What was even tougher to take, she then
went to Chicago and sang "Goody Goody" over WLS, the
Prairie Farmer Station.

But a week later, none of this mattered anymore, because
I was invited to Chicago by some friends of the Gibsons to
play for a private party at the Palmer House. I was only ten,
so Mildred went with me. We spent the night with friends
of hers who had a house on the South Side that sported a
jukebox in the dining room, an odd touch that was never explained. But I fed it nickels the next morning, and we had
music with breakfast.

After that trip, I no longer considered myself an amateur.
I was now a professional; I had played at the Palmer House,
and I had been paid eight dollars for my performance, plus
traveling expenses. And when we got back to Danville on
Sunday afternoon and my mother ran down the porch to
greet me, I suddenly wanted no part of the big embrace, the
hugs and the kisses and "my baby boy." I'd had enough. I
was no longer to be treated like a child.

After that, I began barhopping with a vengeance, and it
was understood that Bobby Short was to be paid for every
appearance. No more going around just to be seen. A cup of
hot chocolate or a Coca-cola would no longer be sufficient

after an impromptu show for someone's visiting relatives or out-of-town guests.

Several colored bands came to Danville regularly to play for dances. Fess White. Fess Williams. Walter Barnes, who came so often his boys had girl friends in town. Floyd Ray, whose boys were great basketball players and would get into a game whenever they were around. Some of the name bands of the thirties also made it to Danville, or at least to some town in the area. It was nothing to drive fifty or seventy-five miles to hear them play—Benny Meroff; Ben Pollack, the drummer, who took a group on the road for a while; and Anna May Winburn, a pretty colored girl who had an all-male orchestra and endless costume changes. She was a colored version of Ina Ray Hutton, although some people still say Ina Ray was a quadroon or mulatto from the South. Who'll ever know? Who'll ever care?

Paul Blair's band was a local outfit (white), which later became Eddie Mack's orchestra. Eddie was the piano player, who took over when Paul Blair stepped down. I was their mascot from time to time, and went around with them as a featured entertainer at various parties. This was the band that played at the Harrison Pavilion dance given by Mildred's etiquette club, The Social Aristocrats.

We also had Jimmy Rachels' band. Jimmy's father was Dr. Rachels, a colored doctor who lived out in Rabbit Town in a large house with extensive grounds. And thereby hangs a footnote. When Dr. Rachels was negotiating to buy the house in the 1920's, Rabbit Town was pure white. Word got around, and a meeting was scheduled to discuss *what* should be done about the new neighbors, this colored family who were about to move in. Dr. Rachels learned of the meeting, strolled in unannounced and uninvited, introduced himself, said that he had indeed bought the property and planned to live there with his family and practice medicine. He disarmed everyone. Nothing overt was said after that, and within a few years, many of his patients were from the surrounding neighborhood.

Jimmy Rachels formed an orchestra. He changed his name to Raschel, pronounced as though it were French, and called his band "Jimmy Raschel and His New Orleans Ramblers." Arthur, his younger brother, later joined the orchestra as a saxophonist. Whenever times got too bad, the New Orleans Ramblers, who were headquartered in Detroit, took up temporary residence in Danville, most of them staying out at the Rachels' house in Rabbit Town. And while they were around, they'd play for a lot of local dances and parties. From that group came Clark Terry, an ace trumpeter and a big jazz figure today, as well as Milton Buckner, the piano player who starred for a long time with Lionel Hampton. The Ramblers didn't mind being stranded in Danville. It was a pleasant place, the people were nice, and the girls pretty enough. When the band eventually broke up, some of the boys migrated back, settled down and became hometowners.

It was almost impossible to hear jazz then as you can hear it now. There were jazz records around, true. But you couldn't buy them in most local music stores; they usually sifted into town from a big city. So we hung on the radio broadcasts from Chicago. One program starred Cleo Brown, a jazz figure of the day, who played and sang and recorded for Decca. Another Saturday-afternoon program was devoted to old jazz records. And on many evenings there were broadcasts from the Grand Terrace, a famous Chicago South Side cabaret, which featured the big colored orchestras—Earl Hines, Claude Hopkins, Duke Ellington, Jimmy Lunceford, Count Basie. The male vocalists broadcasting from Chicago included Orlando Robeson, a smooth tenor; Walter Fuller, a trumpet player who sang with Earl Hines; and Arthur Lee Simpkins, also with Hines, who later stepped out as a single performer, added a few semiclassics to his repertoire, and made quite a career for himself on the West Coast. Back in the Earl Hines days, he sang "Sylvia," always in a tenor that was almost a falsetto. Hines' theme song was "Deep Forest," written by Reginald Forsythe, also colored, who was a very stylish and sophisticated composer. "Serenade To A Wealthy Widow" was Forsythe's. He later moved to England, where he stayed for the rest of life, becoming an English gentleman in every way.

Valaida Snow was another big-timer who appeared at the Grand Terrace, singing and playing the trumpet, and it's been said that she was second only to Louis Armstrong. Fabled Valaida Snow, who traveled in an orchid-colored Mercedes-Benz, dressed in an orchid suit, her pet monkey rigged out in an orchid jacket and cap, with the chauffeur in orchid as well.

I'd heard all about Chicago's South Side from Mildred. She'd gone up there to live for a while in 1933, because she was ambitious, young, and attractive. She knew typing and shorthand and thought she might find a job there that pleased her. Mildred stayed with Mother's cousin Ruth at what was probably the most swank colored apartment house on the South Side—the Rosenwald, built by the philanthropist Rosenwald family. Cousin Ruth, in fact, so enjoyed the luxe of Chicago that she didn't like to visit Danville, because, as she once remarked, it had no conveniences.

Chicago was the center in those days for black-and-tan clubs, where Negroes and whites freely mingled, all part of the big "sin" scene. In any day-to-day situation, Chicago was sewn up tight as far as Negroes were concerned. It goes without saying that Negroes were not allowed in any of the downtown clubs or in the big hotels. Chicago's South Side, however, led the field with black-and-tan clubs like the Grand Terrace. New York's Cotton Club in Harlem, on the other hand, with all-colored entertainment and considered the boss colored nightclub in America, was restricted to whites only. But like the Cotton Club, the Grand Terrace put on shows with scores written especially for it and a line of ten to fourteen chorus girls, two orchestras, singers, comics, and dance acts. A complete hour-and-a-half revue, comparable to a Broadway show. And Mildred had been to the Grand Terrace.

Another black-and-tan club was the Club De Lisa, named for the Italian family who owned it, known for its late, late Saturday night revue, which began around four in the morning and lasted till dawn. Mildred had been to the Club De Lisa. The Cabin Inn was a notorious drag nightclub, where the performers were colored men turned out in women's clothes, with names like Joan Crawford, Jean Harlow, Carole Lombard; they put on a fantastic floor show. Mildred had been to the Cabin Inn.

The Regal Theater on the South Side, one of the Balaban and Katz chain, played vaudeville, always with the best and the biggest of the colored entertainers. Mildred had been to the Regal when McKinney's Cotton Pickers were on the bill with Claude Hopkins. And Mildred had been to the World's Fair—The Century of Progress. Mildred had gone everywhere and done everything, and I made her tell me her Chicago stories over and over again.

The white orchestras broadcasting in those days were those led by Dick Jergens, Hal Kemp, Horace Heidt, Shep Fields, Lawrence Welk, Orville Knapp. Later on, the College Inn at the Hotel Sherman broadcast colored orchestras as well. But until then, most of the music we made in Danville was strongly influenced by the big-band sound of the white orchestras and the singing styles of their vocalists. That's what we heard the most, and that's what we imitated. And we always had to be right up on all the hits of the day, the words and arrangements.

But one thirties hit, "The Object Of My Affection," sent us into shouts of laughter. The opening lyrics, "The object of my affection can change my complexion from white to rosy red," were clearly not written with us in mind. Whenever a crowd of kids was singing, we made it a game to come up with a new set of words. One version went: "The object of my affection can change my complexion from brown to inky black. . . ."

The radio at home was turned on first thing in the morning. Before Mother shook down the stove and started a fire, she would tune in one of those programs that gives the time and weather, with a couple of songs in between. When Barbara and I were little, we loved Ireene Wicker, the Singing Lady, who was on the air for Kellogg's corn flakes. And with all the ballyhoo about Ovaltine on the Orphan Annie Show, we were always asking for it, but Ovaltine cost too much money. Eddie Cantor was on the air, and Joe Penner and

101

Fred Allen and Major Bowes. I spent half my time dreaming about getting on Major Bowes' Amateur Hour. We listened to Milton Cross and his children's show every Sunday morning ("We'll have a happy landing, a happy landing. We're coast to coast on a bus. . . .") He had a passable tenor-baritone and tended toward selections like "On Wings of Song," which Mama liked to hear, and she felt he had a pleasant voice to start off a Sunday. The Southernaires, a quartet of Negro singers, came on after the Cross show, and Mama tuned in their program religiously. I have a feeling that the Southernaires, along with our lengthy prayers at Sunday breakfast and our Sunday clothes, were a definite part of our Sabbath.

XII

All of us were avid movie fans. My movie-going career began when I was very small, trailing after my sisters and brothers to a Saturday-afternoon show. Cash for such pleasures was scarce, and often we got in on the free coupons one local baking company gave away with their "lucky loaves." The same went for other pleasures, such as the pony rides in an empty lot in Vermilion Street; we occasionally won a free coupon from the bakery for this special treat. The movie theaters had their giveaways, too—free dishes with each ticket, or occasionally, a Bank Night, when you might win fifty or even a hundred dollars if you were in the theater during the drawing.

Although free movies were given each Sunday night in Lincoln Park (lots of Tarzan films), I much preferred sitting high in the balcony at the Palace or the Fischer, the only two theaters in Danville whose doors were open to Negroes at the time. Interestingly, they were the two best theaters in town. The Palace, the less elegant of the two, was done up in the art-deco style of the day. But the Fischer, next door, was very plush, very posh. It had chandeliers and deep carpeting, and in the lobby there sometimes was an elaborate exhibit along one wall—a glass window rigged to give the illusion of a huge aquarium. Inside sat a pretty girl in a mermaid costume, smiling and waving—and completely at our mercy. We'd stand in front of the tank and make faces at her and stick out our tongues.

The first show at the Fischer was always preceded by music. And the same piece, an ancient recording of "There's Danger In Your Eyes, Chérie (But I Don't Care)," was played, always at full volume, for years. Then the lights went down, the great curtains swept open, and there was Hollywood land. On weekends there might be a stage show, the curtains opening to real music from a real orchestra, and dancers, singers, comics, and jugglers. A host of wonders. Once, when I was about nine, I made it my business to go backstage and introduce myself to the M.C., a man named Monk Watson, who was traveling with the unit. I played the piano for him, and he was very kind and encouraging, and gave me a pass to see the show again the next day. I remember a lovely girl who sang "Hold My Hand." The last line was, "Say the word and make me understand . . . Hold my hand," and she walked off the stage extending her hand to the audience—and thrilled me to the heavens. By then, I was affluent enough to go to the movies almost every weekend. I'd take twenty-five cents of my earnings and spend five cents for the bus, five cents for a candy bar, ten cents for a movie ticket, and five cents for the bus home. If I bought two candy bars, I walked home. Sometimes, instead of the candy bars, I bought a bag of Karmel Korn at a shop between the Fischer and the Palace—the sweetest, most enticing smells wafting out the shop door.

We always sat in the balcony—that was a theater rule, except for Mrs. Chavis and Mrs. Frazier, the fashion plates of Danville's colored society. Ruth Chavis and Anne Frazier would wheel up in their chauffeur-driven cars, breeze into the theater in their furs and pearls and perfumes, and sit right down in the mezzanine with no further ado. And there they stayed. The two ladies were so grand, no usher dared challenge their right to sit where they wished. Meanwhile, up in the balcony, we lesser lights sometimes had the company of a Danville lady, known as Black Henrietta. I don't know the rest of her name or anything else about her. She was just Black Henrietta, and she was in love with Cesar Romero. Anytime Romero came on the screen, we always knew if Black Henrietta were there, because she'd holler, "Yeah, that's my man! That's my man! My man!" He was Black Henrietta's man.

My favorite films were the musical comedies. I immediately picked up and played the hit songs from the scores, most of which were written by Robin and Rainger or Gordon and Revel. I knew everything sung by Alice Faye, Dick Powell, Kitty Carlisle, Bing Crosby, and all his leading ladies. And the musicals with Lily Pons, Gladys Swarthout, and Grace Moore; Grace Moore singing "Minnie the Moocher" in her operatic soprano: "She sings hot. Hi-de-hi-de-hi. She sings sweet . . ." and here Miss Moore threw in a line from "Depuis Le Jour," from Louise.

One musical, however, I missed when it first came to town —Gold Diggers of 1933. We were forbidden to see it because Mother was put off by the title, probably because to her, "gold diggers" could only mean peroxided chippies and sugar daddies and fancy sin in the big city.

Ginger Rogers and Fred Astaire were shining in their musical comedies, always with a story line that involved a million dollars worth of evening clothes, penthouse apartments, and side trips to the Riviera. They were Hollywood's solution to hard times. Give the masses a glimpse of the rich, cheer them up with a peek at high living. No one was ever broke in an Astaire-Rogers film. Cole Porter's "Night and Day" survived the journey from Broadway to Hollywood and was included in *The Gay Divorcée*. The rest of Porter's score for the original show was scuttled. "Night and Day," as a matter of fact, was the only Cole Porter song we knew of out in Danville. And as for Hoagy Carmichael, so far as we knew, he too had written only one song—"Star Dust."

My other big favorites were the cowboy crowd—Hoot Gibson, Ken Maynard, Buck Jones, Hopalong Cassidy. And Thorne Smith's *Topper* series, the Marx brothers, Norma Shearer's costume pictures, Jack Oakie, Joan Blondell, Lyda Roberti, Clark Gable, all of Carole Lombard's movies. And *Frankenstein,* that was the big killer, and *Bride of Frankenstein,* with Elsa Lanchester and her electric hairdo. But of all of these, Bing Crosby was the reigning favorite in Danville. Every boy in town with any talent whatsoever tried to imitate his crooning and his whistle. Mama was fond of him, too, and spoke of him familiarly as Bing, because he was her own kind of boy, a *nice* boy, who behaved well in his movies and sang pleasantly.

We saw every Shirley Temple movie that came to town. The theater lobby would have a display of Shirley Temple dresses—copies of her wardrobe from the current film, and usually on sale at Meis Brothers' department store. Mother got one for Barbara, and I remember Barbara in her Shirley

Temple dress, her hair in Shirley Temple ringlets, singing "On the Good Ship Lollipop" at a church entertainment. There was my mother looking so proud, and there was my little sister up on the stage, skinny as a rail, looking mean as could be, and hating all of it.

I adored Mae West. She turned me inside out. I'd sit in the movie theater and watch her all day. Some girls in our crowd couldn't walk in a normal fashion after they'd seen Mae West walk. I still get a kick out of her old films. I remember phrases, whole songs, everything she did. One song I added to my repertoire when I was eleven, I first heard rendered by Miss West—"My Heart at Thy Sweet Voice" from Saint-Saëns' *Samson and Delilah*. This was in *Going to Town*, in which Miss West played a social-climbing lady who bought a tremendous house in Southampton; to prove to her high-hat neighbors that she had culture and plenty of it, she threw a soirée and entertained her guests with opera. The clincher was Mae West stepping out to sing "My Heart at Thy Sweet Voice"—in French! Marjorie Gateson, who played the ruling grande dame, was stunned (so was I), and Miss West was instantly welcomed into high society.

We were always excited by any movie that came along featuring colored players—actors such as Mantan Morland, Ben Carter, Stepin Fetchit, and Willy Best—Willy "Eats and Sleeps" Best. We'd learned to laugh at the part they played—the stereotyped shuffling Negro servant whose eyes rolled wildly when a ghost was mentioned. Eddie "Rochester" Anderson arrived in a Bing Crosby picture, and playing with him was a pretty colored girl, Edna Mae Harris. Miss Harris also appeared in *The Spirit of Youth*, a third-rate film that starred Joe Louis in a chronicle of his early years. It didn't have a wide enough appeal to play one of Danville's best theaters, but was shown for only a night or two at the Colonial, a jitney house that usually operated for whites only. That film gave me my first (and last) glimpse of the seedy interior of the Colonial.

Etta Moten, the Brown Thrush of Song, was featured in *Gold Diggers,* and one of the songs, Hollywood's tribute to the World War I veterans, was "My Forgotten Man." Busby Berkeley filled the screen with thousands of marching men, and Joan Blondell half-sang the lyrics. Then Etta Moten came on the screen to sing the song in full. She was talented, good looking, and had a marvelous walk. Someone once said, after seeing her on tour, that he hadn't cared if she sang an encore or not. All he wanted was to see her walk across that stage just once more. And there was Nina Mae McKinney, who preceded Fredi Washington and Lena Horne on the screen as the pretty colored girl who wasn't always just a housemaid. Among the colored actresses who were relegated to playing maids in every other film that came along were Ruby Dandridge, Louise Beavers, Hattie Noel, and, of course, Hattie McDaniel, who won an Academy Award for her Mammy role in *Gone With The Wind.* Ellington made several movie shorts early in the 1930's with his orchestra and such stars as Billie Holiday and Snake Hips Tucker, the dancer.

But it wasn't often that we had a chance to see a movie that dealt with colored people as anything more than servants or clowns or entertainers. A Negro film maker, Oscar Micheaux, brought several of his works to Danville. I remember one called *God's Stepchildren,* shown at Armory Hall. The title was from a line in the script, when a pretty mulatto, faced with the sticky complexities of passing for white, exclaimed: "We're not God's children. We're God's stepchildren!"

But Micheaux's movie paled next to *Imitation of Life*. Produced early in the 1940's, *Imitation of Life* was based on the 1933 Fannie Hurst novel. The book had caused a lot of talk in our community, because it dealt with a colored girl who passed for white, an audacious theme in those days. Edna Ferber had wrestled with the problem in *Show Boat* and had consigned Julie, her octoroon, to a life on the skids. Not so Miss Hurst. She let her heroine "pass," and she let her marry a white man into the bargain. The movie part was played by Fredi Washington, who was very fair-skinned and could have passed for white herself.

Fredi and her sister Isabelle had both entered show business as dancers, and both danced in a show called *Singing the Blues*. Shortly after that, Isabelle married Adam Clayton Powell. Fredi kept on with her career until the 1930's, when she married Lawrence Brown, a trombonist with Ellington's band. I saw Fredi about that time in one of Ellington's movie shorts, *Black and Tan Fantasy*. She played a dancer who collapsed on stage from an obscure but clearly fatal illness. And as beautiful Fredi lay a-dying, Ellington's orchestra gathered around the deathbed and played "Black and Tan Fantasy" for her, for the last time.

Fredi was a good actress, and in *Imitation of Life* she really strutted her stuff as the "white" daughter of Louise Beavers, an enormous, dark-skinned colored woman, who was also a fine actress. Claudette Colbert was the star lead in the film, and Rochelle Hudson played her daughter. Having read the novel when I was about thirteen and having seen the movie when I was eighteen, I have *Imitation of Life* fixed forever in my memory. The story, basically, was of the trials and tribulations of two widows, one colored, the other white, each with a child to support. To me, it's a classic example of the colored world as interpreted by whites, an interpretation intended as high drama. But seen from *our* side of the fence, it succeeds only as high comedy. *Imitation of Life* was a dilly.

As the movie opens Claudette is hard put to support her little girl. She's struggling along in her late husband's business, peddling a line of food specialties for restaurants and hotels and using his name—B. Pullman. One morning when Claudette is rushing about trying to get to work and get her daughter to school, she hears a knock at the back door, and there is the black, smiling face of Louise Beavers. Her name is Delilah, and she's looking for a job to support herself and her little girl.

"But folks jes doan seem to like ma baby. Her name is Peola." With that, she pulls Peola into view. To the astonishment of Miss Colbert and everybody in the theater, Peola, aged six or seven, is as white as Claudette's child. Miss Beavers hastens to explain that little Peola's father had been very light colored. (I imagine my black-skinned Great-grandmother Basset must have explained the presence of her fair-skinned child, my grandmother, in much the same terms.) In no time at all, Louise Beavers has worked her way into the house and into Claudette's heart.

"Ah'll make you-all some breakfas'. Doan you worry 'bout a thing, honey. I'se here to take care of you." Then she asks Claudette's name.

"My name is B. Pullman."

110

Louise Beavers decides to call her Miss B., which resolves that social impasse. In the meantime, Louise whisks up a batch of pancakes, and Claudette raves over them.

"What's the secret?"

Louise Beavers cackles and says it's an old secret her mammy taught her. "But ah'll tell ma secret to you, Miss B.," and she whispers something in Claudette's ear.

The audience never does find out what the secret is, but the two ladies are about to make their fortune with Louise Beavers' pancake recipe.

In the next big scene, Louise Beavers is living in the house with little Peola, and Claudette announces that they should open a restaurant—a pancake restaurant on the Boardwalk. (All of this takes place in Atlantic City.) They find an empty shop, clean it up, and get to work, with Louise Beavers behind the counter making pancakes. They are an overnight success and soon have more business than they can handle.

"What am I going to do?" says Claudette one day to their best customer, played by Ned Sparks, whose trademark was his sour face and nasal twang.

"Box it," says Sparks.

"What do you mean?" says Claudette.

"Box the pancakes. Make the flour. Do the whole thing."

In a flash, the ladies are in business on a grand, Quaker-Oats scale, and Louise Beavers becomes a national celebrity. She is known the country over. Her name and picture are in lights on top of the complex of buildings that house the pancake empire. The relationship between Miss Beavers and Miss Colbert continues, however, just as it was in the beginning. When Claudette comes home from a day at the factory, Louise still rubs her feet as she did in the old days and still refers to her as Miss B. They have bought an enormous house in the swank section of Atlantic City, but Louise refuses to live upstairs. She knows her place, by golly. She and little Peola have a nicely furnished apartment in the basement.

But not much thought has been given to the fact that little Peola is a colored child. She goes off to school with Claudette's daughter, and no one tumbles to the fact that Louise Beavers is her mother. God knows where the neighbors have been all this time, but Peola has already passed as white among her schoolmates. (The name Peola, incidentally, was immediately picked up by Negroes as a slang expression for a very light-skinned colored person.) The day of revelation, however, is at hand. A bad storm sweeps Atlantic City, and Louise appears at the classroom door with Peola's galoshes and raincoat. She knocks, and the teacher comes out.

"I'se brought ma little girl's galoshes and raincoat. Her pap died from bronchitis he cotched in jes' such a storm."

"But you must be mistaken," says the teacher kindly. "We have no colored children in this school."

"Oh yes, you do. Thass ma baby right ovah der."

Baby Peola, of course, is squirming away for dear life and fit to be tied.

"Yassuh, Ma'am, thass ma baby in the third row."

With that, Peola jumps up. "I hate you. I hate you!" she screams and runs out of the classroom.

And that is the first big stab in the heart of Louise Beavers, who adores her child more than life itself. She unburdens her sorrow to Claudette, who is no help at all.

Years go by. The girls are grown up, and at this point the child actresses are replaced by Fredi Washington and

Rochelle Hudson. Claudette is now coping with a suitor, played by Warren William, as an ichthyologist. (There was no ichthyologist in Miss Hurst's novel. This was a Hollywood addition that gave Louise Beavers the opportunity to offer such lines as, "Ick-thee-*what*, Miss B.? Ah sho' nevah heard no word like that befo'." And after Claudette explains that an ichthyologist is a person who studies the habits and habitats of fish, Louise Beavers mumbles "Hmph," and "Dat's too fancy fo' me," and so on.)

Peola's problems too are obviously getting bigger and bigger. She can't face the fact that she is colored but looks white. There is a scene that stands out in my memory very clearly. It's at a lovely party at the house, with an orchestra, and cocktails are being sipped. Louise Beavers, her hair marcelled, is wearing a floor-length gown. Fredi, as Peola, is as white as any guest there and wearing a dress as pretty as any dress at the party. But she is not allowed to mingle. No rule has been laid down, nothing that crude, but it was just "not done." She was colored and had to keep her place on the sidelines. Fredi, of course, admires all the comings and goings of the various attractive guests and wonders why she can't be part of it. Things reach a nasty head.

Peola turns on Delilah. "Mother, look at me. I'm white. I'm not colored, at all. I'm white, I tell you."

"Peola, doan call me Mother. I'se yo' mammy. Ah ain't no white mother. I'se yo' *mammy*."

"Oh, Mother! Stop saying that. If you don't leave me alone, I'll run away."

Which she does. Fredi bolts and cannot be found, which leaves Louise Beavers in a terrible state.

Next we see Claudette, sitting in the back seat of her

limousine, with Rochelle Hudson. In front is the driver, and beside the driver is Miss Beavers. (The film was dazzling in its bluntness.) They pull up in front of a restaurant, and there behind the cash register is Peola, smiling, making change, and saying thank you very much and come again—passing for white. Louise Beavers stands respectfully outside, while Claudette goes into the restaurant.

"Your mother is heartbroken, Peola. Won't you please come home with us?"

Fredi leaves the restaurant, mother and daughter are re-united, and there's a fortuitous fade-out before we see the seating arrangements in the limousine for the trip back.

This scene is followed by a painful conversation between Fredi and Louise.

Louise says, "I'se gwine send you South, Peola, to one of dem fancy colored schools. You won't have nothin' to be 'shamed of. They'll make you jes' as grand as anybody's baby in dis world."

But Fredi was utterly scornful. "Mother, I must tell you for the last time, I am going away. Don't come for me. If you see me in the street, don't speak to me. From this moment on, I'm white. I am not colored. You have to give me up."

At this point Hollywood rewrote Fannie Hurst's novel. In the novel, Peola goes west and works as a librarian, passes for white, and to any questions about her family, answers that she is an orphan. Lo and behold, Peola falls in love with a white boy and he with her. He proposes. She accepts. The possibility of black babies is neatly taken care of; clever Peola has quietly had herself sterilized! The young couple will be living in the wilds of Brazil, where he has been offered an engineering job. He needs Peola; not only did he lose part of a hand in World War I, but he was gassed in the trenches and his health is uncertain. Peola, Miss Hurst reasoned, was certainly entitled to *half* a white man. She would be living in a jungle, anyway, and there would be no babies. Peola may pass—let her go, and God bless her. The chapter ends with Delilah gasping, 'Black wimmin who pass, pass into damnation," as she sinks to the floor in a mountainous swoon. Several chapters later she dies.

Now in the movie version Peola runs away, and her mother goes into a deep decline.

"We'll get the finest doctors in the world for you," says Claudette.

"No, Miss B., ain't no doctor in the world gwine help me. I'm crossin' Jordan now."

And indeed, at that very moment, the Hall Johnson Choir breaks out with "Swing Low, Sweet Chariot." As the music swells, Louise Beavers says, "When ah die, Miss B., I want those colored folks' eyes to burst outta der heads. Ah doan want no gasoline at ma funeral. Ah wants to be drawn by six white horses. An' Ah wants a white hearse. Ah wants all de lodges to turn out. Ah wants de bands to play. Ah wants to meet ma Jesus in style."

Needless to say, she dies.

The next scene is the most magnificent funeral ever staged in the movies. The funeral, held in Harlem, has all the white horses and the white hearse and all the lodges turned out in costume. The streets are lined with people. Everyone is there, because headlines across the nation had announced the passing of this famous mammy, and as the cortege comes down the street, the bands play "Flee As a Bird to the Mountain," a minor dirge that is an old-time colored funeral song.

(It was always played in Danville, along with another funeral song, "Come Ye Disconsolate," and is still played in New Orleans as the brass band marches to the graveyard.)

When the church service is over and Louise Beavers' coffin is being carried out to the hearse, a little figure is seen pushing her way through the crowd. It is our Peola, distraught, crying, and carrying on. Everyone thinks she's out of her mind. Who is this white girl, sobbing and hysterical? Claudette Colbert, Warren William, and Rochelle Hudson look over and see that it is Fredi.

Fredi is screaming, "I've killed my own mother. I've killed my own mother!" She has come back, a penitent colored girl. The film closes with Claudette and Rochelle and Warren taking Fredi into their arms, into their hearts, and into the limousine. . . . *Finis.*

Fredi Washington made another film with Sally Blaine and Bill Robinson called *One Mile From Heaven.* But her career in the movies was limited because of her complexion. She was so fair that it was difficult to cast her as colored, but at the same time Hollywood was uneasy about casting her as white. I'm told they even darkened her for the movies because she photographed altogether too white to be true. A number of colored people in Danville were so sold on Fredi's performance in *Imitation of Life* that they truly believed she must have been anti-Negro to do the part of Peola so well. In reality, Fredi was one of the first in the fight for equal rights and never hid behind her white complexion.

XIII

Early in 1936 my father became ill, down in Kentucky. He had been working in a safe job at the mining company's bathhouse, much to my mother's relief, but for some reason he went underground again, and after all his years of survival in what is one of the most hazardous occupations in the world, disaster struck. He was felled by mine gas. I remember the letter he wrote to Mama from the hospital in Lynch. It began "Dear Wife," as he always addressed her, and it was written in his own hand, the precise and elegant handwriting of his generation. The letter said he was not feeling so good, that he had had some trouble in the mine. ". . . I'm getting a little weak now, and I'll write you again tomorrow."

Now, in the afternoons when school was over, a crowd of us would walk home together, talking and laughing, dropping off at our various streets or stopping for a glass of soda pop before we went home to change clothes to play or do our chores. On this spring afternoon, when I reached the corner with my little sister Barbara, who was also at Garfield School, Naomi was there waiting for us.

"Come straight home," she said. "Don't fool around another minute."

We knew something terrible had happened, because all the family was there when Barbara and I came in. Then Mother told us she'd had a wire from Kentucky saying that Papa was seriously ill and to please come at once.

Such a trip was a major effort for our family, just getting the money together, having to go to anybody you could think of to borrow train fare—a few dollars from one neighbor, a dollar from another. Mother didn't want to go alone, so she was taking Bill, who was then about sixteen, and money had to be found for two train tickets. Phone calls had to be made and telegrams sent, suitcases packed, and plans made for the children left at home—all this further complicated by the fact that our telephone was disconnected, which meant running back and forth to a neighbor's house. By evening, however, Mother and Bill were on the train to Kentucky. And, although she still didn't have enough money, we got more together after they left, and Mildred went out late that night to wire it ahead. A few hours later a second telegram arrived saying that our father had died.

"I *knew* Papa was dead," Mildred told us. "I saw a falling star when I went out to send the money." It was a long and sad night for all of us at home.

There was no way of getting in touch with Mama, and when she did at last hear about Father's death it was from a stranger in a taxicab. Mother and Bill arrived at the railroad stop nearest the little town of Lynch, and from there they were driven by taxi. Some colored people who were going in the same direction were riding in the taxi, too. One of the ladies fell into conversation with my mother.

118

"Where are you going, may I ask? Are you here for a visit?"

"I'm going to Lynch," said Mama.

"Why, how nice. I have many friends in Lynch." And she gave Mama her name.

"My name is Short," Mama replied.

"Oh, really?" said the lady. "You aren't related, by any chance, to the Mr. Short who died yesterday, are you?"

Mother arrived in Lynch in complete distress and despair. All that kept her together after that was her determination to see that Father was treated properly and gotten out of Kentucky as fast as she could get him out.

Now my mother, like so many women of southern background, believed in the powers of prediction, but she was afraid of fortune tellers. She would not have her fortune told, either by the cards or by tea leaves or by having her palm read. She did not approve of anybody who dealt in that sort of thing. Nonetheless, Mama had lots of dreams, and her dreams were predictions. She told us later that the night before my father's wake she had had a mysterious dream, in which she had seen nothing but snakes. (I suspect that my mother didn't like anybody or anything in Kentucky. She may have been born there, but she'd grown up in Illinois, and she didn't like the whole idea of Kentucky and the Dixieland way of life. Also, I know she wasn't fond of my Uncle John Will and his wife.) The trip must have filled her with foreboding, to begin with. And so she dreamed about snakes.

But one of the snakes in Mama's dream had a great head with an elaborate sort of headdress, and as she told us the story later, many many times over (Mama loved this story): "The next night at your father's wake, I came down to join

119

the ladies and gentlemen who had come over to pay their respects. And there, in that very room, sat a woman with a headdress exactly like the snake in my dream. She did not speak to me. I did not speak to her. No one had to tell me a thing. I knew, without a word being said, who that woman was and where she fit into your father's life."

It was bound to have happened. Father was away from home for a long time. My brother told me later that while they were in Kentucky, he had done his best to hide from Mama any evidence about my father's personal life down there, anything at all that would have upset her. But she knew. And yet she didn't know and didn't *want* to know the details of Papa's life away from home.

Back home, the Allen girls from next door, lovely, well-brought-up girls, had come over and cleaned the house and done everything that had to be done before Mother got back and before the relatives began to arrive. This was the way, among neighbors, in time of death. Earlier, when the Allen girls' mother had died, and several years later, when their father died, the neighbors went to them, in turn, and took over the cares and chores of the household.

All the uncles and aunts and cousins came to the funeral, from both sides of the family. In those few days, I saw more food being prepared and eaten than I had ever seen before in my life. For the wake, there was a feast of baked ham, roast chicken, casseroles of macaroni and cheese, scalloped potatoes, and dishes of every sort, all to feed the mourners who came to the house that night and stayed, as was the custom, till dawn. But there was no drinking, Mama would not allow drinking. Every morning enormous frying pans of scrambled eggs and great pots of coffee were on the stove, and rashers of bacon and sausages and hot biscuits. And dinner was again some enormous amount of food.

This was the one and only time I saw my Grandfather Short, a tiny black man who arrived with plans for my brothers and me. We were to be trained in good, honest, old-time country trades—blacksmithing, horse-doctoring, and so on. I only remember his plans for us—I wish I could remember our reactions. When he died a few years later, his third wife, our stepgrandmother, wanted to send us his razors as a sentimental legacy from grandfather to grandsons. This, too, was an old-fashioned country tradition. But we were sophisticated city boys by then. We weren't interested in any of that and refused the bequest. I imagine they were rather special, or she wouldn't have made the offer—hollow-ground steel straight razors with engraved or ivory handles and set into a fitted, plush-lined case. I'd like to have them now as a memento; my grandfather's razors.

Papa was laid out in the front room for two days, the coffin open, surrounded with flowers and wreaths. I remember when the Gibsons came to pay their respects, they brought a big cake and offered their cars for the funeral. During these two days I was forbidden to go in to the front room and play the piano, but when the grown-ups were away from the house, if only for a few minutes, I would steal in and quietly play songs I had learned at school and at church, songs I felt were suitable. But in truth, I was not playing for my father, I was playing for my own pleasure. I hadn't known Father well. At first he had come home twice a year, then once a year, and finally he had come home in a box. The grief I felt (and the grief my little sister felt) was a reflected emotion; Barbara and I wept because the others wept.

But my clearest recollection of the funeral was the concern shown for Mama by her sister, my Aunt Rosie. Their family had always been close, and I saw this clearly and touchingly at the service, and understood it for the first time just in the way Aunt Rosie said Mama's name and the way she took her hand.

After the service, we got into the limousines and cars, and the funeral cortege drove out to the cemetery. Mama, a great planner in anticipation of death, had long before bought a plot at the Atherton cemetery, where both colored and white were buried. When Father's funeral procession arrived there was a macabre moment when Mama, who had collapsed at the end of the service, rallied long enough to realize that the grave dug for Papa was not in the Short plot. There was nothing for it but to turn the long line of cars and drive back into town. The next morning the cemetery people phoned, with abject apologies. The grave was now ready in the correct plot. This time the family drove out alone and watched as Father's coffin was lowered into the ground. Mother had never called my father Rodman. She always called him "Short," modifying the old-fashioned custom of formal address between husband and wife, which would have been "Mrs. Short" and "Mr. Short." Mother had just abbreviated this to "Short." It was the last thing she said when he was put in the ground. A few flowers were thrown onto the coffin, and my mother whimpered his name, "Oh, Short, Short."

Aunt Nancy, Father's younger sister, had come down to the funeral from Detroit. She and my mother were the chief mourners, like twins in their black mourning clothes and long black veils. After the burial, Aunt Nancy stayed on in Danville for a while, accompanying my mother to and from the

122

bank and other offices where necessary business was being transacted. They made an odd pair, both draped to the ground in black and wearing veils, on the streetcars and up and down the main streets of town. Mama's spring coat, a black number with a small fur collar, was stripped of the fur at once, leaving it a perfect base for her weeds.

I'm not ambivalent in my feelings about my father. As I remember him, not having known him really well at all, I admire him a great deal. I admire the kind of person he made of himself. I don't know what went on inside his head, so I cannot make an objective judgment. But it seemed to me that my father did what he had to do to preserve his self-dignity and take care of his family in the best way he knew how. Reg's feelings *are* ambivalent. He knew my father better than I did, because he was older, lived with him longer than I, and felt his affection. Father cut Reg's hair, often dressed him, and took him to school. But Reg felt that Father did us a bad turn. My older brother Bill had the most benefit of Father's presence, yet he was often an angry and difficult young man, fighting it out against God-knows-what demons. Our oldest sister, Naomi, was totally devoted to my father and profoundly affected by his death. She was perhaps closer to him than the rest of us were ever privileged to be, because she was the first born and had been given trips to Kentucky to visit Father and Grandfather Short and Great-grandmother Basset. The family and family ties were very dear to Naomi's heart. Mildred was fond of Father, because he'd been attentive to her even though he was away from home. She used to send him crossword puzzles in the mail, and he would correct them and send them back. He wrote speeches for her and sent her books to read. He helped her with her studies as much as he could. So Mildred's feelings about him were just fine.

But Barbara and I, being almost a separate family altogether, had none of these benefits at all. In the past, his name had been brought up too many times as a threat. If we behaved badly, Mother would always say, "When your father gets here, he'll take care of you for doing that. Just wait. He'll straighten you out." And one day I had answered this by saying, "He's not my father. Mr. Gibson is my father." And that was another time I got a smart slap from across the table.

One thing, however, I've never forgotten. The number of my father's post-office box in Lynch, Kentucky. It was box 573.

XIV

Mother was always deep in insurance, and she liked to do business with Metropolitan Life. The local agent was a thin, quiet man of German descent, Mr. Roth, who came around to collect the premiums. I remember a couple of times he bought magazine subscriptions from Reg, so we'd have money to pay the month's bill for Mama's policies. Then, just to prove she wasn't prejudiced, Mama took out a policy on me with a Negro firm in town. But all this insurance was not a matter of getting big money at the death of a loved one; it was to assure that funeral and burial expenses could be met. Getting a loved one into the ground has always been a concern with the poor, and a few pennies weekly on an insurance policy was a practical way to make sure there would be no panic or embarrassment when the time came.

My father, as the head of a household, was insured with Metropolitan Life for $5,000, a hefty sum of money in 1936. Even now this sum surprises people, because it was commonly believed in those days that no large insurance company would issue a policy for that amount to a Negro, particularly a coal miner. And many Negro-owned insurance companies capitalized on the general belief that white firms would not insure Negroes.

Also, at the time of Father's death, we thought that the mining company in Kentucky would pay us from the fund they had for just such accidents. But Mother had no legal assistance and was unable to make any headway with Father's employers. Although he had died because of conditions in their mine, that was of no further concern to them. Metropolitan, however, came through according to contract, and the first bill Mother paid was the undertaker's. She next cleared a remaining bill for my sister Ruth, who had died nine years earlier, and settled a few small debts that had gathered here and there.

For a while, Mother was terribly distraught about my father's death, and then she got herself together and set about her banking business, still dressed in deep mourning with black veils down across her face. She opened a checking account, which was an entirely new venture in her life. She made a sizable down payment on a new house at 627 North Oak Street, signed on for a mortgage, bought new furniture, some clothes, a fur coat, and had her teeth fixed. The house was in a North End neighborhood that was white except for two other colored families on the block. Mother bought it from a man named Eli Brown, a fairly successful Danville Negro, who had moved to California but kept the Oak Street property to rent out. He had been a friend of my father's, and Mother felt that buying a house from Eli Brown was a good idea, because she always put stock in old friends, old customs, old ties.

The house was not grand, but Mother was always very proud of it, and she wore that house like a Paris hat. She loved telling about the day she was cleaning and polishing her beautiful new house, an apron around her waist and a cloth around her head, when a salesman who came to the door mistook her for a maid. "May I speak to the lady of the house, please," said he. Mother, with great hauteur, whisked the dustcloth off her head and showed her waves and replied, "*I* am the lady of the house."

There was a nice green lawn, a big front porch, and inside, the usual complement of rooms, with the extra touches of a small library off the dining room and a staircase that curved upward from a landing—a pretty fancy-looking affair. In the backyard was a small building intended as a laundry and at the far end of the property was an old carriage barn. I remember an elderly colored man who lived in our laundry house for a while. He'd taken to the road, as so many men did during the Depression, on the way from no place to no place, and persuaded Mother to let him stay there until he could gather his forces to move on. Once he came to the kitchen door with a beef kidney and asked Mother to cook it for him. Mother had no idea how to cook a kidney, so he gave her his recipe—boil with salt and onions—which she did, and he took it away for his dinner.

Mother's garden, her vegetables and flowers, was planted as soon as we moved in. Morning glories covered the screen on the back porch, and there were zinnias, hollyhocks, roses, dahlias, peonies, snapdragons, marigolds, nasturtiums, sweet peas, and ragged robins, Mama's name for bachelor buttons. Barbara once won a flower-arranging contest at grade school with a bouquet of Mother's marigolds in a green vase.

It is now the summer of 1936. We have buried my father.

127

We have moved into the new house, and we have a mortgage to pay. Mildred had found a good secretarial job with the Vermilion County Emergency Relief Corps, an enviable position for a young colored woman in Danville who hadn't gone to college. With her salary, we always had the money when the mortgage came round. Bill and Reg had odd jobs after school, and Mother was out working in service. When she put on her hat and left the house, Naomi was there to take over. Barbara, of course, was still too little to have any kind of job, but she was getting straight "A's" at school, which was her job of the moment; Barbara, my skinny little sister, with her pretty heart-shaped face and wide eyes, who hated to have her hair done in the morning. "Barbara Louise, stand still!" And Barbara would go through conniptions, while Mother combed and brushed and braided her hair.

I was out working every chance I got and bringing home my share of household expense money. By the time we moved to Oak Street, I'd become established in Danville; everybody knew who Bobby Short was. One day I discovered, to my astonishment, that I could even get credit. I'd gone down to the Goodrich Appliance Tire Store, which sold Goodrich bikes, and said I'd give them a down payment if they'd hold the bike for me. No, they said, take it home. That's all right. Pay us by the week or pay us by the month. So, I now had a beautiful new bike of my own, the bike Leona Rouse mentioned in my yearbook inscription in 1942.

On the nights when I didn't have an engagement at a private party, a roadhouse, or whatever, I was still being taken from bar to bar by various Danville men. Lord knows I wanted to earn the extra money, and now it occurs to me that maybe they did too. I always came home with a couple of dollars, but certainly they must have taken some share of the collection that we picked up in our tours. They were the ones, after all, who steered me around town and got me to the piano wherever we walked in off the street. This was something I couldn't have done by myself, as a small boy—wander in and out of bars, singing and playing. But money was never discussed. I took what they gave me at the end of a night's outing, brought it home, and no questions were asked.

That summer the American Legion held a convention in Danville. The town turned itself wide open, and people made money hand over fist. The hotels were filled, the restaurants and cafés were filled, and people were renting out bedrooms to the Legionnaires. It was hoopla for the better part of a week, with all sorts of noisy pranks and tricks played on the local public—palm buzzers, whoopee walking sticks, toilet paper streaming out of hotel windows, water bombs dropped on passersby below. And parades every day. They always started out in orderly enough fashion with the mayor, city and state officials, Legion bigwigs, and Gold Star mothers—and models of French railways cars, the "Forty and Eight" that held forty horses and eight men. Bands played. Flags flew. But as the long files of Legionnaires marched down the street, the parade disintegrated into a procession of disorderly drunks, out of step, out of line, and out of control, ricocheting from curb to curb.

And late at night, there'd be spontaneous parades: hundreds of World War I vets marching through Danville, howling and staggering, a surprising number dressed in ragtag bits of female attire, brassieres, wigs, corsets, some of them waving boxes of sanitary napkins at whatever crowd was gathered to watch. These men, all of them heading into middle age, many of them broke and disillusioned, were just raising hell in someone else's town. The bonus had not yet come through, and the bonus marchers had been routed out of Washington. For most of the veterans, those two years in France had been the only free-wheeling excitement of their lives. It was convention time, and if you can't have the glamor of another country, you can always stir it up a little bit in Danville, Illinois, and try to recapture the bad old days. And there was plenty of sin available; the convention was a field day for the sporting element. Whores and gamblers moved into town to get their pickings, the bartenders were cleaning up. Everyone was into the Legion's pocket.

And night after night, I was out in the midst of all this, taken from bar to bar by a man named Porter Hudson, who looked more Mexican than Negro. Besides the established bars in town, a lot of impromptu ones had been set up for the quenchless veterans. These were called dugouts, a nostalgic nod to the dirty days in the trenches. Several dugouts had been improvised in the Hotel Wolford. One in the ballroom provided professional entertainment along with the ceaseless flow of liquor. Among the professional out-of-town talent was a young man who sang, named Leonard Rosen, who looked like a short version of Dick Powell. Porter managed to battle me up to the piano, and I played and sang, while Porter passed the hat. Afterward, the young singer asked me my name and exclaimed over my performance. I thanked him very much, and Porter and I pressed on. Before the night was over, I was sitting up on an old steam-driven circus calliope out on the street, and I was playing and singing all my songs in the middle of a swarming, careening

130

crowd of Legionnaires and all the others who were downtown on a drunk. I felt enormously professional. For all in-
tents and purposes, I was in show business. When I went
home that night, I was ready and waiting for a call from
Warner Brothers or Twentieth Century or M-G-M. I would
be right there when the phone rang, with Mr. Goldwyn on
the line saying, "Bobby, we need you out here."

ON THE ROAD

ON THE ROAD

XV

The next morning was one of those innocent summer days. It was July, and there's nothing to beat a July morning. School is out, and you have nothing to think about but what you're going to do that day—play ball, go to the woods, have a picnic, ride your bike. And we were living in the new house, which made us all happy.

At about ten o'clock a young man came to the door with another man. "My name is Leonard Rosen," he said. "I heard you sing last night at the Hotel Wolford." Of course, I recognized him immediately. "I was very impressed with your performance, and we wanted to talk to you and your mother about taking you to Chicago."

Well, I was all ears—as high as a jackass' ears. He introduced me to his friend, who was quite swarthy and much taller. This was Julius Jay Levin, or "Bookie" Levin, as everyone called him, the agent from Joliet who'd booked Len Rosen into Danville for the Legion convention. I explained that my mother wasn't home; she was at work. Mother was then doing a half day for a maiden lady on Vermilion Street, so I put on a clean shirt, and we drove over to see her. While

I stood there, agawk at their sales pitch, the two men told Mother how talented her son was, what a promising future he had, and, Mrs. Short, think of the money he could be sending home! Len, it seems, had been so excited when he heard me play and sing that he'd called Bookie Levin that same night. Bookie had got into his gray '36 Chevy and driven right down to Danville. I could see that Mother was interested. But she told the men this would take some thought, that she would be back at the house about five o'clock, and if they would come over for dinner, we could discuss it further.

The men were staying at the Wolford, and I went back there with them for the rest of the day. And when I wasn't showing off, talking and playing the piano for Mr. Levin, they took me to the drugstore for chicken-salad sandwiches, chocolate malts, ice cream, and candy bars.

Late in the afternoon we went back to the house. All the family was there, and the men mapped out the plans for my mother. We'll take him to Joliet and Chicago for a few weeks, and we'll see what we can do. If Bobby doesn't like it, if *you* don't like it, he can come right back here to Danville in time for school and forget the whole thing. There were quite a few successful, young colored performers around at the time: Buck and Bubbles; Chuck and Chuckles; and the Nicholas Brothers, Harold and Fayard Nicholas, a dance team that starred at the Cotton Club, in the movies, and on all the big bills, and who were later listed by Langston Hughes in his Golden Dozen of Negro dancers. My two benefactors had equally grandiose plans for me—nightclubs, radio, movie contracts, the top vaudeville houses.

I could see that Mother was questioning herself and look-

136

ing to *me* for some sort of decision. (I was eleven going on twelve.)

"Do you want to go?" she asked.

Of course, I wanted to go. I wanted to go anywhere.

"All right, you can go."

After dinner, Mother packed a suitcase for me, gave me some money and a big kiss. "Now, you be careful. You can take care of yourself, I know that. . . ." Then all her midwestern, Protestant attitudes came to the fore, and she said. "But don't forget. These men are Jews."

We drove directly to Joliet. I remember stopping at the Woodruff Hotel, where Bookie had some business to attend to. Len and I waited in the lobby. Two elderly ladies, summer visitors with crimped white hair and print dimity dresses, noticed us.

"What a cute little boy," one of them said. "Do you live in Joliet?"

"I'm going to work in Joliet, ma'am. I play the piano and sing."

"How sweet. He plays the piano and sings. Would you play a piece for us?"

Why, yes, I would be delighted to play a piece. Now, my taste in songs didn't have a thing to do with my age. I sang anything. "Sophisticated Lady" for one, not having any idea at all what I was singing about—deep, chic lyrics about disillusion in your eyes and I see you now, smoking, drinking, never thinking of tomorrow, but "nobody is nigh, you cry." So I went into the cocktail lounge with the two white ladies, and I don't know what they expected to hear, but what they got was "Love is like a cigarette . . . You held my heart aglow between your fingertips . . . I never felt the thrill of love until

I touched your lips." And thus it went on about love burning down to ashes of regret, and being flipped aside like an old cigarette. Whatever they thought of the song, they clapped politely and oohed and ahed, and I was very pleased with myself.

In Joliet I stayed at first in Len's apartment, where he lived with his family. I was given his bedroom, and Len slept on the couch. The Rosens were delighted to have this little boy—the *Schwartz-Wunderkind*—who played the piano and sang and would make lots of money for everyone. Mrs. Rosen, a widow, who'd been the daughter of a rabbi and still spoke in a deep, old-country accent, was thrilled at her son's being in show business and having found me in Danville. And no exception was ever made about my being part of the family. One sister, Etta, was married to a man who owned an auto-mobile-accessory store. Another sister, Bernice, was still single and living at home, and a brother, Dave, was keen on boxing and athletics and worked, I think, for the city.

But it was crowded at the Rosens' apartment, so I was moved over to the Levins' house—quite a large and grand house, Bookie's father having been a highly successful to-bacco importer. Mrs. Levin, Bookie's stepmother, was as kind to me as Mrs. Rosen had been, and I was given Bookie's old room. He had moved out years before and now lived at the Louis Joliet Hotel in a single that also served as his office. Julius Jay Levin, with the accent on the second syllable, was the prototype for what a show-business agent is supposed to be—hands in motion all the time, nervous, abrupt, with an impatient manner—and he called me "the kid." It was always "the kid," as though we were working our way through the script of a B picture. "So, how's the kid? How'd the kid do?"

Bookie was still a small-time agent, whose business was limited to cities and towns around Illinois—St. Charles, Aurora, Joliet, Springfield, Danville, and so forth. But not Chicago, he was not yet in the Chicago league. The bookings he handled were largely cocktail-lounge entertainment, small groups of musicians, piano players, girl singers, and what were known in those days as "strollers"—musicians who played portable instruments, accordion or guitar. That was his business. And with his experience he was going to promote his new find, Bobby Short.

For starters, they had a suit of white tails made for me in Chicago. Then we got to work sorting out the material I had. What was suitable and how would it be presented? What kind of act would it be? How long would the act last? What new songs should I learn? We spent a number of weeks polishing our material, so I could sit down for an audition and offer a finished routine.

My first song, an "up" song, "It's A Sin To Tell A Lie" was the opener for a long time. Next, a ballad. Next, "My Heart At Thy Sweet Voice," Mae West's *Samson and Delilah* aria that had bowled me over in the movies. I'd play it through classically, and then I would call to the audience: "Shall I swing it?" But we found that the audience didn't always respond to this. So we changed it. Instead of asking them, I now told them: *"I'm going to swing it!"* And I'd go into a hot version of the song, with the orchestra behind me. "Rhythm in My Nursery Rhymes" was often part of my act—and "Rainbow on the River" or "Rosalie" or "Shoe Shine Boy," perfect for me because of the imagery. Len and Bookie were always on the lookout for new material, something appropriate for a child—songs about rhythm or swing, or a little love song

139

that didn't sound like midnight at the Club Zombi. "Sophisti-cated Lady" and "Love Is Like a Cigarette" were dropped from the repertoire. All of this was put to the test at the Louis Joliet Hotel, where Bookie was the house agent. I sat in with various groups appearing there, and I also went around with Bookie to neighboring towns to put in an appearance with his other units.

Much of the time I was singing in the wrong key for the pitch of my voice, but my piano playing had not reached the point that I was able to transpose. So I would cheat, singing above my range, which made a much more interesting sound. It's brighter and clearer to sing above one's range rather than below it, naturally. But the result was a continuing round of sore throats and laryngitis and doctors' visits. One doctor, baffled by a sore throat that wouldn't clear up, came to the medieval conclusion that it must be caused by excessive masturbation, which would drain away a growing boy's energy and cause him to fall ill. You could go blind. You could lose your mind. So I was given a brisk rundown on the facts of life. All well and good, mighty interesting to a twelve-year-old. But I still suffered from sore throats and laryngitis. A singing teacher or voice coach would have known immediately what was wrong.

Child labor laws were loose and relaxed. We had no prob-lem about my performing at night in a cocktail lounge or bar. Len was present at every performance I gave, as close to me as he could without being on stage. He stood in the wings with a big grin on his face, telling me to sell it—and to smile. "Sell it! Sell it! Sell it! Smile! Smile!" When I came off, he'd be right there directing my bows and my encores, keeping everything going. He was intensely involved—I was *his* discovery. Len was no mere shadow on Bookie's trail; he knew the ropes and was out there pushing.

Little by little, I began to pick up the rudiments of performing professionally, and I made new friends—other entertainers in Bookie's stable who took me under their wing and were very protective about me. Eddie Fritz, an accordionist who headed one of Bookie's units; Marjorie Coles, who sang with Lee Bennett's orchestra; and Lee Bennett himself, who'd earlier been a vocalist with Jan Garber's orchestra. All were very kind to me.

Joliet was large enough and close enough to Chicago to have week-long vaudeville bills with big stars. George White's Scandals came through that summer, with Helen Morgan and George Dewey Washington, a colored man with a fine voice, who sang "Brother, Can You Spare a Dime?" Helen Morgan was going through her number then, appearing some nights, but on others they'd play the overture nine times and she still wouldn't be up on that piano. She was backstage, half seas over and sailing into the wind. Then Olsen and Johnson came through town to play a big vaudeville date—complete monkeyshining, wild and crazy buffoons. I didn't know who Olsen and Johnson were, at the time; but when they went out to Statesville, the penitentiary outside Joliet, to put on a show for the prisoners, Bookie got me on the bill.

The Olsen and Johnson unit included the Peters Sisters— three enormously fat colored girls who sang and danced. Fat! One of them alone would have been startling enough, but such a trio, and really quite pretty despite their size, was a sight to behold. Their act opened with the first girl coming out on stage and saying, "I can't sing until my little sister is

141

here." Then the second girl appeared, heftier than the first, and said, "*I* can't sing until *my* little sister is here." And then the third girl appeared, the heftiest of them all. The men at Statesville, thousands of them, in their prison uniforms, roared and whistled and stamped and applauded. The Peters Sisters eventually wound up in Paris—"3 *Faibles Femmes*"— the three fat Peters Sisters, dressed in aviatrix costumes and lowered to the Folies Bergère stage, strapped to balloons.

Getting me into a vaudeville house or a bona fide night-club was a big step for Bookie Levin in those days. He hit his stride later, in the 1940's, with Lord Buckley, a stand-up comic who was the Lenny Bruce of his day. Bookie then got into an office with two or three other important agents and handled a number of top orchestras. But back in 1936, when Bookie's business was small potatoes, he had to contact other agents—the Chicago agents, Jack Malcheim, James O'Malley, Doris Hertig. And Leo Sulkan, always referred to in unsavory terms, one of the many crooked agents who existed before AGVA and other unions were organized to protect the per-former.

We spent a great deal of time in Chicago, day after day after day, back and forth from Joliet, talking to agents and hanging around the Wood Building in downtown Chicago, which, like the Brill Building on Broadway, housed every major music-publishing firm. Widmark, Chappell, Craw-ford, Harms, Irving Berlin all had offices there, and each office had at least one piano, sometimes two or three. All the singers came down to hear the newly published material. I was around those offices from morning to night, picking up new songs, meeting people, playing the piano, talking to publishers, trying to impress the right people and get the

142

right jobs. Two of my best friends in Chicago were Irwin Burke and Hy Cantor, at Chappell. They were both young, working hard to get ahead, and trying to get me a few breaks along the way. It was at the Chappell office that we saw a new song that had been written by Anna Sousenko for her protégé, Hildegarde—"Darling, *Je Vous Aime Beaucoup*," which we added to my repertoire. It was a nice touch, a colored child singing in French.

XVI

At the end of the summer we went down to Danville. After being away so many weeks, I was homesick. But I told my mother that I still wanted to go back with these men and become a star. We drew up a contract—I was then nearly twelve—a nine-year contract to last until I was twenty-one. My sister Mildred wrote it out in longhand, and in Joliet a lawyer looked it over, had it typed, and sent out copies to be signed all around.

Bookie and Len worked together to arrange my jobs, but Len took care of me. I was his responsibility. He saw to it that I was clothed and fed, that I had haircuts, that my laundry was done, that there was a place for me to stay when we were on the road, and this wasn't always easy. As the late Bert Williams once said, "It's no disgrace to be a Negro, but it can be very inconvenient."

Up to that time, we hadn't sent any money home. Now we were prepared to tackle Chicago: I had my white tail suit, I had my repertoire down cold, and we would get my career rolling. But first we had to do something about my schooling, and we had to find a place for me to live in Chicago. We

144

couldn't all live there, Bookie and Len weren't able to afford that. So we looked around a small colored neighborhood just off Roosevelt Road, the route we'd driven day after day into Chicago from Joliet. I believe an uncle of Len's, a doctor who had his office in that part of town, suggested this neighborhood. It could be called the West Side. It wasn't the South Side, the big colored area in Chicago, and God knows it wasn't glamorous. It was my first glimpse of the tenement life Mother had always dreaded. When she'd talked about how bad it could be to live in Chicago, this was what she'd meant—close quarters, no place to play but the streets, third-rate schools.

Originally Jewish people and other middle European immigrants had lived there, and many still were. But as these groups made it and moved on, the Negroes moved in—the next rising minority on the ladder. It was now a predominantly Negro community, a ghetto of sorts, but the people who lived there were hard working. This was no part of the South Side slums, with their overwhelming, abject poverty and catch-as-catch-can living in rotten, rotting surroundings.

We checked the public schools in the area and discovered that the school officials were not going to look kindly on a little boy who would be absent for as long as a week at a time. They didn't care that I was a half-year ahead of my class. They simply said they would not tolerate a child who was absent for reasons other than illness—which made sense, I guess. Then someone suggested we try a Catholic school. They were private; we'd pay tuition, and the nuns might look more favorably on my professional commitment. In the search, we found St. Joseph's School, which had been founded as a mission and school for the colored children of that area. St. Joseph's was staffed by the Sisters of Nazareth, most of whom seemed to have Polish or Lithuanian backgrounds.

We had a long talk with the Mother Superior, who was charmed instantly. But I felt she was persuaded partly by the sheer brass of my two representatives. Not only did they ask that I be given time off whenever professional engagements came along, but they also wanted me to start in the eighth grade, not the last half of the seventh, and to graduate in June. To this, the Mother Superior said, "We'll see. It depends. If he can keep up, he can graduate. But I can make no promises on that score." So I started in the eighth grade, and I made up my work, despite being out of school for a week sometimes and doing extra jobs at night. My tuition was paid on time, which kept me on the good side, and my agents were always thoughtful about donations. At Christmas time, for instance, they brought fifty pounds of hard candy to school.

The nuns even found a place for me to live. They told us about a colored family in the neighborhood whose son was a year behind me in school. Their name was Schanette, they were born Catholics, and they came from Louisiana. Perhaps they'd take me in for five or ten dollars a week. We went right over, spent an hour or so, and it was all taken care of. I moved into the Schanettes' apartment. Every morning Joseph and I were fed and packed off to school together. On mornings when Mrs. Schanette had to be at work early, we'd fix ourselves hot cereal and a pot of hot chocolate. The Schanettes took me unto themselves as though I were their own child.

At St. Joseph's we had catechism every morning; catechism

was part of the curriculum. I went through all the rituals and learned all the dogma. I went to Benediction each day and very often to Mass on Sundays. The nuns, I knew, wanted me to turn Catholic; they hankered after every nonbeliever, because that's what it's all about. I was a nice child in their midst; so why shouldn't I be confirmed and be an altar boy and all the rest of it?

Our religious backgrounds were thoroughly checked out. How many children in this class were born Catholic? How many are converted Catholics? How many belong to other faiths? It was like the revival meetings back home: "How many have been saved? Brothers and Sisters, raise your hands if you've been saved." And if you hadn't been saved, you'd better get busy and sign up, right on the dotted line. But I remained loyal to the Methodist Episcopal Church, and my mother didn't seem to worry about me, despite warnings from her friends that I was in the clutches of Rome and would be lost to Allen Chapel at any moment. Had I converted, I think Mother might have offered a few words of protest, but after the initial surprise and chagrin, she wouldn't have minded for more than a day. Meanwhile, as a child, I was captivated by the music, the clothes, the adventure of it.

Looking back, I realize how impoverished the neighborhood was and how much the nuns tried to help. There was a bakery two or three miles away from school. One afternoon I was sent with another boy to pick up several cartons of day-old nickel pies to be distributed among the poor children. And the nuns knew of a shoe outlet on Roosevelt Road where we could go with a slip from St. Joseph's and get a decent pair of shoes for half price. And we could also earn coupons for running errands and doing helpful chores. These coupons were called "clavers," in honor of Peter Claver, the patron saint of slaves—a Jesuit who worked as a doctor among the African slaves in South America in the early 1600's. Every now and then the Knights of Peter Claver would sponsor a party and a sale at St. Joseph's, and you could buy things with your coupons—rosaries, small cases with miniature statues of saints, medals, candlesticks, crucifixes, chains with a little decoration. Always religious objects. At night bingo parties were often held to raise money, and often the children put on skits or musical revues. I always took part, and I played for dances, too.

All the nuns were nice. Some were stern, but none was mean. I doubt that many boys and girls at St. Joseph's left without feeling the kindness and concern of these dedicated women, the Sisters of Nazareth. Our classroom teacher in the eighth grade, Sister Presipia, had been transferred to St. Joseph's from a school in a different part of town. She was in her forties, I'd guess, a quiet, sweet lady, and I'm sure we were her first all-colored class. And a colored class from a semi-slum, at that. (I've no idea how some of the students paid their tuition—probably it was never paid, because St. Joseph's was first and foremost a mission.)

Sister Presipia was fascinated that I was an orphan.

"Your father is dead, Bobby?"

"Yes, Sister."

"Oh, my dear child. Then you're a little orphan."

"But, Sister, I'm not an orphan. My mother isn't dead."

"Well, you're half an orphan. . . ."

And in our eighth-grade catechism, when Sister Presipia was discussing the doctrine of the Virgin Birth, it wasn't unusual for one of the girls (who was possibly fourteen or fifteen, and a woman in every way) to say, "What you mean, Sister? A virgin birth! Aw, c'mon. . . ."

"Now, Juanita. I'm sure you think Mary was a bad girl. But Mary wasn't a bad girl at all. Jesus was the son of God."

"Hunh! I'll never believe *that* story, Sister!"

Now, Sister Serafin was a strong sister who put up with no nonsense whatsoever. Nor did Sister Eugene or Mother Superior. But Presipia, a pink-and-white and naive woman, was not equipped to deal with children who would take advantage at the least chance, the girls slouching in the back of the room with their coats on—often their mothers' old coats with shabby fur collars. And they'd come back from noon hour with half their lunch, a pickle or a hot dog or a candy bar, still eating and carrying on. If Sister Presipia asked them to stop eating in the classroom, they wouldn't stop. If she asked them to be quiet, they couldn't be quiet. If she asked them to take off their coats and hang them up, they wouldn't obey. They vexed her beyond thinking. They harassed and goaded Presipia with dozens of little crudities and rude ways. Often Presipia would get so upset at her unmanageable students, that she just sat there and cried. One day, when she'd been weeping at her desk, she suddenly got up and shouted, "I don't care what you do. I don't care what you do. You're nothing but a bunch of little snot-nosed niggers!" And she fled the classroom.

I also remember a young lady named Ronnie, from the local diocese, who volunteered to come to St. Joseph's and take us through modern dance, a Martha Graham type of movement. But it wasn't just a question of the boys resisting modern dance; everybody resisted. Nothing could have been done, short of horsewhipping the class into order. "Oh, damn all of you!" said Ronnie one day, and left.

As for the schoolwork, it was easy. No homework at all, as there had been in Danville. I was far ahead, anyway, because of the Danville school system; I had already gone beyond the work they were still going toward. And the nuns were fascinated by a student who went off and played in night-clubs. They were proud of all their "talented" pupils—the ones who could sing, the ones who could dance, the ones who recited nicely. And whenever the Mother Superior had visitors in her office (visitors, I presume, who would make a donation to the mission) she would call in her talented pupils to perform. One afternoon I was invited to play and sing for a lady who turned out to be the aunt of comedian Morey Amsterdam. Afterward she complimented me, but followed this with a word of warning. I must always remember that flattery was like perfume—to be sniffed lightly but never to be swallowed whole.

I repeated this aphorism later to my managers, and there was a sudden sharp inquisition. Where'd you hear that? Who told you that? Now, I'd been strictly forbidden to play or sing for anyone connected with show business, and to my young mind, if the lady's nephew were a comedian, then the lady was connected with show business. I hemmed and hawed, said I couldn't remember who told me that flattery was like perfume. But Len and Bookie were continually on guard against my being appropriated by another agent or some fast-moving impresario. To keep my mother from being found and coaxed into other arrangements, Len and Bookie would give out my home town as Springfield, Illinois. They didn't want anybody else nibbling on the pie.

The Schanettes were my introduction to the Creoles of Louisiana, quite a few of whom had settled in Chicago. Historically, of course, the Creoles were actually whites of French or Spanish descent, but they picked up with the Negroes, as everyone has always done, and the resulting breed called themselves Creole, too. Some of them didn't look any more "Creole" than I do, but they spoke in the patois and they had French names. The Schanettes fell into this group, Paul and Daise Schanette. They lived with a cousin named Anne Alexander, and both ladies did day work. I don't remember what Mr. Schanette did—it was the Depression— pickup jobs, I suppose. He was a handsome man, and his wife Daise was energetic and pretty. They cooked all the richly spiced dishes, all the gumboes, all the bisques, things I never had at home, shrimps, oysters, and crab. Roasts were garlicked to the point of divinity. (We didn't have garlic in Danville.) Lots of thick soups, lots of okra, lots of food at all times.

The Schanettes spoke in the Louisiana patois when they didn't want the children (me and Joseph) to understand, and they often swore in this patois. I remember a funny little song they sang that was traditional to Mardi Gras, and in those days Mardi Gras was separated—the Zulu Mardi Gras and the white Mardi Gras. In Creole patois, the words of the song sounded like this: *"Blanc dans lit, mulatta sous lit, negé regardé. Ai ya ya. Mo' pas l'aimé ça."* ("White man in the bed, mulatto under the bed, negro peeping. Ai ya ya. I don't like that.") But the song was good any time of the year, and in New Orleans as you passed under a window you might, on the spur of the moment, just sing the verse as a taunt, a sly message from the streets.

151

The Schanettes also told wonderful stories—Louisiana stories about the animals, the tar baby, and the devil baby who was a trickster, always handing out smart advice and scheming to get everyone else in trouble. And there was a story that explained why dogs and cats are enemies. The tale is an ancient one, solemnly recorded nowadays in one form or another by anthropologists and sociologists rummaging through the West African coastal countries. Well, *I* heard it from Daise Schanette in Chicago. And she told it charmingly.

Once upon a time, it seems, the dog and the cat were married.

One fine day, the cat said to the dog, "Husband, I have good news. I'm going to have a baby."

Yes, that certainly was good news, said the dog. And he had good news too. He had found a large pot of lard and hidden it down in the cellar. When winter came, they would have plenty of food in the house. So, the days went by, and one evening the dog was rocking on his front porch, playing his banjo and singing some little Creole song.

And he turned to his wife, the cat, and said, "Well, wife, have you decided on a name for the child?" And the cat just couldn't think, so she licked her lips and she said, "Yes, I've decided to call the child Top Off."

What a strange name for a child, thought the dog, but he kept on rocking and singing.

A few weeks later he again said to his wife, "Have you thought of a better name for the child?"

The cat couldn't think, so she licked her lips and said, "Yes, Half Gone." A few weeks later, the cat said "All Gone" was the name of the child.

Then the dog went down cellar to find that the pot of lard

was empty. "Now I know where you got those names—Top Off, Half Gone, All Gone!" So he chased the cat out of the house. And ever since that day, dogs and cats have been mortal enemies.

XVII

My career took form very slowly. We began with what are called "club dates," which means one-night stands, usually at hotels, or for a convention, a lodge get-together, or a business group meeting in town. A show would be organized with three or four acts and an orchestra for dancing.

Early in the game we discovered that James C. Petrillo was going to give us trouble; Petrillo at that point was head of the Chicago Musicians Union and had control over every musical act in town. (I might add that there were two unions, colored and white, as there were in nearly every city in the country.) Petrillo turned thumbs down on me right off the bat. I could not join the union until I was sixteen. Furthermore, if I were allowed to perform, I'd be putting a grown-up out of work. (There was a wire from Len to my mother reading: "Just missed chance at the State Lake Theater because of union troubles.") However, Petrillo did suggest that if we could see our way to paying the union, *his* union, one hundred fifty dollars a week, then something might be arranged. The rules could be waived and the big theaters opened to me—the R.K.O. Palace, the State Lake, the Oriental, and the Chicago, as well as the Regal, the colored vaudeville house on the South Side. But we couldn't afford to pay the one-five-o. I was lucky to get that much a week in salary. And Petrillo also had union fees set up for outlying theaters.

Meantime, I was playing club dates at the Sherman Hotel, which was one of the best in those days, always with lady singers in a blue spot, giving their gallant all to such numbers as, "Be still, my heart . . . I hear the pounding of the drums. They bid him come and he must go. He's leaving me and leaving you for someone new, and though we'll miss him so, we'll never let him know . . . Be still, my heart." They paid thirty-five dollars, sometimes fifty a night, so we were meeting expenses and even able to make a little money. With my club dates at the Sherman, I also got a meal—entertainers always had dinner served to them, if they wanted it, and I was eating all sorts of new things. I'd already been introduced to Creole cooking at the Schanettes', and now I was ordering filet mignon with mushrooms or a pepper steak, and *coupe St. Jacques* for dessert. The Sherman also had a Balinese Room, with Balinese maidens drifting about, though it was strongly rumored that they were really high-yellow girls from the South Side. A pastime at the Sherman was to test the maidens with colored dialect and slang and wait for them to crack up. And so they did.

I also played club dates at the Ambassador East, the Stevens, and the Congress. There were out-of-town engagements, like one in Grand Rapids, where we were invited to a party afterward by the head porter at the hotel, a colored man who had a car sent to take us to his house. There was a grand piano, I played and sang for them, and it was almost like being home again. On the Grand Rapids trip, Doris Hertig traveled with us. I'd always known Doris as an agent, a tall, pretty, *zoftig* blonde who handled bookings in the office. But when it was time for the show to begin, Doris, in a diaphanous royal blue dress, went on and did a complete acrobatic turn—splits, contortions, walking on her hands, and double-jointed I-don't-know-what-all. This was her old act, *her* number. And the next morning, back to her telephone, her typewriter, and her desk.

My managers made an effort to get me around Chicago to see other performers. And if they were colored or people I especially wanted to meet, Len often got me backstage and I'd usually wind up playing the piano and singing for them. Apart from my eagerness to see and meet name entertainers, it was all helpful to me in learning how to put an act together. The more professionals I saw at work, the more professional I became. At the Black Hawk restaurant, I heard Red Norvo and Mildred Bailey—"Mr. and Mrs. Swing," as they were billed in those days—and I was taken to meet them at their hotel. Mildred Bailey had her dachshunds along, she always had dachshunds; Mildred Bailey, so funny and comfortable. She loved to cook and loved to eat. I played the piano and sang for them, and when it was time to go she gave me an autographed picture, and Red gave me a little set of xylophones. He was and still is one of the best jazz xylophonists in the business. Her big song at that time was "Rockin' Chair"—"Old rockin' chair's got me . . ." It wasn't until years later that I appreciated the tender care she took with every lyric she sang; plaintive and sensitive and always true to the composer's line.

I was taken to Scholler's Swingland, a black-and-tan club

on the South Side, which ran a complete revue with a good tenor and the girls parading around. "When Did You Leave Heaven?" was a feature number the night we were there, done in a Broadway manner with great style.

Another fancy Chicago nightclub was the Three Deuces, a sacred jazz temple down in the Loop. I was allowed through the door one evening in the wake of my white managers. Roy Eldridge, a top trumpet player, often appeared at the Three Deuces. So did Art Tatum. And Cleo Brown played there; Cleo Brown, the brilliant colored singing pianist, whose weekly broadcasts we'd waited for back home. She had a fantastic left hand, a sexy whispering voice, and one of her best songs was "The Stuff Is Here And It's Mellow." (That title showed up in Danville one Sunday as the theme for a sermon preached at the Shiloh Baptist Church by the Reverend Dixon. "The stuff is here, brethren, and it's mellow. . . .") The night we went to the Three Deuces, Gladys Palmer was on, a tall, handsome, brown-skinned girl who could play only in the key of C. Her show was special to me because Gladys Palmer sang a low-down version of "Trees," my Arbor Day hit from the first grade, and at the end she gave the final phrase her own knocked-out lift—"But only God, oh baby, can make a tree!"

Art Tatum, who was partially blind, was a phenomenon until the day he died. Some people swore that Tatum was a made-up name, that he was really two piano players being recorded at once. But Tatum was never fully appreciated. Still, Len Rosen was aware of Tatum, and wanted me to hear him play. So one day Len took me into Lyon and Healey's music store to listen to a Tatum record. His technique was like Horowitz's. He was a wizard. I listened to the recording, and I was shocked to hell! When it was finished, the salesman said, "Do you play the piano, son?"

Yes, I did.

"Would you play for us?"

I crossed over to the piano and sat down, and because I was so impressionable and depended on my ear for so much, found that I couldn't play the piano at all. Not a note. Tatum had undone me to that extent. I could not get my fingers to react to my mind, because my mind was suddenly overflowing. I'd been stopped in my tracks.

And here we come to a problem that has never been resolved. I depended on my ear. Should I learn to read notes? Or should I continue playing as I did? We asked a lot of people we thought were important. A famous pianist in Chicago named Lee Simms recorded, played in concert, and played on the radio with his wife Ilomay Bailey, who sang. They were very popular performers. In those days a piano player and a singer could go out on a stage or a nightclub floor and completely hold an audience. It wasn't necessary to have eighty-five chorus girls with ten changes of costume. You went out, sat at the piano, played and sang, and you were a big star. Lee Simms had reached that point. To enlarge his career, he had patented a Lee Simms Piano Method with printed charts and guides, and he'd established a studio in Chicago. We asked the person in charge there whether I should take lessons or not, but got noncommittal answers, like "Wait a few years." We talked to Roy Bargey, who had been the pianist with Paul Whiteman's orchestra back in the days when the Teagardens were with Whiteman and they played "Rhapsody In Blue." Bargey said, "I don't know what you should do. I don't know if you should study or not."

Only one person was firm. And that was John Hammond, the first blue-blood American to take a deep interest in jazz. John Hammond, now head of Columbia Records' jazz division, discovered Count Basie in Kansas City, and introduced Basie's orchestra to New York and Chicago. With all his erudition, he had plowed into jazz as an art form. And like Van Vechten, who was so involved with Harlem's literary group in the twenties, Hammond in the thirties became involved with blues singers and jazz instrumentalists, and he brought to the fore some enormously talented people who wouldn't have had such a chance without his help.

He was in Chicago one day at a publishing office, and I played the piano for him. I was a little bit spoiled because in most cases people would say, "Oh, my God, he's darling . . . he's the best in the world . . . he's a genius. . . ." Not John Hammond. Hammond said, "This young man obviously has some talent, but why is he working?" And my manager said, "Why? Because he's talented—he's making a lot of money." John said let him forget about this work altogether, let him be taught the piano properly, let him be taught to read notes, and one day he'll emerge as someone really outstanding. He was totally negative. Well, not totally. He did say the boy has some talent; but, don't fool around with it. Get him into a music school. Get the right teacher. Make him work four or five hours a day at the piano.

Of course, I didn't want to hear any of that kind of talk. I didn't like John Hammond one bit. But then, as the world goes, many years later, John Hammond was the first person to offer to buy my first LP, which I'd made independently and which he wanted for Vanguard, his own recording firm.

Shortly after John Hammond delivered that blunt message,

I received another blow. Bob Crosby, Bing's brother, had a big band, and while they were at the Congress Casino, his pianist, Joe Sullivan, had come down with TB. Crosby had replaced Sullivan with Bob Zirke, whose versions of "Yancey Special" and "Little Rock Getaway" were jazz classics at the time. Well, one Sunday the Congress Casino put on a big benefit jazz performance, proceeds to go to Joe Sullivan's wife. All the big stars came to play—Roy Eldridge, Baby Dodd, PeeWee Russell—and as an extra kick they had little Bobby Short. *Downbeat,* in those days the Bible of jazz musicians, covered the concert, and what they said about my performance was less than flattering. The review said I had a pleasant enough voice, but that I played flamboyantly and had a disjointed style.

But John Hammond's comment was the big shock. He's a fan of mine now, and now I understand what he meant in Chicago in 1936. I've made several attempts to learn to read music, but I've never mastered it. And this to my regret, because there are many composers I'd like to play, just for my own pleasure. The list, in fact, has grown over the years, and it's nearly impossible to name them all. But I have a fondness for the crisp and delicate works of Mozart, and I'm drawn to Ravel, Mompou, Tcherpnin, and Francaix, even to the almost saccharine but beautiful compositions of Rachmaninoff. Delius has written several dazzling works for the piano, and so the list goes on.

Downtown in Chicago one day I met an agent named Joe Glazer. Joe Glazer's biggest claim to fame was that he was the first agent to take Louis Armstrong seriously, and together they had become millionaires. Glazer set up a whole

booking agency around his ace-in-the-hole, Mr. Armstrong
—the Associated Booking Corporation. He heard me play,
was intrigued, and without any introduction at all challenged
my managers' ability to do anything for me. And as proof of
what *he* could do, James C. Petrillo notwithstanding, Glazer
instantly booked me on a one-night show with Louis Armstrong; and as further proof of his power, Glazer had me
photographed for the Chicago *Defender*.

Armstrong's lead song that evening was "Pennies From
Heaven." Also on the bill were some of the female imperson-
ators from the Cabin Inn, that Mildred had told me about.
Suddenly, backstage, I was face to face with those odd trans-
vestites tricked out in women's clothing—I was scared out of
my wits. But that was a big night for me.

The next day my managers and I went to Joe Glazer's office, and he made his sales pitch. He had all kinds of plans,
to which we listened very carefully, but we didn't go with
him. That speech was important, however, because I've
heard the same speech two other times in my life—once in
1953, when I did sign with him (for six months), and once
again as recently as 1965. Never say die. It was the same
speech each time; that was Glazer's speech, and he never rewrote it. "I can triple his salary tomorrow. I can give him
this kind of lesson, that kind of coaching. He should be wearing this sort of costume, he could be singing that sort of song.
He can be playing every big house in the country. He's a
genius. He should be a big star. He *is* a big star. I can make
him a *very* big star." Now, we encountered this quite frequently. People would step in, overpowering, sometimes
overbearing people, and tell my managers that they weren't
equipped to handle a talent like mine.

We got that once from Ethel Waters, backstage at the R.K.O. Palace. In 1938 she was in her prime as a singer and had a matchless command of the stage. I remember her that evening as a regal figure in black velvet, who brought to her music the dramatic quality for which she later became so famous in the legitimate theater. And that night she sang the song everyone had come to hear, "Am I Blue." She was the top. And she was impressed by a small boy who played the piano and sang. But she was also in a very irate mood, as she so often was. She was a tall woman and very domineering. She too challenged my manager immediately. What can you do for this young man? What can *you* do? What power do you have to further his career? What are your plans for him? Where does he go from here? Where has he worked? What do you have in mind? She had with her a boy about my age named Teddy Hale, who tap-danced. "I've got Teddy Hale with *me*. I'm a star. At least he's in a big theater performing."

I didn't know then what bad times Ethel Waters had been through, that she did not trust whites, that she did not trust white managers. It took great discipline to be successful and colored. You had to watch your step, watch your tongue, mind your manners, give no offense, and even as a star you couldn't find a place to sleep or eat in some parts of the country. I've always shunned bookings in those parts of the country where anti-Negro attitudes are strongest, because I've felt I couldn't take it. Once in 1945, against my better judgment, I signed a contract for a club in Phoenix, where Negroes and Indians and Mexicans were all beyond the pale. I hadn't been in town twelve hours before I was ready to clear out. And on opening night, I walked into the club and gave them my two weeks' notice. But if I'd been as famous as Ethel Waters and had worked as hard as she'd worked, and I were *still* given third-class treatment, I too might have been abrupt and imperious.

In those days, however, as a small boy who'd had a fairly easy time of it in the white world, I didn't understand her angry questions. She frightened me. And as far as I was concerned, there was no need to listen to Miss Waters' fierce criticism of Len and Bookie. And there was never a question of going with Joe Glazer. I didn't know these people, and I didn't like their high-powered talk. I knew Len and Bookie, my mother knew them. I was happy, I was in school, and my career was moving along beyond my craziest imaginings. Other important people I met around Chicago didn't make colossal promises or bad-mouth Len and Bookie. Louis Armstrong was complimentary and friendly, so was Cab Calloway, who remembered me from Indianapolis. And both of them left it at that. So did Fats Waller.

The day I met Fats Waller—that was a fine day, one of the finest. Fats Waller had been an idol of mine for as long as I could remember. We'd gone backstage at the Palace. I'd talked to the men in his band, then gone into the rehearsal room and played the piano. Fats Waller heard the music and came in all bubbles, smiles, and bourbon. He marched right over, picked me up in his arms, and hugged me. "You could be my son," he said. "You even look like me a little bit. . . . Say, who's your mother?"

Then, "Play some more. Play one of my songs."

I played. I don't remember now what it was—"Honeysuckle Rose" or "I'm Going To Sit Right Down And Write Myself A Letter" or "Ain't Misbehavin' "—but it was one of his songs, and when I'd finished he reached into his pocket and gave me a five-dollar bill. That was big money for me, that was folding green.

"Now, where are you going?" he asked.

I said we were going home.

"Don't go home. I've got one more show and we're going out . . ."

I stood in the wings while Mr. Waller did the last show, then he changed his clothes, and we went off to the Grand Terrace. The Grand Terrace! I lived for a chance to get into those South Side nightclubs. I knew the names and careers of every performer, the tops in colored show business. Of course, we had a ringside table and all the commotion at the door. "It's Mr. Waller! Good *evening*, Mr. Waller. A table down front for Mr. Waller and his party. Right this way please, Mr. Waller."

Earl Hines was the star of the revue that night, a show written by Buck Ramm, who had a mild success as a songwriter. And Mae Johnson was appearing. Mae Johnson, a comedienne and singer, who also acted for a while. The last time I saw Mae Johnson was in *Stormy Weather*, the film with Lena Horne and Bill Robinson, in which she sang "I Lost My Sugar in Salt Lake City."

But at this point in the show Fats Waller had put his chair on top of the table, and was right into the performance with the dialogue flying. "Sing it, Mama . . . Oh, sing it, baby!" And I'm at the same table, out of my mind with excitement. Mr. Waller couldn't sit in because of his contract, but the next thing I knew, my name was announced and I was out on the floor. When I finished playing I made a little thank-you speech, rather than doing another number, because I thought it wouldn't be nice to do too much. And in my speech I used words like "The acceptance you have given me this evening . . . May I express my gratitude . . . I thank all of you very much." When I got back to the table, Mr. Waller said, "An' ya talk good, boy. Ya talk good, too!"

I took the five dollars he'd given me and bought Christmas presents for my brothers and sisters. My managers came through with an electric mixer for Mother, and I went home for the holidays. Christmas night, I took my sisters downtown to see *Jungle Princess* with Dorothy Lamour and Ray Milland. We went in style in a limousine from A. H. Brown's Funeral Parlor, which doubled as a livery service, naturally, with all those fine automobiles on hand.

It is now the winter of 1937. I'm still enrolled at St. Joseph's School with the kind and patient Sisters of Nazareth; I have a crush on a girl named Lucille, and I've been introduced to Billie Holiday's recordings by a classmate named Beatrice, who sang all the songs exactly as Billie Holiday sang them. I'm living with the Schanettes in the heart of Chicago's Creole world and behaving like any kid on the block—delighted with a free Saturday, when we'd go to the Globe Theater for the day: a double feature, a serial, news, short subjects, and on holidays like Hallowe'en or Easter, favors and candy, all for a dime. And on Sunday I'd go with the Schanettes to Mass at the Holy Family, an enormous church, about eight blocks away, where Mass was a magnificent production.

At the same time I was doing club dates and learning my trade on the job. Petrillo had cut us out of big-time Chicago vaudeville, but we were making it in our own way. We managed another date at the Regal, a Sunday with four shows, memorable to me because of a colored tap dancer named Bob Downey, who held a table in his teeth and danced to "You Took Advantage Of Me," a song I hadn't heard before. We also had an appearance at the Howard Theater, part of the Balaban and Katz chain, a try-out house way out on the North Side across from Rodgers Park. But I couldn't take the next step into the downtown theaters without paying the union one-fifty a week.

Throughout the winter, I often got down to Danville, only two hours by train. The Chicago and Eastern Illinois also ran trains that went on through, down the Mississippi to New Orleans, and there'd often be colored people in the coaches who were going the whole distance for a visit home, their accents identifying them immediately as newcomers to Chicago. I must admit, having been born in the North, I didn't like that deep, deep southern dialect. If a Negro were speaking, to me it meant illiteracy. If it were a white, the accent conjured up lynch time. Once on this trip, a colored woman sat next to me. I recognized the deep, dark South in her voice, and I was bored and impatient with making conversation, didn't want any part of this. And then she asked me (and God knows I felt ashamed at having been so high-hat) if I would walk with her to the drinking fountain at the rear of the car, because a crowd of white men was sitting back there, and she didn't want to have to pass them by herself. Mind you, it was not assault she feared, but insult. So I escorted her to the drinking fountain and back again, and nothing was said to us. I don't know if the men would have insulted her if she had walked past them by herself, but that was what she'd been brought up with and that was what she'd been led to expect. It was one of the first times I saw and heard and understood what it was all about. She wasn't a snappy little dish, she wasn't even young. Just a plain, middle-aged lady. And she was afraid.

XVIII

About this time I got into radio in Chicago and did quite a bit of broadcasting; it became second nature. N.B.C. put me on several programs. One, called Piccadilly Music Hall, with an English-sounding M.C. to present the performers, was a network broadcast and of course went down to Danville. The night I made my debut on radio everybody at home tuned in. Now, the maestro on the program was a man named Al Short, so the M.C. said, in his British accent: "Our next performer this evening, a young man who will play and sing for you, is named Bobby Short. Oh, no. He is no relation to our maestro, Mr. Al Short, but is a charming little pickaninny." Which, I guess, left no doubt about the color of my skin. Then I sat down and did my number, "Never in a Million Years," and my little sister told me later they'd all been gathered around the radio, my mother sitting on the edge of her chair, the volume turned on as loud as she could get it, and the minute I started to sing, Mother got up and galloped around the room, clapping and shouting, "That's my boy! My boy!" She didn't hear a note or a word of the song. "My boy! That's my boy!"

But with the Piccadilly Music Hall, it was firmly established in Danville that I indeed was not just away twiddling my thumbs. I'm sure some people thought I was earning thousands of dollars with each program. But I'm also sure many hearts at home were settled; here was proof positive that I was not just fooling around. I was broadcasting for a national network. And oh, the grandeur and the high tone of broadcasting in the thirties! It was very doggy. You dressed up for work, wore the finest clothes you had. In the solitude of the studio, with no audience at all, the ladies would be wearing hats and silver foxes. M.C.'s wore dinner clothes, and striped trousers were not an oddity. And I, of course, was in my white tails.

There were rumbles from N.B.C. about having me sign on as a sustaining artist. In those days, if you had your own show you were called a sustaining artist and were paid one-fifty, two hundred, or two-fifty a week, and they could also call on you to fill in on other shows. Some advertising genius had projected an hour-long program to be sponsored by Quaker Oats, with Morton Downey as the star, and featuring all the Quaker Oats characters. One of these was Aunt Jemima, and I was going to be Aunt Jemima's son, who played the piano and sang. So we made the audition, and I remember going into the board room afterward. The officers of N.B.C. were sitting around in their great leather chairs, having just heard the trial broadcast, and trying to decide if they could sell it to Quaker Oats. Evidently they couldn't, because the project fell through.

Early that spring, however, we had a sudden flurry of vaudeville dates in good out-of-town houses. Contracts were more or less standard, no matter what the agency, with nine-teen clauses in fine print that covered everything, from a pro rata wage in the event of "fire, casualty, public authority, strikes, or any cause beyond the control of the theatre," to manners and morals; "If the Artist shall be guilty of conduct likely to bring discredit upon himself, the vaudeville profes-sion or any of said theatres, this contract may be cancelled forthwith without notice." You paid your own traveling ex-penses, and you were expected to supply clean and complete orchestrations for the conductor, two stands of first violins, cello, bass, flute, clarinet, first trumpet, second trumpet, third trumpet, French horns, first trombone, second trombone, drums, piano, first alto saxophone, second tenor saxophone, third alto saxophone, and banjo. At the foot of each contract was the cautionary message in boldface type: DON'T TRAVEL BY MOTOR—LATE ARRIVAL WILL RESULT IN SALARY DEDUCTION.

Our first contract, in March, was for a week at the St. Louis Theater. This date was a landmark to us; this was what we'd been after—to get on that coast-to-coast circuit.

The bill was headed by Johnny Perkins, a round, jolly man, an old vaudevillian, who sang a few songs, executed a few dance steps, and held the shows together. There was a splen-did acrobatic team, Park and Clifford, who came out in white leather straps and tights and did contortions and turns to "The Waltz of the Flowers" from Tchaikovsky's *Nutcracker Suite*. There was a juggling act, Van Cello and Mary; she in her tights, would pass him the Indian clubs or a ball then after one of his tricks, she'd step around, smiling, bowing, acknowledging the applause. A young man on the bill named Jack Prince was the winner of an amateur contest; a week at

170

the St. Louis Theater was part of his prize; Jack, who was later on Broadway, in *Guys and Dolls,* for one, had a fine tenor voice and sang "The Night Is Young and You're So Beautiful." The comedy act was Freddie Lightner (brother of the famous Winnie Lightner) and Freddie's partner and straight girl, Miss Roscella. There was a line of girls from New York, a road company of the Roxy chorus line, all of them very sweet and some of them very young, as evidenced by the presence of mothers who traveled with them. Several nights we were invited by a pair of young ladies to have dinner at their place; they had serious eyes for Len Rosen, unattached and in his mid-twenties, so they cooked for us. Len liked all that; he liked the ladies a lot.

The girls' big production number was "Speakeasy Bolero," done against a Venetian-blind backdrop, and the girls in Grecian dresses boleroed down a flight of stairs. They also danced to "Swing High, Swing Low," from Burton Lane's score written for the movie of the same name with Carole Lombard and Fred MacMurray. (He was a trumpet player, she was a singer with the band, and of course they were in love.) The movie was still playing in town, and the theme song had been immediately incorporated into our revue as the smash, swing production number.

Swing was the word. You didn't say jazz anymore; it was swing. Ella Fitzgerald was "The First Lady of Swing," Benny Goodman was the "King of Swing," Norvo and Bailey were "Mr. and Mrs. Swing," and even I was billed as "the Miniature King of Swing" or "Bobby Short, the Singing Swing Pianist."

St. Louis was a southern town, but Len found a rattletrap white hotel that let us stay there together. Usually, though,

I had to eat in my dressing room. It was too much of a hassle to get to the Negro neighborhood for every meal. And late at night, if I was hungry after a show, Len would get food from a nearby restaurant and I'd eat in our hotel room.

St. Louis was a sentimental week—my first week-long appearance in a big vaudeville house. And I cried on closing night. Everybody made a fuss over me and spoiled me, and I didn't want to leave my new friends. I went around saying good-bye—crying, shaking hands, kissing people, and asking everyone to write in my autograph book. Everyone, Ula Mason, the old wardrobe lady; Frank Dine's electrical crew; the stage manager, Harry Arthur, who wrote: "Bobby—A miniature edition of Duke Ellington, Cab Calloway, and all the rest rolled into one. He has stopped every show for us."

And it was a successful week; *Variety* gave me a good review: "Bobby Short, a nine-year-old Negro youngster, is an ivory tickler and warbler and wows 'em by warbling 'It's a Sin to Tell a Lie' and a piano number from *Samson and Delilah* and, for an encore, 'Rhythm In My Nursery Rhymes.'" I don't know where they got the "nine-year-old," unless my managers were using that in publicity releases.

In April we had a split week in Kenosha, Wisconsin, with Faith Bacon at the top of the bill. Faith Bacon had been a Ziegfeld girl, a tearing beauty, known for her beautiful body. And she danced. She wasn't a stripper; it was very classic and artistic and high-minded. While the orchestra played such numbers as "Temptation," she frisked about nymph-like and naked as a jaybird, behind a cellophane drop.

The Stroud Twins were also on that bill, Clarence and Claude Stroud, attractive boys who did comedy routines and eventually went on to Hollywood and the Kraft Music Hall with John Scott Trotter and Bing Crosby. I'd met them before on club dates, and we'd also been given screen tests by Twentieth Century Fox on the same day. Len had picked me up at St. Joseph's and hustled me down to the studio. I did my routine for the camera from five in the afternoon till eleven that night, togged down in the white tails at a white baby grand with a set of white palm trees behind me. When I saw the test months later in New York, I didn't like myself on the screen. I was forced and rushed. And not for the first time, either. A nun at St. Joseph's had taken movies in our classroom one day when I was leading calisthenics. I'd been amazed, when I saw the film, at my stiff and self-conscious manner, which must have come through in every performance I gave, although I was never aware of feeling self-conscious or ill at ease on stage. But at any rate, Twentieth Century had given me a screen test, and the Stroud Twins had been scouted at the same time. So in my autograph book from the split week in Kenosha, the Stroud Twins wrote: "We'll see you in Hollywood. Your contract is in the bag."

The movie playing between stage shows that week was *Top of the Town*, with Ella Logan, the Three Sailors, and Gertrude Neissen. To me, Gertrude Neissen was the epitome of what a nightclub torch singer should be, both in looks—the pageboy hairdo, the bangs, the stiletto eyebrows—and in the way she sang. I went out front to watch the movie every chance I got. Neissen's songs in that film were "Where Are You?" "Blame It on a Rumba," "Top of the Town," and "Jamboree."

What's more, I got offstage early.

As we'd originally rehearsed the finale, the band played,

the line, the Murray Brown Girls, danced on, and each act came out to take a final bow. Faith Bacon, the star of the show, appeared last. And appear she did, high upstage on a revolving platform with a pillar on top, and as the platform revolved, there posed against the pillar was Miss Bacon, completely naked except for three strips of silver tinsel draped low on her hips. That was her number. I was out on stage with the rest of the cast, and as the last chords of music sounded from the pit, the entire ensemble turned and gestured upward toward the vision on the pillar. After the first show, however, the manager took me aside and said he'd rather I left the stage immediately after my final bow. "It doesn't look good," he said, "to have a child out there with a naked lady."

At the end of April, we had a week at the Riverside Theater in Milwaukee. This was a privilege. Fletcher Henderson and his orchestra starred; Fletcher Henderson, a top-notch arranger for the big bands, a college-trained musician, and as a Negro, a pioneer in the field. He arranged for the Dorseys and for Benny Goodman, when his orchestra was king-high in the thirties. I've heard that Henderson died a frustrated man, having never truly achieved his potential. The last time I saw him, he was Ethel Waters' accompanist, a job he'd held at the beginning of his career, back in the twenties.

I had an instant admiration for Henderson, and I began to realize what it took to keep thirteen or fourteen musicians together, to create and maintain a first-rate band. One of his stars was Chu Berry, who played tenor saxophone and was rivaled only by the late Coleman Hawkins. (Chu is dead too.) Fletcher's brother, Horace, also starred. Horace played

174

the piano and had a solo called "Stealing Apples." One day, watching from backstage, I had a vignette of Henderson's ability and savoir-faire. He announced "Stealing Apples," turned around and saw that Horace wasn't there—so, without hesitating, Fletcher walked back to the piano, sat down, and played the solo himself. I cherished those glimpses of a real professional at work. In between shows, Fletcher found time to work with me at the piano on modulations, phrasing, harmonic variations, and his arrangement of "I Surrender, Dear." And he taught me an introduction, a lead that could be used for any number of songs. It was one of his own, and he'd played it for years. The next show, I came on with that introduction and dumbfounded the band, who weren't expecting the new kid in the revue to slip in one of Fletcher's trademarks.

Dorothy Derrick was his vocalist, a sweet lady who sang every song he'd written. I particularly remember "It's Wearing Me Down." And backstage one afternoon, Dorothy taught me to make a proper exit. I'd been doing a stiff, childlike nod and shuffle. "The way you're bowing just isn't making it, baby. I can show you in two seconds." So she taught me how to get offstage and then come back just outside the wings to take my bows in a smooth and professional way.

Chuck and Chuckles, the song and dance team, were also at the Riverside—a solid and well-established second attraction to have on a vaudeville bill. Any theater owner could count on them for a hit. They were the sort of successful young Negroes in show business that my managers had had in mind when they knocked on the door of our house in Danville. Chuckles was tall and thin, Chuck had a marvelous grin, and they both danced like fiends. We spent a lot of time

175

together between shows. Because they had money to spend, they traveled with a phonograph and a complete collection of the latest records. Chuckles died in Paris a few years ago, but Chuck appears now and then in tap-dancing revivals. I saw him again, after all those years, at a Newport Jazz Festival. And he starred recently in *The Hoofers*, an off-Broadway show.

That week, the Riverside cashed in on *Red Hot and Blue*, the current Cole Porter show with Ethel Merman. Our vaudeville revue was advertised as *Red, Hot, and Oooh*. And I now had special billing in the Milwaukee newspaper ads, a little box announcing "An Extra Added Attraction—Bobby Short, the Miniature King of Swing," and my name was up on the marquee.

In May we had a week at the Fox Tower Theater, Kansas City, Missouri. The bill was headed by the Three Stooges—"The Gentle Maniacs"—in this instance, Garner, Wolff, and Akins. I list their names because there were several sets of Stooges out on the road, all with the same routine, the bizarre haircuts, the dumb one getting the fingers in his eyes—just as there would later be several traveling troupes of "Inkspots" with the falsetto tenor and the talking bass; "Honey Chile, Ah'll never smile again. . . ."

Harlan Christie was M.C. at the Fox that week, with Judy Conrad's orchestra and Lester Harding as the male vocalist. The second-string star was Harry Savoy, then a well-known nightclub comic. His straight girl, Louise Tobin, was a good singer as well, who later sang with Goodman's band; when we met Louise on the street in New York a year later she told us she'd married Harry James, one of Goodman's trumpet players. I was billed after Harry Savoy and Louise. After my billing was Toy and Wing; he was Chinese, she Japanese, and they had a dance routine with a few little songs. "Limehouse Blues" was the classic number in their act, but they then swung into the jitterbug routine to show that they could be Western as well as Eastern. They dressed next door to me, and I remember their little dog named Ho-Choi, which meant "Good Luck." They were friendly and charming, good performers, a nice vaudeville act—an Oriental act was always attractive. House performers were in and out of the revues from one week to the next; there was the line of girl dancers, of course, and between shows a feature movie. And the fare for all this was twenty-five cents.

The movie that week was *Hit Parade,* in which Duke Ellington and his orchestra had a featured sequence. I must have sat through the film twelve times, and I knew that sequence by heart. The star of it all for me was Ivie Anderson, Ellington's vocalist and my favorite singer—not only then, but for all time. As the band played, she sang, "I Gotta Be A Rug Cutter," and she sang it as no one else could sing it. She was given a lot of trashy material by Irving Mills, who managed Ellington in those days, but Ivie carried it off. Like Gertrude Lawrence, she could sing the worst songs in the grandest way. And she had a rare gift. She was a popular singer who listened to the lyrics and stayed within the character of the song. She was into the words and music at a time when most girl singers flounced out and warbled lyrics about heartbreak and despair with bright smiles on their faces.

We played Kansas City for a week, and by now I was feeling at home backstage and sopping up attention from the cast and the production crew—always spoiled and pampered beyond measure. Kansas City, again, was a locked-up southern town, but the Whites Only restaurants and no hot dogs from the five-and-ten rolled right past me, because I was getting plenty of applause and loving kindness at the theater. I couldn't have bought a ticket for the show, but I had only to step in through the stage door, and I was everybody's darling. *Variety* gave me another good review, but with a small dig about the arrangements, which were mine:

Bobby Short, a ten-year-old Negro, Ellingtons a piano and thin-pipes the vocals. Alert youngster with plenty of showmanship; his dental flashing on completing a tricky keyboard passage has plenty of what it takes. Arrangements are all from the same stamp, however. This is the act they talk about on leaving the house.

XIX

It is now graduation time. Mother came to Chicago and stayed with Clara Blakeley, another Kentucky-born lady, and Kentucky folk stuck together like kin; Clara Blakeley, who lived in the best section of the South Side and whose opening remark when she saw my part of town was: "Myrtle, how can you let your baby son live in this dreadful neighborhood!" But Mother wasn't quite so critical, and she liked the Schanettes immediately.

Graduation ceremonies at St. Joseph's were divided into two parts—a religious service, and then a show for the parents, with skits and songs and acts. I did "Sing, Baby, Sing," an Alice Faye hit, and the girls in our graduating class had a special production number that had been rehearsed for weeks, "Moonlight and Roses." I don't remember who was responsible for choosing that number, but I do indeed remember that in the second chorus, the girls had been given some swing-and-sway movements to set off the lyrics. At the final rehearsal it was decided that "Moonlight and Roses" was not coming across as had been intended—the swinging and the swaying had got a little loose, a little bit too broad

179

for the occasion. There was a certain amount of distress about their performance, but the crisis was resolved by Sister Presipia. "Well," she said, "I think there's no reason to learn a new song. What we can do is just say, 'Moonlight and roses, *Mother* . . . bring wonderful memories of you, *Mother* . . . My heart reposes, *Mother* . . . ,' and it will be all right." And so it was.

The boys were asked to wear navy-blue jackets with white trousers, which we all did, somehow. The girls were asked to wear yellow organdy dresses, little white hats, and white shoes. They all went along with that, except Juanita, the class rebel (she who had questioned the doctrine of the Virgin Birth). Juanita refused to wear an organdy dress. She said the girls in the public school were going to have a dance and would be wearing formal gowns, so she would compromise with a floor-length yellow silk dress. And that was the dress she wore and the dress she was photographed in for our graduation picture.

Mother was on her knees at Mass graduation morning, then sat there very nicely and watched the exercises and was proud that I had finished school. She was all dressed up in her best, the mother of the child prodigy, the little vaudeville star. I don't know what her thoughts were; it was June, 1937, and my father had been dead for over a year. I guess she was adjusted to this. She was in the pink, living in a lovely house she had just bought, with new furniture and lots of new clothes. Pretty clothes were her only addiction. I remember one Sunday after church in Danville—Mother in a big blue hat, white gloves to the elbow, print silk dress with pearls. She stopped to chat with two of her equally spruce lady friends, and Dorothy Taylor, who'd founded the Social Aristocrats, stepped out of church, viewed this group of ladies, and was driven to say, "Oh, such stunning widows!"

In May, shortly before graduation, Len had said, "I've got a secret. You and I are going to run away from Bookie." I was fascinated. Every child is fascinated by intrigue and derring-do. . . . I'd never run away from anyone, anywhere. And now we were going to run away from Bookie. I didn't see Bookie very often; and when I did, he was curt and gruff. "Hi, kid. How's it goin', kid?" While Len took care of me and was always there on our out-of-town appearances. He was the one who brought me something to eat in my dressing room or hotel room in towns like St. Louis or Kansas City; he was backstage giving me encouragement; he saw that the white tails were dry-cleaned, my hair cut, a doctor called in when I hit one of my sieges with sore throat and laryngitis. If Len said we were running away from Bookie, then, indeed, we would run away from Bookie.

So when school was over, Len came by, we paid off our debts to the Schanettes, and tiptoed out of Chicago. We were stealing away from Bookie, running off to Ohio—all the way from Chicago, Illinois, to Cleveland, Ohio.

Jules Stein's Music Corporation of America, MCA, had a Cleveland office because of the vaudeville houses, radio stations, nightclubs, hotels, and dance halls in town. There was business. The night life was great, there was a lot of money around, and all the tourist trade, of course, from the Great Lakes Exposition, Cleveland's own world's fair on the shore of Lake Erie. At MCA one of the agents said yes, he had a spot for us, not too much money, but one of the best rooms in town, and he thought he could get us a decent deal. He took us to the Hollenden Hotel, then the top hotel in Cleveland, and I was hired. We lived at the Hollenden and got one meal a day and seventy-five a week, as I recall.

We opened in the Vogue Room, where the band leader and M.C. was Hugo de Paul. There was a friendly dance team from Cuba, Raoul and Eva Reyes, and a trio called "Major, Sharp, and Minor," two men and a lady—one played the piano and all three sang, and their arrangements were first class. But the lady, stiff and haughty and well past her debutante years, who walked on like Nellie Melba, was immediately outraged by my presence. She could not tolerate a small colored boy sharing the same bill in the Vogue Room. Now, there's an old saying in show business: "Never follow an animal act, a kid act, or a colored act." I was both a kid act *and* a colored act, and Major, Sharp, and Minor had to follow me. Perhaps that's what unsettled her. She did everything she could to upset my performance and make me unwelcome around the hotel, even to complaining to the headwaiter about my color. The trio's pianist, however, was extremely kind and was a fine musician as well. I was trying to work out a new arrangement for "Shoe Shine Boy," and he spent a good bit of time working with me on it.

Things went well at the Hollenden, despite the sniper fire from Madame, and I stayed on for three or four weeks. We worked up a new introduction. During the M.C.'s spiel, in comes Bobby Short, wearing white tails and a bellboy's red cap and carrying a tray with a note on it.

"Paging Mr. de Paul! Paging Mr. de Paul!"

"Just a minute. I'm Mr. de Paul."

"I'm paging you, sir."

He'd take the note off the tray and read it aloud: "This is to introduce Bobby Short. He plays the piano and sings." Then he'd say to me, "Are you Bobby Short?"

"Yes, I am, sir."

"How about giving us a sample of what you can do?"

"All right, sir."

So I'd sit down at the piano and go into my act with a small microphone pinned to my lapel, a new device at that time. And a new song in my repertoire was the one I'd heard Ivie Anderson sing in the movies—"I've Gotta be a Rug Cutter." A very successful engagement, all told.

The Exposition was my principal entertainment during our stay in Cleveland—we saw the midway attractions, the rides, all the displays featuring The Future, and Billy Rose's Aquacade with Eleanor Holm. Two songs that Rose had written for the show, "Happy Birthday to Love" and "At a Perfume Counter on the Rue de la Paix," were popular that summer, and Major, Sharp, and Minor had already included them in their act. I pestered Len continually to take me into this sideshow or that arcade, to buy me this, to buy me that. And he usually did, if only to keep my mouth shut. I insisted, one day, on seeing a child advertised as having one head and two bodies. I remember the come-on: "A baby, a real live baby, one head and two bodies. Step right up, folks. A baby, one head and two bodies. . . ." Inside, it was a horrifying sight— a pathetic seven-year-old, riding around on a tricycle, and when enough of a crowd had gathered, everyone gaping at the child, he was told to lift up his sweater, and there indeed was the lower part of another body growing out of his chest. I also begged to see the peep shows—a nickel in the slot and turn the crank. One of them was titled "Time On My Hands," and featured a naked lady judiciously holding a clock, quite a large desk clock, with pillars, over her privates. I ran into her again, years later, in a peep show at Venice, California, and there she was, still juggling that clock. I also demanded and got an Indian beadwork kit, with the wires, the tiny multicolored beads, and directions for making rings, bracelets, and so on in various patterns. I became totally absorbed in beadwork. It was my after-hours diversion, whenever there was nothing else to do but sit in the hotel room. I made dozens and dozens of beaded doodads. Later, when we got to New York, I demanded a new kit and again took up my beadwork to kill the long, empty offstage hours.

One day our phone rang at the Hollenden Hotel, and Bookie Levin was on the line. He had discovered, without the least difficulty, where we'd run off to. Len must have expected Bookie to find us. But I was still child enough to believe one could vanish into thin air, simply by moving to another town. What Len had done, however, was to show Bookie that he—Len—could handle me himself, that he was fed up with splitting fees with Bookie, that he was doing all the work, that Bookie wasn't paying enough attention to my career. What's more, Len had set aside his own singing career and invested his time in Bobby Short, while Bookie had other irons in the fire.

"All right," said Len. "Levin will be here over the weekend to have a long talk with us and to see what can be done about our arrangements together." Then he explained that he might have to say some pretty strong things to Bookie, things that might upset me. He might, for example, have to ask Bookie just how much *he'd* like to live with a little colored boy every day of his life. I said I wouldn't get angry. Anything Len wanted to tell Bookie was fine. I was in cahoots with Len; Bookie was bad, and Len was good.

The men talked for two days. I don't know what was said or what arrangements were finally agreed upon, but we were back under Bookie's long arm and on our way to Toledo for a week at the Rivoli, where an all-colored revue—"Harlem on Parade"—was scheduled, with Don Redman and his band at the top of the bill. Len sent the local reviews to my mother. They read glowingly:

The Redman revel is thumbs-up all-colored fare all the way. . . . Redman features his own arrangements—and rightly so. They have a distinctive and catchy swing and in several instances novel ensemble singing is effectively employed. The stars of "Harlem on Parade" are Bobby Short, called "the miniature Fats Waller," and the show-stopping steppers, Gordon and Rogers. . . . Master Short certainly is a youthful marvel at the piano keyboard, and his playing of syncopated melodies, plus an appealing singing voice and winning personality, make him an immediate favorite. . . . Gordon and Rogers, the dancing funsters, really "go to town" with their stunts. . . . Extraordinary dancing, climaxed by acrobatic antics as wild as their costumes. . . .

The "novel ensemble singing" mentioned by the Toledo critic was a Don Redman innovation. The orchestra was used as a choir and sang in counterpoint, melody and words, behind the lead vocalist. The most famous, I suppose, of the jazz choir arrangements is Tommy Dorsey's recording of "Marie." In the thirties the men in a band were often featured as entertainers, not merely as music-makers. Few orchestra leaders went as far as Kay Kayser and his College of Musical Knowledge, but most bands had several numbers designed to show off the extra talents of their personnel.

There was much rising and shining—all the saxophonists on their feet, for example, dipping and swaying with their instruments. Jimmy Lunceford's band, for one, had a snappy version of "Rhythm Is Our Business," which gave each member of the band a chance to rise and shine individually, and Ivie Anderson's singing "conversations" with Cootie Williams' trumpet were standard vaudeville fare with Duke Ellington's band for many years.

Redman, whose arrangements were famous, used the choral background for such songs as "Stormy Weather," "The Man on the Flying Trapeze" (of all things), and "Sweet Leilani," sung that week in Toledo by his pretty vocalist, Louise McCarroll. A trombonist nicknamed "Butter" also sang in a tenor falsetto.

The red-hot hoofers that so delighted the Toledo reviewers were Freddy Gordon and Timmy Rogers, a clever and successful team. They broke up their act a few years later when Freddy became a producer at the Club de Lisa in Chicago. Timmy, who went on as a single, is still going strong. Again, they were the sort of successful young performers who had inspired my managers to promote my talents.

During that Toledo week, Joe Louis had another championship fight, the match with Tommy Farr at Yankee Stadium, which went fifteen rounds. We had a radio backstage, and as the fight went on, round after round, the cast at the Rivoli was in an uproar. When you were on stage you couldn't tell what was happening at Yankee Stadium, so Redman's drummer, Big Sid Catlett, would relay the news. Someone would steal out and whisper to Sid, "Round five," and you'd hear the count on his cymbals, very quietly, ding, ding, ding, ding, ding, in the middle of someone's song or the

M.C.'s patter. Round five had been signaled, the fight was still on. Joe was still in the ring. And as long as you knew it was round five or eight or fourteen, the match wasn't over. And with the fifteenth round, when Joe won, "Harlem on Parade" broke loose backstage.

Away from the theater, the week in Toledo wasn't so good. We'd been on the road only a couple of months, and suitcase-and-hotel living was a seedy scene. It always is, for anyone on the road, but for a child it's really thin pickings. When the excitement and concentration and intensity of the show are over, the day is over. We had an apartment with a little kitchen at the Algeo Hotel, and Len would often cook me supper when we got back from the theater, see that I got to bed, and then go out, on a date or somewhere. He was the only person I had. I didn't have friends, and there was no place for me to go or other people for me to pass time with. I'd read a book or thread my Indian beads and then go to sleep.

When Len chose to go out and stay out late, as any young man would do, I felt that I'd been abandoned. Oh yes, I was the abandoned twelve-year-old in a strange city, and I started a little game to show just how abandoned I felt. I'd wake up the instant I heard Len's key in the lock, and when he walked in I'd be hanging half out of bed, my head and arms dragging on the floor, as though I'd had a nightmare or were sick and in a coma. I don't know *what* it was supposed to look like. As he dragged me back into my bed, I would feign deep sleep. And sometimes I'd fall out again. It was a very interesting performance. But I'd become possessive about Len Rosen and his time, where he went and whom he saw. I was surrounded by adults all the time. Not that I

187

particularly craved to be around children, but I did want someone. And the grown-ups around had other things on their mind, God knows, besides the company and entertainment of a small boy.

We had one busy evening at the Algeo when a bat flew in the window of our little kitchen and clattered and clanged among the pots and pans. On this occasion Len was down in the bar with the hotel manager, so I called to say there was a bat upstairs. Len and the manager made several trips back and forth from the bar; the moment the two men would step into our kitchen, the bat would fold itself away in some dark corner. I saw their exchange of glances. Clearly I was crying wolf. But finally the bat took off on a flapping tour of the apartment. I was delighted. See what happens? Leave me alone, and I'm beset by vampires!

About this time, Len started sending my mother weekly accounts, scrawled in pencil on sheets of lined yellow paper. Mother saved them all. For the week in Toledo, I see that we arrived from Cleveland with forty dollars in Len's pocket. My salary at the Rivoli was one fifty. The budget read as follows:

Hotel	$21.56
Laundry	.46
Telephone	3.00
Food	30.00
Postage and papers	3.00
Commissions	22.50
	$80.52

Leaving a balance of $109.43.

At the end of the engagement, Bookie came by in his gray 1936 Chevy sedan. "So how'd the kid do?" We loaded up the music, the trunks, and ourselves, and set off for New York.

XX

We took a suite of rooms at the Somerset Hotel on West Forty-seventh Street. Through the Board of Education we found a tutor, Miss Mahr, an attractive young colored woman from New Jersey, who would take me through the first year of high school, at twenty dollars a week (they talked her down to fifteen dollars). We went to Bruno of Hollywood for some new photographs, to Karnak, a custom tailor on Broadway, for a new suit of white tails with a vest, then to Macy's for stiff-bosomed shirts, size 12 neck. I also had a new overcoat made for me, tailored after one I'd seen worn by Harold Nicholas of the Nicholas Brothers—almost ankle-length, wraparound camel's hair coat, with a tie belt like a bathrobe. Harold Nicholas' coat had two side pleats; mine had one in back.

So here I was walking around New York, my coatails flapping around my shins, with Len and Bookie, trying to get a job. Trying to get someone to listen to me, spending hours waiting in agents' offices or sitting at the hotel, where I was again plagued with nothing to do. I read all the papers—Charlie Chaplin had seduced Joan Barry in his stocking feet;

Ruth Etting was getting a divorce from Colonel Moe Snyder; Belle Baker was getting remarried; the Waldorf was new; the Rainbow Room was fantastic; the International Casino had revolving stages with all the trimmings; and Billy Rose had the French Casino. The rest of the time I listened to the radio, made Indian bead rings, and drew a lot.

An audition was at last arranged at the Cotton Club, which by then had moved down from Harlem into the theater district, but was still Jim Crow. I remember being taken over on a hot, hot afternoon in late September, in my new white tails. "But can't I change when I get there?" I'd asked at the hotel. "Don't be silly, kid—come on, let's go!" Off we went, I in costume, flanked by my two escorts. I must have looked as though I were in custody. Even out of costume, people turned to stare at the three of us on the street, wondering what that concoction was all about, I suppose. At the Cotton Club (decorated with lots of colored cupids flying about), after the audition, they said they were sorry, but they couldn't do anything with me. That was a bitter disappointment.

Club and smoker dates, however, began to come along. I played one evening with Avis Andrews, a beautiful colored woman with a lovely high voice who was appearing at the Cotton Club. I played another date with Bill Robinson and then went on a radio show with him. He sang and tap-danced, I played the piano and sang—and he ignored me throughout. But the columnists were quick to report that Bill Robinson, the dean of colored performers, the beloved entertainer, had taken me under his wing. All of which was hokum; Bill Robinson was in no way concerned with my career. He was "Bojangles," the cock of the walk, a boastful

and difficult man. The nicest thing about him was his wife
Fanny, so pretty, and always at his side—until he divorced
her for a younger woman. Robinson evoked either admiration or dislike—the old-guard colored show-business con-
tingent reverently called him "Uncle Billie," the new breed
was coldly unimpressed by his braggadocio and overbearing
ways. But no matter; our names were linked in the columns,
and through that I landed my first decent job, an October
engagement at the Frolics Cafe.

The Frolics was very smart. It was over the Winter Garden, where the Hawaii Kai restaurant is now. There were two
orchestras; one played society music, one played Latin music.
Joe E. Lewis was top banana—the M.C., the stand-up comic,
and singer of a few songs. Parodies were his forte: "Sam, you
made the pants too long" burlesqued "O Lord, You Made
the Night Too Long." "The Merry-Go-Round Broke Down,"
an innocuous ditty of the day, became "Mary Brown broke
down. Mary went to town. She told her dad that she was
bad. And then she add, 'Ooh, Papa, ooh, Papa! . . .'" and so
on. In 1938, when Joe Louis was rematched with Schmeling, a Lewis take-off closed with, "I'm yelling, don't bring
Schmeling. That's why darkies were born." And the audience
cheered. Almost no one was rooting for Schmeling, the German. Few Americans wanted the title to leave the States,
even though it meant having a colored fighter as world
champion.

It was no secret that Joe E. Lewis was a heavy drinker,
but he was an amiable drinker—he liked everyone in the
show, we were his buddies. A stunning blonde named Joan
Abbott sang "Love Is On the Air Tonight" for openers, and
then "The Loveliness of You" and "The Lady Is a Tramp,"

from *Babes in Arms,* a Broadway hit that year. A funny team, Gerry and Turk, did a dance act, and they danced well—they danced like a colored team. Their act always closed with Gerry, a small woman, her hair frizzed into what would be called an "Afro" today, singing "Black and Blue." She did a mean blues, and Joe E. Lewis, with more than enough under his belt, would get into the act, sit down beside her, mimic her gestures and react to the plaintive lyrics. Or ask her how come she got so black and blue, or was it true she combed her hair with an eggbeater?

I was held over at the Frolics for another two weeks, this time with Lou Holtz as top banana. *Variety* reported his salary to be $3,500 a week. His straight girl was Manya Roberti, who turned herself out à la Brenda Frazier, played the guitar, and sang in Polish. Holtz was into everything throughout the show, interrupting performers, swapping gags with them, insulting them, insulting the audience, knocking them out with his Jewish dialect stories, British dialect stories, and dirty stories. He also sang parodies. One, to the tune of "Never in a Million Years," ribbed the WPA— "A couple on relief were blessed with a baby boy, so it appears. Do you think the little jerk will ever go to work? No, never in a million years. . . ."

The WPA spoof was typical of the times. The Roosevelt administration and the Roosevelts themselves were an unending source of material for nightclub acts. There was a surfeit of Fireside Chat imitations, the cigarette-holder cocked in the teeth, the FDR grin, and "My friends. . . ." Mrs. Roosevelt, of course, offered a field day for fluty-voiced take-offs or rotten jokes about her looks. All so bad. Even the little dog, Fala, was dragged in for laughs. Roosevelt himself

192

popped up in more popular songs than any other President we've had. In Jimmy Van Heusen's "How About You?", in Vernon Duke's and Ira Gershwin's "I Can't Get Started." And one of the star-spangled production numbers in *Sing Out the News* was Harold Rome's "Franklin D. Roosevelt Jones." There was even an allusion to the NRA blue eagle in "Coffee in the Morning, Kisses Every Night"—another Depression song expressing the cheerful sentiment that we may have been broke, but we sure were happy. . . .

But back to the Frolics and Lou Holtz, and a few words from *Variety* on his style: "Holtz still carries the cane but he's quit using it for any but orthodox purposes, and the gals no longer are so hypernervous. . . ." And a small colored boy coming out in tails evoked endless witticisms from Mr. Holtz.

"Years ago," he would say, "when Healy and Cross were making their debut in show business, Cross became ill one night and Healy went out to Harlem and had a tryst with a dark uptown beauty. A child was born. Years went by, the child was given piano lessons. And tonight that child is here. Ladies and gentlemen, I give you the son of Healy and Harlem Hattie. . . ." Or I'd be introduced as the son of Broadway Rose and Bojangles Robinson. I was told not to be upset by this. That was show business. So I'd go out and sing "Darling, *Je Vous Aime Beaucoup*," "Gone with the Wind," "You're Not the Kind." And the audience loved it.

But *Variety* wasn't altogether smitten by my performance. "Bobby Short, pickaninny type, is a colored singer of hot songs for which he plays his own piano accompaniment. He may have a better chance of climbing the ladder by turning to different song material. Is the kind of a colored kid type who should be doing ballads or sweet melodies rather than a strictly Harlemish torch. . . . His style of delivery makes it sound like he belongs in a Harlem cellar cafe."

Before the Frolics engagement was over, I began doubling at La Grande Pomme on the East Side, taking taxis back and forth to make the next show at one place or the other. But this brought my weekly take to $225—$100 at the Frolics and $125 at La Grande Pomme. This last was a small room with a few tables and a tiny piano pulled out on the stage. A sophisticated, rather special room, with splendid drawings by Zito on the walls, a relaxed and easy atmosphere, and a quiet, well-dressed clientele, obviously well-heeled people who were amused by a small boy playing the piano and singing, who listened and enjoyed it, and asked for more. No screaming or yelling from the audience, and I didn't have Lou Holtz to contend with. I was the only one on the bill, there was no orchestra, and I performed for twenty or thirty minutes at a stretch, the show running smooth as cream. I liked La Grande Pomme, but when the night was over, I was a very, very tired child.

Curiously, during that entire New York winter I didn't see a single Broadway production; curious, because Len made such an effort to have me see the best of vaudeville and the best nightclub acts, introducing me to whatever was new and good in music. Not only had he taken me to a music shop in Chicago to hear Art Tatum on records, but as soon as we got to New York, he'd taken me to the Famous Door on West Fifty-second to hear Tatum in person. But it never occurred to anyone to take me to the theater. Or to the Statue of Liberty or the zoo or the Natural History Museum, for that matter, instead of hanging around the hotel room between engagaments. So I didn't see *Babes in Arms* or *I Married an*

Angel, both of which opened and scored that winter. Or Kitty Carlisle, who was playing in Oscar Strauss' *Three Waltzes.* All this I picked up from the newspapers. I followed all the columns and the reviews. Gertrude Lawrence was starring in *Susan and God,* Bette Davis in the film *Jezebel.* Jack Buchanan took a full page in the holiday issue of *Variety* to say Happy New Year. Seeley and Fields finished a record-breaking twelve weeks at the Chez Paree in Chicago; Blossom Seeley, who traveled with monogrammed slip covers for the chairs she used backstage, who opened each show wherever she played amid clouds of Shalimar; her audience was overwhelmed by her jewels and wardrobe—and her perfume.

Variety took a stand on civil rights that winter, reporting a bill introduced in Congress by Harlem Democrat William T. Andrews. The proposal said, in effect, that a cafe or restaurant that has a legal license to sell liquor has no legal right to turn away customers because of their color. The bill fizzled, but it was an interesting approach, an early stab in the right direction.

I was taken to see Judy Garland at Loew's State. She was perhaps fourteen or fifteen years old, charming and completely professional, her voice steady and clear and lovely. But more than that, she had an innate sense of what to do and how to sing. Every time you turned on the radio that winter, you'd hear her recording of "You Made Me Love You." Another top record at the time was *"Bei Mir Bist Du Schön"* by the Andrews Sisters. I'd played a benefit with them early in the fall at the New Yorker Hotel, the sisters draped about the piano like the three Muses, and nobody really cared. Then suddenly, they had a new manager, a new arranger, *"Bei Mir Bist Du Schön,"* and fame and fortune.

Again at Loew's State I saw Ella Fitzgerald and Chick Webb. Ella was the new singing star, and everyone was picking up her style. She sang so smoothly, with an unequaled sense of phrasing. I listened to each record she made, and studied the arrangements for any phrasing or tempo that I could possibly incorporate into my own performance. In the show at Loew's State she sang "So Rare" and "Don't Be That Way," and of course she hit the big charts with "A-Tisket, A-Tasket." Chick Webb, one of the great, great drummers, was crippled, so rather than being his own M.C., which was customary for an orchestra leader, an attractive colored man named Bardu Ali served as M.C. And in Chick Webb's rhythm section, incidentally, was a young bass player, Beverly Peer, who now plays bass for me.

Eddie South was around, a colored jazz violinist who had great success abroad, particularly in Germany where he was known as the "Black Angel"—the *Schwarz Engel*. Snub Mosely was also around, a colored man who'd written his own theme, "The man With the Funny Horn," which he played on a cut-down trumpet. Tiny Bradshaw had an orchestra up in Harlem, and Gladys Bentley was at the Club Ubangi, singing her ludicrously filthy songs—"The Last Time I Saw Harris" and "She Went Back to Alice and He Went Back to Fred" and "Christopher Colombo"—so dirty, they were sheer nonsense. The Nicholas Brothers were covering the town, at the Cotton Club and then in *Babes in Arms* with Mitzi Green, so I ran into them often in the Broadway neighborhood: hence my wraparound coat like Harold Nicholas'. One of his songs that year was "I'm Mammy's Little Brown-Skinned Angel, I'm Mammy's Little Pumpkin Pie," and my manager, always in the market for new material, thought perhaps I should learn that song. But it didn't appeal to me. That sort of sentiment left me cold, even though the *Variety* reviewers who didn't like me at the Frolics might have been happier if I'd gone in for the pickaninny bunkum. There was still a surprising dose of the Uncle Tom syndrome in show business. I remember one agent, who had on the wall a plaque given him by his colored performers. It read: "To our Great White Father." Again, joking on the level.

One day in Irving Mills' office, I met Duke Ellington. He was in the throes of writing the score for the next Cotton Club revue, in which he was to be starred with Mae Johnson and Peg Leg Bates, the colored tap dancer with a wooden leg. Ellington's Cotton Club score had some very attractive songs—"Scronch," the name taken from an earlier dance step, and "I Let A Song Go Out Of My Heart," and "If You Were In My Place," which Ivie Anderson recorded. And I believe that in that same revue, my fat lady friends, the Peters Sisters, sang "It's Always Springtime in Honolulu."

But after all those classroom speeches on My Favorite Famous Person, when I actually met Ellington, it was like meeting anybody. He had a graciousness about him that put me immediately at ease, that Ellington graciousness and openness that has always been first nature with him. In Irving Mills' office that day, I said to myself, "This is easy," and I wasn't nervous at all.

It was a strange winter. We had success, but not the success my managers had expected. As the season went on, conflicts began to flare between Len and me. (Bookie had cut out for Chicago; he had other things on his mind, and the hopscotch search for the next job made him nervous.) One eve-

ning, for example, I was taken to Ethel Merman's by a man
named Harry Link, one of her beaus whom we'd met at the
Irving Berlin publishing office. She, too, was charming and
delighted with my piano playing and said so. And in a letter
I wrote home later that night, I quoted Miss Merman: "She
said I was great," for which Len slapped me down. How dare
I be that "self-conceited!" So I changed it to read that I had
met Ethel Merman and she thought I sang very well. The
revision passed the censor.

To add to our problems, we fetched up against another
high-powered agent like Joe Glazer in Chicago. This time it
was Nat Nazarro, who ran and literally owned a stable of
colored performers, including Chuck and Chuckles, Moke
and Poke, Buck and Bubbles, and Avis Andrews. They were
all working under long-term financial contracts that allowed
them a certain minimum percentage of their earnings; the
rest was invested or put in trust by Mr. Nazarro. He held all
purse-strings, and who knew what fancy bookkeeping was
afoot; not to say that Nazarro was embezzling salaries, but
his organization was run on a perform-now-and-collect-later
basis. He was a formidable character, and after I'd played for
him in his office, he immediately told my managers to go to
hell, they didn't know what they were doing. He said he'd
take me on right that minute and turn me into a veritable
Fats Waller; he'd pay my expenses and send me out on the
road with Fats Waller for six or eight months; I would live
with Fats Waller and learn to mimic everything Fats Waller
did. Then he showed me how he, Nat Nazarro, had shown
Mr. Waller how to flip over a page of music with a stagey
flourish. "That's what I can teach *you*," said Nazarro, "and
if you pattern yourself after Fats Waller you can become a

star. . . ." Well, we had our reservations about Mr. Nazarro, so I didn't sign. The last word on Nat Nazarro was a recent television exchange between Moms Mabley and John Q. Bubbles. Moms, all admiration for Mr. Bubbles, asked him about his old manager. Bubbles replied that Nazarro had died, and Moms' response was: "He died? Thas' good . . ."

Much serious thought was given to changing my act, not along the lines laid out by Nazarro, but into and including tap dancing. And why not? I was a colored boy, I was supposed to have that innate sense of rhythm. But I could never loosen up enough to do much more than fumble through a self-conscious dance step of perhaps six measures. I visited a studio not far from the Somerset, and the instructor, a colored man, said that for five hundred dollars he'd throw the book at me and in no time at all I'd be a dancing fool. But we didn't have the five hundred, and it would have been wasted anyway. Still, I was always intrigued by dance routines, hanging in the wings to watch what was to me the most intricate and difficult of show-business trades, far more complicated to master than juggling or knife-throwing or acrobatics, certainly more difficult than piano playing and singing. I was continually amazed at the girls in the chorus line who could learn and remember new choreography every week, all of them crackling out the steps in unison. For me, tap dancing always remained a mysterious, fourth-dimensional art.

All right, we'd done a few broadcasts, worked a Broadway nightclub and La Grande Pomme, gotten some mentions in the columns. And at Irving Mills' office, I'd met Leonard Feather, a jazz critic from the *Melody Maker* in London, who went back to England and published a piece on me. The

Cotton Club had turned thumbs down, so when the Apollo Theater in Harlem became interested, Len and I went up there several times to scout the lay of the land. If hired, I'd be appearing before a sophisticated, mostly colored audience; apart from brief appearances at the Regal in Chicago, I hadn't played to a Negro house. We weren't certain that I could carry it off with the Harlem audience.

Lucky Millinder and his band were regulars at the Apollo. And Moms Mabley was there, doing the same sort of act she does today, the rasping voice, the down-to-earth, raw humor. Out she'd come, dressed like an old scrubwoman, and flirt with Millinder, in his best pearl-gray tuxedo, hair slicked back. And she'd say, "Lucky, you sho' are lookin' fine. That suit Ah bought for you fits you well. . . ." And the audience would roar.

Pigmeat Markham was another headliner with his "Here Come De Judge" and "Open De Door, Richard"—Pigmeat, locked out of his house, knocking at the door, up on a ladder knocking at the window, saying "Richard, open de door!" He was a genius, just by using the name Richard instead of another name. Another Pigmeat favorite was "The Businessman's Skit." The straight man comes out and says, "Listen, I want to be in show business." And Pigmeat tells him, "Sure. We've got a skit here. All you have to do is take this briefcase and walk across the stage like a businessman." Whereupon the straight man with briefcase minces across the stage. "Wait, Wait! I said to walk like a businessman." So off goes the straight man with the briefcase and crosses the stage a second time in the same mincing walk. "Now, just a minute, there. We told you to walk like a businessman." The straight man then puts his hand on his hip and says, "You don't know what my business *is* . . ." Blackout.

Andy Kirk's band—"Andy Kirk and His Clouds of Joy"— were also regulars at the Apollo. Pha Terrell was the male singer, and Kirk's pianist and sometime arranger was Mary Lou Williams, still a great light in jazz.

Amateur Nights at the Apollo were famous. And ruthless. If you didn't make the grade, you'd be booed off the stage. If you were terrible, you'd be shot off (prop guns with blanks), sirens would sound, the hook would come out. I saw an Amateur Night from the wings. It was crude and brutal and hilarious. The audience was just waiting for the kill.

Sometimes the contestants couldn't even speak intelligibly, and the M.C. always began with a put-on. "We have a young lady for you now . . . an eye-filler. . . ." And the audience would howl. That's all they needed. They knew it would be an enormous, fat housewife, who'd shamble on and shake the boards.

"Step right up, Sister. What's your name?"

"Pearl Jones." (A low mumble.)

"What? Speak up, Sister."

"Pearl Jones."

"Where do you come from, Mrs. Jones?"

"Ah'm from Georgia." (Screams from the audience.) "But ah'm from Brooklyn, now."

"What are you going to sing for us, Mrs. Jones?"

"Ah'm goin' to sing 'Blessed Jesus . . .'" (Mumble mumble mumble.)

In no time at all, more screams from the audience, boos, sirens, the shot gun, and sometimes the hook. All of it was unbelievable. But the best and worst tried out there. Ella Fitzgerald began her career on just such a night. She walked onto that stage, and she sang "Judy" by Hoagy Carmichael and was magnificent. In no time at all, she was starring with Chick Webb's orchestra.

All of this, then, was the Apollo theater, one of the big houses on the vaudeville loop played principally by colored artists and catering to colored audiences. Other big theaters on this list were the Howard in Washington, D.C., the Regal in Chicago, and the Lincoln in Los Angeles, with stops in between. The colored vaudeville and nightclub circuit was so busy that some performers never played the white houses —Pigmeat Markham, Sandy Burns, Moms Mabley, Butter Beans and Susie, Dusty Fletcher. Each theater had a permanent or semipermanent staff of M.C.'s, production singers, and chorus line, as well as ex-chorus girls who helped out backstage or would occasionally do turns as straight girls in the blackout skits.

When the Apollo decided to hire me, I was petrified. But the producer had me come up one night, went over my material with me, and selected what he thought would be best for the audience. Everyone told me I was great, that I had nothing to worry about. So the big day arrived, and I was given a featured billing. The orchestra that week was Louis Russell's. He was a fine musician who frequently took over Louis Armstrong's band when Armstrong was doing something else. Russell had a trombone player named George Washington, whom I'd met earlier with Fletcher Henderson's orchestra in Milwaukee. It was like old times to see him, and of course this began to happen more and more. I started recrossing paths with people I'd played with in other theaters or clubs in other towns, as one inevitably does, but it made me feel tremendously professional. I, too, was now part of the fraternity.

I learned a few lessons in my first two days up at the Apollo. We did well, we never did poorly, but we didn't come within miles of what we thought we were going to do. When my old friend, Timmy Rogers, came around, Len told him, "Bobby's doing all right, but he's not killing them." Timmy explained that the Apollo customers had seen so much— they'd seen everything—and they were a difficult audience. He said I was too "downtown" for them, that they didn't care about my size or my age, but were interested only in my ability. And this was being measured in terms of my familiarity with the hit songs of the day in Harlem.

I changed my whole format immediately and began to sing songs that were popular in Harlem. And my show improved altogether. I recall singing "Love Is the Thing, So They Say" —an Ella Fitzgerald hit—and the audience, totally forgetting that the provocateur on the stage was a child, just leaned back and clapped as though I were a thirty- or forty-year-old blues singer. They didn't care who was doing it, so long as it was being done.

Throughout that week at the Apollo, Miss Mahr came to the theater every day and gave me my lessons in the dressing room—French, English, algebra, and so on. Sometime during that period we ran into trouble with the city about child-labor laws. This was a real threat to my career, but Bookie solved it by having one of his henchmen go to the Joliet City Hall and extract a birth certificate for a sixteen-year-old colored boy who had died. Whenever I was asked my age, we'd flash this birth certificate and explain that Bobby Short

was only my stage name. We had a few token visits and inquiries here and there from the authorities, but a theater
manager or a producer would say, Sure, he's sixteen. Go talk
to him, you'll see how old he is. Or, Go call his mother. She
was there. And then someone else would say, All right, move
along. Show's on. Out of the way, let's go. And that would
be the end of it.

Something else is happening about this time. I'm getting
more sure of myself. I'm beginning to realize that I am the
breadwinner. I am the gimmick around which everything is
revolving. I'm beginning to appreciate how powerful I am—
I can make or break an audition, an engagement, a meeting
with someone important. So I begin to speak my piece, more
and more. Len and I had an open conflict about a cot that
was rented for my dressing room. I decided that since I was
the one who was out on stage performing all afternoon and
half the night, I should have first crack at the cot for a nap.
My salary was paying for the cot (a two-dollar rental fee),
I was doing the work, and I was the one who'd lie down on
that cot and go to sleep between shows.

Then one of the house staff, a lady named Vivian Harris,
who worked backstage and took parts in blackout skits as
well as burlesque routines, said to me, "Where'd you get
those awful shoes? Why don't you get that shiftless manager
of yours to buy you some decent shoes?" I'd never presumed
to question any part of my stage wardrobe, but now I did.
Len took me down the street to a shop that sold dancing
shoes, and I was bought a beautiful pair of white kid pumps
to wear with my tails.

On the bill during my engagement at the Apollo was Sonny
Woods, who sang with Louis Russell's orchestra and stopped

the show with "Empty Saddles." Bobbe Caston also sang with the band. Pigmeat Markham did two or three of his marvelous skits with Jimmy Basquette as his straight man; Jimmy Basquette, who later played Uncle Remus in the Disney film, *Tales of Uncle Remus.* Every now and then they brought in a white act, and that week it was the Little Johns. The Little Johns, four or five men and one woman, juggled—and they drank. They used bowling pins, knives, hatchets, performing in front of a dark blue velvet drop that hid the grand piano all set up for my act. Many a time, if the piano hadn't been behind that velvet curtain, they would have fallen flat. One Little John after another would totter into the curtain, blind drunk, grapple with the folds, catch his balance against the piano, and reel back to center stage. The audience didn't care. They were just waiting for the next act, and the next and the next. I felt sorry for the Little Johns, scrabbling through their juggling act. They were "the white act" and obviously at the end of their rope, up in Harlem and nobody went near them.

I learned quickly that week, things I couldn't have learned from Len Rosen in ten years. Sharpen up this . . . don't say that . . . talk longer . . . take your time. Use the microphone properly . . . rush back out there for your bow . . . bow to the M.C. And between shows, upstairs in a rehearsal room, I'd work like the devil on my own new arrangements. I'd composed an opening, for example, to "Love Is a Thing," because of the sophisticated lyrics about love making a fool of me. So to cover the gap between my age and the sentiments of the song, I introduced it with a verse, "Love, love, love. Everybody talks about it. I don't know a thing about it. All I do is go by what they say." From there I went into the

205

verse, as written, and it worked out very well. But Len also had me trying to learn Yiddish. He'd already put "My Yiddishe Mama" into the repertoire, and now he was teaching me "Eli, Eli." But I couldn't get with that German talk at all. Yiddish, like tap dancing, was out of my range.

We worked hard at that theater. There was no movie between shows, just a couple of shorts, then back on stage again. On Saturday we did five shows. But still it was an easygoing week. The feeling backstage was casual. I was impressed by the way people who'd played there were always returning. You'd come off, and someone would be in the wings who'd been there the week before or was scheduled for the week after. I remember Benny Paine coming back—Benny Paine, who'd been Cab Calloway's pianist, the night I'd played at the Circle Theater in Indianapolis.

But every chance I had—between Miss Mahr's tutoring, my Yiddish lessons with Len, my naps on the controversial cot—I'd be in the wings watching the chorus line. In one production number, those lovely *café au lait* girls were on stage with a backdrop of a garden, a trellis and great vases of flowers on the side, and all of the girls in long organdy frocks, picture hats, and little parasols. They were ladies promenading in a formal garden, and for the first chorus they just strolled around, with the parasols twirling on their shoulders. But every now and then a hip would slip, just enough, and a couple of steps would be a little too jazzy, just enough, so you knew they were really the colored chorus line up there doing their number. They weren't strolling on anybody's Hudson estate or Charleston garden—they were the Apollo line, and the audience went wild. And I was in heaven, I was in love with them all.

206

Notice something here. For an awfully long time, only fair complexions made the chorus line. It just wasn't fashionable to have a dark chorus line. This eased somewhat in the thirties, but in old film clips of Bill Robinson, for example, the line behind him looks just about white. Even Josephine Baker was made the butt of many jokes because she was brown-skinned—as brown as I am. Of course, when Josephine became the Empress of France, she showed them all; and she skillfully played up her dark skin by always having as light a chorus as possible. Before one New York appearance in the thirties, she wrote ahead to her producer, laying it on the line—the chorus was to be blonde and fair-skinned; nothing but Nordics would do for Miss Baker. Mae West had the same sense of color contrast, which she used in reverse, always pointing up her blonde hair and pale skin by having other members of the cast, men and women, darker in complexion than she. And always with many Negroes in her films to show off her whiteness. In *Belle of The Nineties,* Duke Ellington's orchestra accompanied her songs, and in one scene she had not one but several colored maids scurrying around her. In another classic Mae West number, a Negro chorus down on the levee sings "Troubled Waters," which drifts through the windows of Miss West's hotel suite, and there she is, white as the driven snow, listening to the darkies: "I'm goin' to drown down in those troubled waters . . . They're creepin' 'round mah soul. . . ."

Well, among the girls in the Apollo chorus line, my special favorite was Annabelle, and Annabelle liked me. She called me her baby, and every morning she greeted me backstage with a kiss, and another kiss at the end of the day. I'd loaf past the chorus girls' dressing room, saucer-eyed at all those half-naked ladies sitting in there.

Down the street, the Braddock Hotel cooked what is now known as "soul food," and the chorus girls would have it sent in between shows—collard greens and chitlings, black-eyed peas boiled down with pork, or red-pepper rice. Len and I used to go to Eddie Green's to eat; Eddie Green, who was a featured comic on the New York stage and on Ed Gardner's radio show, *Duffy's Tavern*, also had a barbecue place up in Harlem. And I remember, when we walked the streets in Harlem on our way to Eddie Green's, hearing Ella Fitzgerald and Ethel Waters records on the loudspeakers from the record shops.

Decca and Bluebird, being cheap record labels (thirty-five cents a record, against seventy-five for a Victor record), led the field in selling colored artists, and the colored entertainment world had a hit parade of its own, quite separate from the white hit parade. The popular songs in Harlem that season were "I'll Get Along Somehow," "Love Is The Thing, So They Say," "Until The Real Thing Comes Along," "This Is My Last Affair," and "If You Ever Should Leave." Decca printed a Sepia Series, and Bluebird called their series Race Records. Unlike today, when any good record store carries a sampling of the current and choice, at that time record manufacturers shipped only certain types of records to specific parts of the country, to specific cities, and even to particular neighborhoods. Race and Sepia records went to Negro sections; country and western to the hinterlands, the South and the Southwest; Cole Porter or Rodgers and Hart show tunes to the more urban areas. And so it went.

XXI

After the Apollo, we had a week at the Howard, in Washington, D.C. It was a run-down theater, the stage patched with tin, which I tripped over on one of my exits, falling headlong into the wings. Backstage the only decent mirror (even it was cracked) happened to be in my dressing room, and everyone came in for a last-minute look at their make-up and costumes. And out front the steam radiators hissed on and off throughout the show. I panicked when I first heard this, thinking the audience was hissing me. But the Howard was as easygoing and relaxed as the Apollo; and even though the theater may have been a little shabby, my salary—two twenty-five for the week—was the very best. I was introduced to crab cakes in D.C., at a colored restaurant called the Little Gray Tea Shop. I ate crab cakes every day for the entire week.

Teddy Hill's orchestra starred; Teddy Hill, just back from London with a sharp array of English-tailored suits. We had the Renée Lamarr trio; Chink Collins, a light-skinned Negro with oriental eyes, as straight man as well as singer; and my old dancing friends from the Frolics, Gerry and Turk. Pigmeat Markham headed the comedy routines and blackouts. He did his In School skit that week, everyone done up in children's clothes, sitting at rows of desks, and Pigmeat with long blond curls. One little girl gets up and says, "I'm late this morning, teacher, because Momma had a new baby." And the teacher says that's very nice that Sally's mother has a new baby. But hasn't Sally's father been out of town for the past year and a half? "Yes, he has," says Sally, "But he writes to Momma every single week." Then Pigmeat in his big blond wig says, "Hmmmm . . . What kin' of fountain pen is *dat?"*

At the beginning of November, we were booked into the Fox Theater in Detroit. The Fox was the biggest house I'd ever played, a castle, and my salary was $250 a week. They'd assembled Bunny Berrigan's orchestra, a troupe of colored Big Apple dancers, a comic or two, and Bobby Short. Berrigan, even then deep into his drinking problem, kept very much to himself, withdrawn and removed from everyone around him. "The Prisoner's Song" was one of his classics at the time, and his theme was "I Can't Get Started With You," one of Vernon Duke's most haunting melodies. Though I stood in the wings to watch every show, it never occurred to me to find out who had composed this song. In 1937, at the age of thirteen, I had little or no knowledge of Broadway's composers and their outstanding scores. I'd heard of Irving Berlin, Sammy Cahn, and Sol Chaplin, and from the movies I was familiar with Gordon and Revel and Robin and Rainger. Another Vernon Duke melody appealed to me in 1937, a song called "Now." But even after *Cabin in the Sky,* I wasn't aware of his name. One day Vernon Duke and I would become friends. And by then of course I'd know he was responsible for so many of the songs in my repertoire—smooth, flowing melodies, always with a highly sophisticated undercurrent of musical complexity.

I became friendly with all of Berrigan's musicians, and his piano player taught me "In A Mist," a Bix Beiderbeck piano classic. Beiderbeck and Art Schefte, as well as two or three others, were writing jazz compositions for piano. I was intrigued by "In A Mist" because I'd heard Teddy Wilson play it on Benny Goodman's Saturday Night Swing Session—a big radio show that also featured the Swingtet: Goodman, Lionel Hampton, Gene Krupa, and Wilson.

Another Berrigan classic I heard that week at the Fox was his arrangement of "Black Bottom," which was an old song and a dance unto itself. It was woven into an accompaniment for the Big Apple Dancers, one of the many professional colored troupes on the vaudeville circuit when the Big Apple was a national craze. Basically the Big Apple was a lindy, and when a couple's turn came to shine, they'd get into the center of the floor and try to out-lindy each other—burning up that stage like a grass-fire, everything going, all the zany gyrations of the lindy hop.

The audience also got a high-flown program of *entr'acte* organ music between the movie and vaudeville show, perhaps the *Poet and Peasant Overture,* or possibly *Rhapsody in Blue.* Here again, Len, with my musical education in mind, saw to it that I was aware of *Rhapsody in Blue* and the *Porgy and Bess* score. Although he had little knowledge of classical music, he was up on the contemporary trend—George Gershwin, Ferde Grofé (*Grand Canyon Suite* and *Mississippi*

Suite), and other American composers who were writing in a semiclassic, semijazz mood.

I see by Len's budget sheet that we sent my mother twenty-five dollars from Detroit. Other weeks we'd only sent ten dollars, and still others, when I wasn't working, we hadn't been able to send anything. What with traveling expenses, commissions, hotel bills, restaurant meals, and the rest of it, we never seemed to get ahead. In Detroit we also bought my little sister Barbara a dress for four dollars, rented the cot for the dressing room, and had my tail suit dry-cleaned, because the concert grand at the Fox had been painted tomato red and I finished the week with dabs of paint on my trousers and coat. So we returned to New York with a balance of seventy-nine dollars to tide us over until the next job. But before we left Detroit, we went to the Flame Club to see Bill Bailey, Pearl's brother, who is another listed by Langston Hughes in his Golden Dozen of colored dancers. There in the line at the Flame Club was Annabelle, pretty Annabelle from the Apollo, and when we went backstage: "Now everybody get away," she said. "Just get away. This is my baby." We had a hug and how are you, sugar, and how's everything going . . .

Around this time we had a random collection of dates. The Folly Theater in Brooklyn, not a good booking, a rag-bag establishment with dressing rooms in the basement and a sign at the head of the stairs that warned all performers not to alter or cut their act in any way while on stage. I could understand the temptation to do so. We did a one-night stand at the Rye Country Club with Henry King's orchestra. Very posh. We did a spot on Benny Goodman's Saturday Night

Swing Session on N.B.C. Bookie set up a weekend at the Père Marquette Hotel in Peoria, and I was given both room and board. Yet four years later, I came up against Whites Only at that same hotel, where I'd once been welcomed without a flicker of an eye. But that's later on.

We played a couple of weekend dates at Laurel-in-the-Pines in New Jersey, through a young agent named Abner Greschler, who years later emerged as the discoverer and manager of Martin and Lewis. "Come on down to Laurel-in-the-Pines," he kept saying—so down we went, just to keep ourselves together. It was a Jewish resort hotel (tobogganing and sleigh rides in the winter months), and strict dietary laws were observed; it was the first place I ever ate a jelly omlette. Len had me primed to meet all trains, with "My Yiddishe Mama."

A young comic named Henny Youngman was on the bill that Thanksgiving weekend, and Eddie Seiler was playing piano with the orchestra. Eddie also wrote songs—one was "Jack Climbed a Beanstalk to Heaven"—and this intrigued me, because I fooled around between shows writing songs myself. Even back in Danville, I'd written a song with one of my neighborhood friends, Betty Morton, and we'd gone so far as to get a copyright. (Where is it buried now?) It was the "hot tamale" theme. My brother Bill had his tamale song, and the tamale man peddled his wares around town, so Betty and I recapitulated all this in yet another version with another tune: "Hot tamales stay in season . . . Listen, I'll tell you the reason . . . Everybody likes hot stuff . . . Some folks just can't get enough . . . Just a nickel, better buy one . . . Just a nickel, better try one . . . Come and get them while you can, from the hot tamale man. . . ."

But Eddie Seiler, down at Laurel-in-the-Pines, meant business. And a few years later he wrote a song called "I Don't Want to Set the World on Fire," in collaboration with Sol Marcus and Benny Benjamin, a young Negro musician from the Virgin Islands. From there on this trio had a series of five or six blockbusters, and they made a lot of money.

I did a vaudeville date at Atlantic City's Steel Pier Theater. Headlining the bill was Eddy Peabody, the Banjo King—a short, ginger-haired man, salt-of-the-earth and old-time America—who indeed played the banjo like a champion. I didn't like Atlantic City at all. It was cold, the boardwalk wasn't very pleasant, and we had a hell of a time finding a place to stay. Our first move in any Northern city was to go to a second or third-class white theatrical hotel, where we usually got a rate and were checked in with never a word said. But this didn't work in Atlantic City. There was a great to-do about my color. After being turned down at four or five hotels, and knowing we had to rehearse that day and open the next night, we couldn't waste any more time. So Len told me to put my hat on to cover my hair and if anybody asked me what I was, I was an East Indian. This I did, and we got into the next hotel.

Len was always worrying about my hair. "Why don't you get it straightened? It looks terrible. Timmy Rogers has *his* hair straightened . . ." But I didn't want to straighten my hair. It wasn't that kinky. Why couldn't I just comb it nicely with a little bit of oil and smooth it down with a stocking cap? Well, every month he took me up to Harlem to have my hair cut—at two bucks a throw, including dressing. He and the barber persuaded me to sit through a "treatment." It wasn't as radical as a straightening job, but was the next thing to it. So I sat there in the chair by the window, and the barber slathered my hair with grease and thick waxes and covered it with a net to make it lie flat. To my acute embarrassment this performance was watched, from start to finish, by a gang of deadpan colored kids who stood enraptured outside on the street.

But after Thanksgiving that year, work came to a standstill. The country was poor, show business was poor, and vaudeville was slowing down to a walk. We were really up against it, going for weeks without paying our rent, doing our laundry in the bathtub. My tutoring was quietly discontinued. Bookie Levin was in again, off again. I think he'd given up on us temporarily. We borrowed money from MCA and from the desk at the hotel, but dead air had closed in around us. Nothing was happening, and Len had a solemn talk with me about Christmas. No Christmas this year, no presents. Very well, no money, no Christmas, and I was prepared to be noble. But at the last minute, Len borrowed again, from the desk or MCA or one of his agent friends, and when we came back to the room from dinner on Christmas Eve, there was a heap of presents he'd bought me at Whelan's drugstore—new books, a game called Big Business, fruit and candy, and a toy typewriter. I took immediately to the typewriter, one with a revolving dial, and typed all my letters home from then on. A merry Christmas after all, and two days later our luck turned. Out of the blue we got an engagement—a theater date in Providence for the first week in January. And the money wasn't bad. One seventy-five, as I recall.

In Providence were the Three Stooges again, but not the

agreeable trio I'd worked with in Kansas City. Sybil Bowan, a mimic and monologuist, topped the bill. Lady monologuists were much in vogue, with heavy emphasis on their elegance and aristocratic ways; Ruth Draper, Cornelia Otis Skinner, and Sheila Barrett made grand appearances at the Waldorf, the Persian Room, and the Rainbow Grill.

One afternoon the show was taken out to the state penitentiary; Sybil Bowan did *her* Eleanor Roosevelt routine for the prisoners. A handicraft shop at the penitentiary sold all sorts of artifacts made by the prisoners from old toothbrush handles. For twenty-five cents I bought a green ring. And this became the object of my first and last show-business superstition. The moment I was announced by the M.C., I made a little ceremony of taking off the ring and putting it in my vest pocket. Thus protected, my talisman at work, I'd walk out on the stage.

But Providence was a bad week for me. Len had jumped on me for swearing—hell or damn it—which was the least of the language I heard around me, but as far as Len was concerned, I suddenly could do no right. He came to me with the news that the Three Stooges said I was without doubt the worst act they had ever worked with, in all their years in vaudeville. Yes, he said, I was the worst act on the bill, and I had the worst manners he'd ever seen, and I was headed down the drain. That was it. We went through a terrible time; we were on the brink of total war. And I didn't want to hear reports on what the Three Stooges had to say. I was performing to the best of my ability and I didn't need a continuing relay of dirty digs from a team of middle-aged vaudevillians. I wasn't as angry with the Three Stooges, as I was angry with Len for reporting their criticisms with such relish. My confidence was shattered, and at that age, I didn't understand what was happening. Now I do. I can understand the situation in which Len found himself. Here was a twenty-eight-year-old man with no personal or private life of his own, shackled to me morning, noon, and night, whether we liked it or not. The summer before, back in Cleveland, he had planned to ask Bookie how *he'd* like it, living with a small colored boy twenty-four hours a day. There was the crux of it—Len was fed up being nursemaid as well as entrepreneur. And he was disappointed—I hadn't zoomed to stardom over night, I hadn't landed a Hollywood contract. I hadn't fulfilled the big dream and the big scheme. We'd go back to New York and probably be broke again within a week, doing laundry in the bathtub and borrowing money from the desk clerk. And that was exactly what happened.

Back from Providence, we paid a few of our bills and then could find no work. Len and I had an armed truce, and I occupied myself with reading and writing letters home and got deeply absorbed in writing a revue on my Christmas typewriter. The revue was based on skits and dance routines I'd seen, songs and arrangements I'd heard. I was going to to take it to Minnie Lee, the head of the community center for colored people in Danville, and with Minnie's help, I would produce my show. I had cast the revue in my mind with hometown talent—who would sing what songs, who would act in what skits—and I'd filled the chorus line—the Eight Red Peppers, as I named them, because I knew at least eight girls in Danville who could carry off the dance routines. Obviously, the thought of going home was in the back of my head, though I wasn't aware of it. So, I worked on my script, and we looked for a job.

Before Christmas we'd been approached several times by Benny Davis, who was putting together a string of new acts. But the pay was bad, fifty a week, so we held out for awhile for more vaudeville dates. After all, it had been two fifty a week at the Fox in Detroit and two twenty-five in the Howard in Washington. But this time around, Benny Davis's fifty dollars was fifty dollars. Davis had written "Margie" once upon a time. And with Fred Cootes he'd done a score for the Cotton Club in the fall of '37, with two outstanding songs, "She's Tall, She's Tan, She's Terrific" and "I'm Always in the Mood for You." So Davis, now a producer as well as composer, booked his revue of young talent into the Yacht Club. We opened there the week after Frances Faye closed —Frances Faye, with her husky voice, her hot piano, and her four-figure salary, who was known as the Zazu Zazu Girl. The Yacht Club was on West Fifty-second Street—Jazz Street, as it was known in those days, several blocks lined with nightclubs and restaurants on both sides, where every jazz musician in town played at one time or another. Leon and Eddie's, the Famous Door, the Onyx Club, the Hickory Club, Tony's, and "21" were all on Fifty-second.

Show business discovered Hawaii in the thirties. Movies appeared with Hawaiian settings, songs were written with Hawaiian themes and Hawaiian words in the lyrics, Hawaiian orchestras sprang up right and left with flowers on their shirts and flowers around their necks, and Hawaiian dancing girls rippled across nightclub floors throughout the country. The Yacht Club jumped on the bandwagon by changing its name to the Hawaiian Yacht Club. They too had the Hawaiian orchestra, and in our revue a Hawaiian girl did a neat hula and sang "Hawaiian War Chant" and "Hawaiian Hospitality."

Most of the performers in the Benny Davis lineup were not much older than I. Margie Knapp, who was about sixteen, traveled with her mother; Margie sang "The Dipsy Doodle" and "The Love Bug Will Get You, If You Don't Watch Out," two of the sillier songs of the thirties. There were the Dorn Brothers and Mary, two boys who played ukeleles while their sister sang. There was Marie Austin, a minute singer, who did "Mama, Oh, Mama, That Moon Is Here Again"—based on Al Pierce's old traveling-salesman gag, "Mama, that man is here again. . . ." Margie also sang "Alexander's Ragtime Band," frothed up into an extravaganza, the type of arrangement that Al Segal specialized in, with changes of mood and changes of tempo, new material added and operatic leads and complicated vocalizing, with the band doing several different layers of soaring and spinning and fiddling. All of this before you got to the song you were going to sing.

These gaudy arrangements cost a lot of money, but you got lots of wear from them, because it could take a couple of years to cover the vaudeville circuit, the nightclub circuit, and assorted radio programs. Today, after two or three television shows, your material is old hat and you've had it. At any rate, Margie Knapp rambled through the elaborations on "Alexander's Ragtime Band," and the audience was enchanted. I, meanwhile, was doing my own arrangements with the orchestra in the background, while Len—I suppose with the idea of enlarging his stable—latched on to a very pretty girl who'd won some beauty contests in the area. She sang, so he got her into the Yacht Club revue and out on the

219

floor for one evening, singing "The Greatest Mistake In My Life." But nothing came of it, just a thank you very much, dear, and we'll call you later.

The Yacht Club was a nice engagement. I stayed on six or eight weeks. The salary was steady, we were keeping up with our bills, as well as eating regularly, and I had friends who were more or less my contemporaries. So I brought in my Christmas game—Big Business—and for the first time had people to play it with. We had a running match going backstage. I also got some good publicity. I was the budding Cab Calloway, a youthful Duke Ellington, a juvenile Fletcher Henderson. Even, for a switch, a colored Bobby Breen. And people were coming backstage to tell me that I was a genius, a prodigy, a fine little showman. All of which boosted my ego. Maybe I wasn't the worst performer in the world, as I'd been told in Providence.

XXII

An agent from the MCA office in Cleveland was after us to accept an engagement at the Lookout House in Covington, Kentucky. This, too, we'd turned down earlier that year, because I felt uneasy about working in the southern states. St. Louis and Kansas City were manageable, with Len bootlegging food into the dressing room, running the blockade, so to speak. But to go below the Mason-Dixon line, to accept a long engagement where the barriers were infinite didn't appeal to me at all. Len understood and agreed. But MCA got in touch with us again: "Come down to Covington." So we took the chance.

Covington was a sin city, a wide-open town across the river from Cincinnati. But the entire area was alive with entertainments of every kind, from the Cincinnati Symphony Orchestra to rollerdromes, to gambling casinos, girlie shows, and dining and dancing nightly at roadhouses up and down the pike. When I was there, George Abbott's production of *Brother Rat* came through. So did *Tobacco Road* with John Barton and Sheila Barrett, "The Mad Empress of Mimicry—direct from the Waldorf-Astoria." Madge Carmyle and Kitty

Ralph were on with the Gayety Traveling Burlesque. At the Club Wonder Bar, Mademoiselle Jean Le Wisse was doing her peacock dance, and the coming attraction was Zorita in "The Wedding of the Snake." At the Topper Ballroom, waltz contest finals were being held, with a silver loving cup for the winning couple.

And at the Lookout House on Dixie Highway was "The Most Sensational Show In Town." I got feature billing and good write-ups—"Bobby Short who pounds a hot piano for encore after encore." Also on the bill were Lynn Nagle and Her Wonder Dogs—little fox terriers, ruffs around their necks, who pranced on their hind legs, jumped through hoops, and did backward somersaults; one of them, the comic in the troupe, trained to frisk around the circle the wrong way or stroll off stage. Miss Nagle came on in a scanty pale blue outfit, high heels, blonde frizz, and lots of make-up. She showed me one of her tricks. You stood in front of the dog with a cane, and if the cane pointed in one position, the dog nodded his head; when the cane moved to another angle, the dog shook his head. "Do you like rhubarb?" I asked the terrier. He nodded. I moved the cane. "Do you like meatloaf?" The dog shook his head. Agreed.

Maidie and Ray had a western act with songs and rope tricks and some of that dry western patter of the Will Rogers school. Ray and a girl friend who lived in another town had written a slight verse that I set to music for him. He was very excited and decided to telephone his girl right away.

"Guess what, honey? I got somebody here who set the lyrics to our song, and we're going to sell it. You want to hear?" Yes, of course she did. "Just a minute, honey," and he brought the phone to the piano. I played the new arrangement and sang for her, in my boy soprano. Ray took the phone back when I was finished. "Well, honey. How'd you like it?"

"Fine," she snapped. "But who's the floozy singing it?"

On the same bill as well were Rose and Ray Lyte, a proper dance team; George Downey, an old clown and trick cyclist; and Billy Snider's orchestra, the Kentucky Colonels. The chorus line was headed by Donn Arden, who wound up producing shows at the Lido in Paris, at another club in Rome, and did shows for the Latin Quarter in New York and hotels in Las Vegas. But at the Lookout House in Kentucky that year, he danced right along with the line. Their opener was a Charlie McCarthy number, all the girls with Charlie McCarthy dolls, the heads waggling and bowing. They also did an exotic interpretation of "St. Louis Blues," Donn Arden again dancing amid the girls, now in white tie and tails; the girls were in black chiffon with lots of slinky shoulder motions and head tossings.

One night there was a piercing scream followed by wild sobbing, which could be heard even downstairs in the men's dressing room. One of the chorus ladies had gone to Cincinnati to have something done to her hair, but her hair had been burned and was falling out, so she'd bought a wig to cover the disaster. In the middle of their head-thrashing St. Louis Blues routine, the wig had flown off, soared across the stage, and landed on someone's ringside table. And in those days a wig was an unmentionable. The young lady could not be consoled. It took a day of sympathy and cajoling to get her back on the stage, in the wig.

Now, the men's dressing room was a rank pit in the basement, everyone jammed together in one large room with no windows. Old George Downey, the trick cyclist, took at least an hour to put on his clown make-up. That was all right, but during that hour and between shows, Mr. Downey coughed and hawked and spit, coughed and hawked and spit. And he spit on the floor. No one had the guts to say anything. They just cleared off to the side and gave him a wide berth. So I wound up as the delegation of one to ask him to stop, "Please, Mr. Downey. Don't spit on the floor," while everyone applauded and cheered.

Also trapped with us in that dressing room was a juggler named Emile, who didn't speak English very well. He was Polish or Russian, and his costume was a middle-European gypsy outfit. Poor Emile! The two Rays—Ray of the western rope trick and Ray of the ballroom dance team—took an immediate dislike to him. They were down in that dressing room night after night carrying on like Faust. Emile was their victim, and they didn't let up for a moment. Torment, torment, torment. In his act, Emile balanced a broomstick on his tongue while juggling a fall-out of flying objects, so one night the two men dipped the end of the broomstick in tabasco. Another night they dipped it in dog pee. They accused Emile of being a eunuch, and on and on. Merciless. Meantime, old George Downey was still spitting on the floor, and we had Donn Arden's distresses with his girls. Arden was a typical choreographer, nervous and anxious, shouting about quick changes and the proper make-up, dark lights and white lights, and oh dear Christ, how will we get through this evening's run!

Away from Lookout House and the snake pit, Len and I split the southern scene—he lived in a hotel in Cincinnati just over the bridge, and I boarded in Covington with an elderly

colored lady named Mrs. Rice. She liked having a small boy
in the house, and I enjoyed her piano. Len and I met for
meals in Negro cafes, as we had in Our Nation's Capitol. I
was stared at in the North when we ate in white restaurants,
where an adult Negro would not have been served. But in
the Southland, when Len joined me at a colored cafe, *he* was
stared at.

Covington lasted three or four weeks. I then went home
for a visit, before going back to New York, where work was
still very, very tight. We did some club dates, but nothing
big. We had one out-of-town booking in the spring, a return
engagement at the Tower Theater in Kansas City. The headliner was Irene Taylor, who'd been with Paul Whiteman, and
all of Whiteman's singers were exceptional—the Rhythm
Boys, Mildred Bailey, Ramona and Her Piano. All of them
got into films and had good radio exposure and good vaudeville bookings. But audiences never seemed to cotton to Irene
Taylor—she was a singer's singer, too sophisticated, too slick,
too dramatic. And she was marvelous. One of her songs was
"There's going to be no horses in races, no rain in the clouds,
no far-away places, on the day I let you get away. I'll shout
out loud . . ." and behind this a stampeding musical arrangement, while she held the last notes and the band galloped on.
It was again the Al Segal type of arrangement so popular in
those days. Her arrangements were written by her husband
Segar Ellis, who evidently changed his style so frequently,
he couldn't remember them all. In 1961, when I played one
of his 1938 arrangements for him, he couldn't believe he'd
really written it.

"I wrote that?" said Segar.

Yes, I said. He had written it for Irene Taylor, and she'd

sung it in Kansas City. "Huh," said Segar. "Sounds like Al Segal to me . . ."

And while we were in Kansas City, Judy Garland came through on her way to the coast and was brought to the Tower Theater to see the show. Len heard she was there and raced me out front to meet her. "Oh," she said. "I think you're terrific." My day was made.

From Kansas City back to New York, and into the doldrums. We've now edged up to summer, 1938. The next break that at last came our way came from Bookie Levin. We were offered the Oriental Theater in Chicago at one thirty-five a week. A year and a half earlier, when we'd fought the battle of downtown Chicago theaters, James C. Petrillo had won. But now someone in the union owed Bookie a favor, and suddenly it was perfectly okay for Bobby Short, non-union and under age, to play the Oriental. All red tape was slashed. Off we went to Illinois. I'd gotten lots of new arrangements and some fine new songs, and I was really steamed up about the Chicago appearance; back to where I'd started and into the Oriental.

Most big vaudeville houses had resident choreographers, usually women, who pulled the show together, amalgamating the performers booked for a week with a slim thread of continuity, using the chorus line as a link between acts. The lady choreographer at the Oriental had plans for me; upon hearing that a colored boy was on the bill, she was inspired to include a shoe-shine number for me. But I had my own arrangement of "Shoe Shine Boy," and it was one of my best. No, no, no. "Shoe Shine Boy" was to be taken off my list, because it was on *her* list. I was to come out, sing the song, the girls would come on, then I was to go down the line with a shoe-shine stand and cloth and polish each girl's shoes, then scamper off stage. The chorus would do a number in their freshly polished patent leathers, and I'd scamper on again to sing the last eight bars. The end. Applause. When the applause had died, one of the girls would say, "We understand you play the piano, too, Bobby."

"Yes, Miss Eileen, I do."

"Gosh, how about swinging a few things for *us*?"

With that, my cue was to say, "All right, Miss Eileen," turn around, sit down at the piano, and go into what was left of my act.

I wanted to wear my beautiful white tail suit in Chicago, but the shoe-shine sequence called for stylized rags and tatters. To top my distress, the rehearsals never quite synchronized my move to the piano. There was a blackout, and from the back of the stage, almost a half a block away, four stage hands pushed the grand piano down front on a rolling platform. That platform shot out of the dark at a different speed at every performance. I'd either be knocked down, which the audience thought was a delicious part of the act, or cracked behind the knees, or I'd turn around to find that the piano hadn't arrived yet. I could hear it coming, but I couldn't see it. The transition was badly managed, clumsy and unprofessional. And I was miserable at the piano in those rags and tatters. They just didn't jibe with my routine.

Len Rosen was doing some backstage wandering again, and had fallen in with a colored porter. He asked the porter what was wrong with my act, and the porter had unlimited stagey advice about what I should be doing. And Len spared me none of it. Furthermore, said Len, the old porter knew what he was talking about. Oh yes, he'd seen them come and go. All of this sounded like a Warner Brothers musical, where an ancient wardrobe lady or tottering doorkeeper steps forward as the production stumbles, and from accumulated years of backstage lore, supplies the magic word. "What the finale needs is six white horses and an amber spot on Miss Marlowe." The old-timer is right, the show is a smash, and everyone's troubles are over. But when I said I didn't care what the old man backstage had to say, Len suggested that I didn't like his advice because he was only a porter. And that I didn't like him because he was colored.

What a bitter week that was. I hated Len. I hated the Oriental Theater. I hated Chicago. *Variety's* review was not unkind, but they felt that my act was inadequate, that I wasn't ready for big-time vaudeville, that my routine needed some serious work, and so on. Len read me the review, aloud, and off we went again into what my act needed. It needed this or it needed that. But I thought to myself, what this act really needs is a rest. I was thirteen years old, and something inside me said, you'd better get out while you can. And you'd better be in school next fall.

So when the week at the Oriental was over, I packed my suitcase, asked for carfare and a few extra dollars, said, "Len, good-bye." I got on the train and went home to Danville.

HOME AGAIN

XXIII

When I'd left home in 1936, the family had been on its feet. We had the new house on Oak Street, there was still some money in the bank, and Mildred's paycheck from her job with Emergency Relief Corps kept the household together. A little poverty was normal for us, the pinch of hard times an old and familiar way of life. But when I came home in 1938, the family was back to normal—we were really poor. We had fallen from grace, and we were still falling.

Reg had left home the year before at the age of fifteen, dropping out of high school, where he was a good student, to join the Civilian Conservation Corps. He had talked Mother into signing the papers that he was eighteen, on the strength of the family allotment; CCC boys were paid something like eighteen dollars a month, and their parents received twenty-five a month, although many parents returned most of this to their sons, young men out to see the world and forever short of cash. Reg, like thousands of boys from the lower middle class, had left school and home in the 1930's to look for something else, somewhere else, hoping things would be better in another town. If you moved on, maybe you'd outdistance the Depression. Take to the road. Ride the rails. One of our friends, a fine colored boy named Reginald Norton, had been killed jumping a freight; he too had gone off on the aimless search, scrounging from town to town.

Roosevelt's CCC camps gave young men a place to go and a job to do—reforestation, construction of dams and new state parks, and projects to halt soil erosion. Reg was stationed near Chicago, and the only bright light during my final week at the Oriental was his visit backstage after a show to say how are you and how's it going. I also remember when he visited Danville shortly after I'd come home, and Reg—in his sweetness and fondness for me—asked me to play something for him. That was always a big compliment, when one of my big brothers asked me to play. After I'd finished, there were tears in his eyes. "Oh," he said, "you've grown up so, and you play the piano so well . . ."

My oldest brother Bill was suffering his own personal torments, driven by a sense of futility and dissatisfied with school. He was a good student and a favorite with his teachers. But what was the use? Where would it take him? The town was full of high-school graduates out of work. Bill looked ahead to nothing, and was discouraged. Fed up, angry. He let school, classes, and homework slide, stood back and flunked out.

Mildred, the breadwinner for so long, was now married and had left her job. Her husband, an undertaker's assistant, was a hometown boy, which pleased Mother. When I returned home, Mildred and her husband and their baby son were living in the back in the old laundry house, now a little apartment. But her husband, the nice hometown boy, turned out to be nothing but a rascal, who finally vanished from the scene. So Mildred, with one small child and a second on the way, closed up her little apartment and moved back in with us.

My kid sister Barbara was still getting straight A's at school, and my oldest sister Naomi still managed the household when Mother was at work. Mother had found a job in a WPA garden—a federal truck farm, so to speak—and from there she'd got a job with a WPA canning factory, at forty-eight dollars a month. Here the women worked in a large basement room putting up Swiss chard, peas, carrots, corn, beans, and soup meat. These canned goods were then doled out to the poor. We also got food orders issued by the relief corps. We didn't get much, perhaps ten or twelve dollars every other week.

In a big city like Chicago, it was easy to pull all kinds of capers, because your case worker didn't know your family and had no way of knowing (the poor are very close-mouthed) if your father were making book or your sister were on the streets. But in a small city like Danville, your case worker knew the entire family, who was working and who wasn't, and there was no fooling around with food orders. These were cut to the limit, and if you ran out of food before the two weeks were up, very well, you ran out of food.

The list (very strict) of provisions you were allowed to buy included staples like beans, rice, fatback, and some canned foods that were high in vitamins and nutritional value. Cookies, Jell-o, and sweets of any kind were off the list, and it was difficult for families with children not to buy a few things their kids craved. But at friendly grocery stores (in our case the "Grab It Here"), shopkeepers would give out a bag of cookies and write it down as a pound of rice.

Our phone had long been cut off. It was a luxury and the first to go. The electricity was off most of the time, also the gas, so we were in hock to a credit store for a kerosene stove. And when there wasn't any cash on hand for kerosene, we cooked in a corner of the kitchen on a little cast-iron monkey stove—an old-time rig with the pipes running through the fire box to provide hot water. The monkey stove, which burned wood, became the center of the household. We cooked on it when there was no other fuel. We huddled around it on cold nights when we had no coal for the furnace. Then the water was cut off, no water for laundry or cooking or the bathroom. We hauled water in bottles and empty lard buckets from a public well some distance away, driving over in the car that Mildred's husband owned (when he was still around) or in Bill's old rattletrap. We saved every possible container we could get our hands on, and when it rained we put all the tubs out in the backyard to catch water. Mother took our laundry down to Aunt Rosie's—she'd had plumbing installed and now owned a washing machine.

Our house on Oak Street had been a big step up, supposedly, but the old house on Robinson had a pump in the yard and a privy—the basics. We'd moved above that, but we'd relinquished the prerequisites of poverty—free water and a privy. With your own water, a privy, and a cast-iron range to cook dinner and heat the house, you're ahead of the system. Not by far, God knows, but you're ahead.

All right, we'd overshot. We'd fallen behind and were in bondage to the utility companies. Barbara took showers at school, I took showers at school. Mother took showers at work. For the rest of the family, it was cat baths and bucket baths. Mother, meanwhile, carried on as though nothing were amiss. She was ardently involved in her church work, her faith always in the Lord and His loving kindness to His children. And her social activities continued apace.

Mother gave teas and entertained the Golden Rod Chapter of the Eastern Star, in spite of everything. But it took careful planning. A meeting at our house would be called for early afternoon so it would be over before the kerosene lamps had to be brought out. We prayed no one would ask to go to the bathroom, but if they did, we were ready with a couple of buckets of water to fill the tank so it could be flushed again. The house was pretty, and Mother had nice furniture and nice china. She could serve tea and refreshments with graciousness, backed up by a certain amount of frantic, behind-the-scenes footwork. It was managed very well. Mother said nothing about her household tribulations, tea parties went off without a hitch, and the ladies departed in peace.

But one afternoon there was a crisis. The bucket brigade had miscalculated, the bottles and lard tins in the kitchen were suddenly empty, and more tea had to be brewed for the party. So while the guests in the parlor chatted on, Mother grabbed a gallon jug and cut out through the back door to a neighbor's house. This particular neighbor was a little addled, a little crotchety, known up and down the street as a lady who'd lost a few of her marbles.

She whined at the door, "Now, Mrs. Short. I gave you two gallons of water last week."

Mother said she was sorry to be any trouble, but this was an emergency.

"No, Mrs. Short. Two gallons last week is quite enough. I

can't give you any more water. No, I can't do it. You had some water last week and that's quite enough. . . ."

My mother, usually so gentle and mannerly, could be fierce when pressed. She turned into a tiger at the door. "For God's sake, woman, give me the water!" she commanded. "Give me the water!"

"Yes. Yes, Mrs. Short." The jug was filled, Mother dashed home through the backyard, and put the kettle on to boil.

That first summer I stayed close to home, a little aloof, a bit to one side; home again and belonging, glad to see my old friends, yet not quite back into the familiar patterns and established rounds. Everyone was pleased to see me. Mother was happy to have me back, and no questions were asked about my quitting show business. My expedition was over, and I was home again. That's all there was to it.

A few weeks later, I wrote the Somerset Hotel in New York and asked them to send my trunk C.O.D. When the trunk arrived, there were a few things in it that belonged to Len—an Eton jacket from his singing days, a plaid muffler, a few odds and ends—and there were clothes I'd long outgrown, some clippings, publicity photographs, several contracts, the toy typewriter, the Big Business game. All of it, except the plaid muffler, which I wore to school, was packed away along with my memories of the highs and lows of the past two years. It was over. I was finished with show business. The vaudeville dates, the radio programs, the nightclub turns bore no relationship to my life in Danville. What's more, I heard not a word from my benefactors, Rosen and Levin. The only message to remind me of Bobby Short, the Miniature King of Swing, the Boy Wonder, the budding Fats Wal-

ler, the youthful Duke Ellington, and so on, was a letter sent
directly to me at the Somerset, not to my managers. The letter, forwarded to Danville, was from a young man named
Don McCray, who worked in Ed Smalle's theatrical agency;
he wrote to say he'd seen me around New York, and had
some ideas for my career. I wrote back that I was out of the
business and planned to enter high school in the fall, and
thank you very much. But five years later, I met Don McCray
in California, and he did indeed have some excellent ideas
for my repertoire, suggesting certain Cole Porter and Noel
Coward songs I should learn, and also suggesting I listen to
serious music and study the harmonics in such orchestral
compositions as Delius' "Brigg Fair" and "On Hearing The
First Cuckoo In Spring."

Except for Don McCray's letter, no other inquiries or job
offers got past Len and Bookie. Evidently, they'd written me
off. I suppose I could have gone back to Chicago, lived at the
Schanettes, and pursued a career of sorts on my own, but that
prospect left me cold. I was going to finish high school, and I
was going to finish it in Danville. So in August I went over
to register as a freshman, presenting my St. Joseph's diploma
to show that I'd completed the eighth grade.

In 1936, before I'd enrolled at St. Joseph's, we'd stopped
at the Garfield School to get my transcript, and I remember
the principal's genuine concern. She said she did not approve
of this move at all, that I had met these two men only a short
time ago, and how could she know they'd be honestly responsible for my education. Still, Len and Bookie had come
through with one year of school, at any rate, and thanks to
the Mother Superior who'd let me enter the eighth grade
instead of the seventh, I'd wound up ahead. But the year I'd

gained in Chicago, I had lost in New York when my tutoring stopped. All this educational backing and filling meant that when I started at Danville High in the fall, I was once more in class with the friends I'd started with in the first grade. Another homecoming.

I was back in the fold and happy to be there. My schoolmates had no comments about my return from the so-called Big Time. Curiously, the only animosity I was aware of, the only envy, came from grown-ups. A condescending look or a remark like, "So you came back to Danville, eh?" I recall an old friend of Mother's saying, "That's a nice suit you're wearing. Where'd you get it?" I told her my manager had bought it for me in Cincinnati and that I was grateful it still fit, because it was the only suit I owned. "Come here and let me see it," she went on. "I bet it says Jewville on it. . . ." I didn't like that! I was disheartened to hear my experiences spoken of in those terms. And there was another cold moment at a neighbor's house, where I'd gone to call someone about a job. She had a guest that afternoon, a woman from out of town, and I overheard the guest ask, "Is that Bobby Short? The musician?"

"Well," said our neighbor, "he tries to be . . ."

But in the classroom, I was pleased to find I remembered all the French verbs and conjugations that Miss Mahr had drilled into me at our backstage tutoring sessions. It was a peppy French class at Danville High. Lots of singing—"*Frère Jacques*," "*Au Claire De La Lune*," and above all, "*La Marseillaise*," which our teacher, Edith Markley, often had us sing at full voice while marching around the classroom. At Christmas time, we sang "*Cantique De Noel*," and "*Un Flam-*

beau, Jeannette, Isabella." Later, I also took Spanish, which stands me in good stead nowadays when Puerto Rican Negroes in New York sometimes assume that I am Puerto Rican and ask me street directions in Spanish. I find this intriguing, I might add. It was a possibility that never would have occurred to any of us when I was a schoolboy in Illinois. Languages were always my best subjects, and I now realize it probably has something to do with my ear for sounds. Just as I could pick up a new melody and its harmonies by ear, I could tune in on and pick up the phrasings and pronunciations of a new language. I also enjoyed my English courses, and ancient history, particularly ancient Egyptian history, but was rotten in math. Glenna Wilkins pushed me through algebra by dint of her sheer good will and determination.

Another fine teacher my freshman year was Almira J. Robertson, who taught elementary economics. Teachers in those days could not resist throwing in a few words of homespun wisdom along with their lessons, and Miss Robertson was given to good, stern, home-style sentiments. "I like my students to work in this class," she'd tell us, "and to work hard. And I'll tell you something else. If you don't work, you can't get ahead in this world. And anybody who thinks he can pussyfoot around these halls and come in here and pass this course has another think coming. . . ." Now, written reports were always a big feature of our classwork, these reports to be in bound notebooks with suitably illustrated covers. Our first assignment from Miss Robertson was to write a report on our life's ambition. It was my first year in high school and I didn't want to admit that my ambition was to be an orchestra leader or an entertainer. Show business was simply not an adequate goal for a serious student. So I raised my

239

sights and wrote a report on my ambition to be a producer. I dug into books to find all I could about the famous ones— Ziegfeld, Garrick, the Schuberts, Harris—and decorated my report cover with theater ads from a Chicago newspaper.

Another time, I was a little too smart about my book-binding decorations. We'd been asked to write a report on *Ivanhoe* for English class. So I drew on the cover the rear view of a horse, with a knight astride it. Across this I wrote I-V-A-N-H-O-E, arranging my lettering so the "A" in Ivanhoe was created by the shape of the horse's back legs. My teacher refused this editorial comment, and I had to redo the illustration.

All told, it was a top-flight school system, and I appreciated that after what I'd seen and heard about public schools around Chicago. While Danville had a few teachers, inevitably, who went about their work in an almost uninterested way, the majority were interested and dedicated to their profession. I liked all my teachers. And I was a good student when I wanted to be, although there was still that game of playing the charming, professional child if it got to a pinch in my homework. I knew how to ingratiate myself if I was late with an assignment or hadn't finished the required reading, though there were occasions when I was unsuccessful.

Once our American history teacher, Fern Haviland, gave us a long-range project for the winter. We were to write an essay on a foreign country chosen from a list she'd compiled. The essays were to be turned in March fifteenth, and any student who did not complete the project by that date would be assigned a second country that Miss Haviland would select herself. I fooled around, letting it ride, putting it off until tomorrow. And then it was March fifteenth.

"Your paper is late," said Miss Haviland.

I offered some winning excuse, but Miss Haviland would have none of it. "Bob Short, you are now assigned to Iceland."

I was still diffident about performing at school, however. I, who had been the first to rush on as a child, front and center at the piano. But one day after lunch, some friends asked me to play for them. Probably just what I'd been waiting for. I eased over to the cafeteria piano and did a few songs. And with that, I received a formal invitation from the senior who was in charge of school entertainment, asking if I would perform at an assembly the following week.

The school assembly was one of the main events of the day, the entire student body—about fourteen hundred strong —gathered for some sort of program. Here, for instance, I heard my first symphony orchestra, a WPA group on tour through the midwest. Several concert pianists also appeared, their music carefully selected for a high-school audience— Chopin's "Minute Waltz," Rachmaninoff's "Prelude in C Sharp Minor." But we were able to see professionals perform on a grand piano, which made a tremendous impression upon me. We also had good speakers and interesting travelogues. And then, we had each other for entertainment—Dick Van Dyke, who was a year behind me, would put on his magic show. Shining lights in the Dramatic Club—Nancy Jo Ramey, Phil Erickson, Ben Davis, and Tom Cavanaugh—would stage skits. Bozo Lete and Lois Jean Connor would zip through a whirlwind dance number. And a little girl with red curls, named Frances Beck, amazed us all with her routine to "Head Over Heels In Love," which she concluded by standing on her head in a special box and tap-dancing on its ceiling, as she sang the last chorus.

I didn't say a word to anyone about being invited to appear at assembly. I still had that tinge of hesitation and withdrawal. Danville High was a big school and I had just rejoined the ranks of students. I was the new boy, I was the prodigal returned, the ex-Wunderkind. I didn't know yet *who* I was. But when I played that first day in assembly, I took encore after encore, and when I walked into my next class, everyone stood up and applauded.

One of the songs I did that day was "Rock It For Me," which Ella Fitzgerald had recorded and I'd done at the Lookout House in Covington. "Rock" was a new word in jazz parlance, so to many of my schoolmates, "rock it" could only mean "rocket." From then on, "Rocket" stuck as my school nickname.

XXIV

Very well, I'd put show business behind me—aged thirteen. I did no work that first summer. Nobody dared approach the returned "star" for a one-night stand at a local roadhouse or a club dinner or a private party. I began to play at Sunday School, but that was quite different, accompanying hymns and children's songs. I got some needling from the family. Why didn't I got out and pick up a few jobs? I'd always done it before, hadn't I? But I made no move to ask for work, and poverty was closing in. It was not until the end of the summer that I snapped out of it and faced the fact that I had no money for clothes for school, no money for paper or pencils or school books. In those days students had to pay cash for their books, whether new or secondhand. So when the first tentative offers finally began to come in—three or five dollars for an evening's work—I accepted, but with great selectivity, working only those jobs I felt were dignified. High-class situations, as Mother put it. At one of my first engagements, a club dinner at the Grier-Lincoln Hotel, we didn't even have a nickel in the house for carfare. There was nothing for it but to get into the suit of white tails and, pride forgotten, walk to work through the main streets of town, my feet aching from the white shoes, now outgrown and agonizingly tight. When I finished my performance, I walked out of the Grier-Lincoln with five dollars in my pocket, called a cab, took off those damned shoes, and rode home in my stocking feet.

The Grier-Lincoln Hotel was managed by Steve Lamphier, who was the town's extra man. All the grand ladies in Danville felt they could call upon Steve Lamphier to be the beau-at-large at their parties, and indeed he was. The Grier-Lincoln lounge was considered one of the "nice" places in town for cocktails and dinner. All this I had remarked and noted in the back of my head as I sat at the piano at various local parties. I needed a steady job, so I stepped forward, enormously professional, aged fourteen, and phoned Steve Lamphier to ask if he'd consider hiring me for his cocktail lounge. Why yes, of course. He'd like to have me in his cocktail lounge. I asked for twenty-five dollars a week, but I think we settled on fifteen.

A new radio station, WDAN, had opened in Danville with several professional announcers to hold the broadcasts together. For the rest, they'd taken on a few high-school students from the dramatic club or who were good at speechmaking to train as alternates. When the call went out for performers, everyone who had anything to offer was given a program of his own. No money changed hands. You appeared for the sheer pleasure of it.

Just back from my grand tour in vaudeville, I thought, why shouldn't I ask for a program too? At my audition, I did a song I'd heard Earl Hines broadcast from the Grand Terrace —"If It's Good Then I Want It." The lyrics of the bridge had a somewhat moralistic twist to the effect that when I was a kid, my mother had told me that I must learn right from wrong. Then the refrain was repeated, "If it's good, then I want it. If it's bad, you can have it. If it's good, then I crave it. If it's bad, then you can save it . . ." When I'd finished, one of the managers delivered a righteous speech on the lascivious thoughts prompted by my choice of song. Furthermore, he told me, I should never sing such a song on the radio. All right, I said politely. I certainly would not sing such a song on his radio station. (Never argue with the chief.)

With that, I was given my own show, ten minutes every Friday afternoon. My announcer was Cody Noble, a bright and fashionable Danville girl. The show began at five after four, so I chose as my theme an old jazz song, "Four Or Five Times." And for as long as my program was on the air our virtuous WDAN manager never remarked on the lyrics. "Four or five times, four or five times, it's my delight doing things right, four or five times . . . Maybe I'll sigh, maybe I'll cry, but if I die, I'm going to try to do it four or five times." Now, those words had all sorts of possibilities. But even after the show, when Cody Noble innocently purred into the mike, "And now, everybody, after that spasm of a theme song . . . ," there was still dead silence from the front office.

We had a solid core of Negro musicians in town, some old pros who'd been around for years and some newcomers, with musical aspirations. After my job at the Grier-Lincoln ended, I played with several outfits put together from this pool of local talent. Arthur Rachels, once a saxophonist with his brother's band, The New Orleans Ramblers, asked me to join

245

a five-piece outfit as their pianist and singer. Arthur, or Nanny, as he was called, played saxophone, Louis Morris was on bass, Bill Dupree blew trumpet, and Abe Outlaw, from the old Edgewater days with Ellyn Treadwell, was usually at the drums. We sounded pretty good and were kept busy at dances both around and out of town.

Now, it was the fashion those days for a man to wear his hair combed back off his forehead, a difficult style for most colored men to follow. Though it depended, of course, on one's hair. Cab Calloway's hair was naturally straight, for instance, while Duke Ellington had his straightened. The usual straightening method was to put on a heavy, greasy dressing, as the Harlem barber had done to me, and then pull on a stocking cap made from the top of a woman's stocking, to flatten the hair down. For women with long hair, there was the time-honored method of pressing it straight with a flat-iron. Pigtails were practical for old ladies and little girls, but any lady of fashion in the city had her hair dressed so it would lie straight. Madame C. J. Walker made a million dollars early in the 1900's from her patented hair-straightening process and wound up living on a fine estate on the Hudson River, up in Roosevelt country. Her daughter, during the twenties and early thirties, presided over the Black Tower salon in Harlem, where the Negro literati gathered, Langston Hughes, Countee Cullen, and the rest.

But the home-brew hair straightener for men, at that time, was "conk," short for Congoline. Nanny Rachels conked his hair and persuaded me to conk mine. This was a complicated process and had to be done exactly according to directions, or you could burn off your hair and scar yourself for life. Len hadn't been able to talk me into this, but Nanny did, so there

I was with a mane of straight hair streaming back from my forehead. Two years later, I said the hell with it, got a short haircut, and simply brushed it down as I'd always done.

For out-of-town dates, the band, with instruments, would squeeze into Nanny's father's Buick and drive off, conked, to the evening's engagement. And this was sometimes a pretty fair distance for the few dollars we'd pick up. I remember one night when we were returning very late from a dance in Attica, Indiana. It was winter and cold, and the heater in the car wasn't working. Freezing and shaking, we finally stopped at a farmhouse on the road. The farmer, who was white, opened his house to us without showing the least trepidation at having a carload of unknown colored boys appear on his doorstep at five in the morning. He was about to go out to the barn to look after his cattle, but he brought us in and we sat around the stove while his wife made a large pot of coffee. This we drank down with sweet farm cream, so thick it had to be spooned into the cup. After we'd warmed up and were given some old burlap bags to wrap around our feet, we got back in the car and went on our way.

Another night during that same bitter cold spell in February, Nanny dropped me off at our house, and as I started in, Naomi threw open an upstairs window.

"Don't let the car go!" she called down to me. "Don't let the car go!"

But before I could shout to Nanny, the car had driven off. What was the matter, I asked.

"Mildred's labor pains have started."

"Well, where's Mother?"

She was at a wake for Leona Rouse's father, so I ran the

eight blocks to the Rouses', found Mother, and told her that Mildred was having her baby. Then I ran over to the Big Four railway station to call Dr. Wilson and then beat it back to the house. I went down to the basement and managed to make a fire in the furnace. Old boxes, old furniture, the last of the coal sweepings, scraps of lumber, newspapers, and rags. Whatever was lying around loose that would burn. And I ignited it all with embalming fluid, highly flammable, a legacy from Mildred's departed husband, who had brought it home for starting fires. I stoked up the blaze till it was roaring and got the temperature in the house up to sixty-five or seventy degrees, so Mildred could have her baby upstairs in a warm room.

Another group I performed with was the Dukes of Swing, an orchestra of aspiring local musicians that Steven and Louis Morris had gotten together. The Morrises were a musical family. Steven played the trombone and piano, and Louis played the tuba and bass fiddle. They had been brought up with music and encouraged by their parents, who thought nothing of having a thirteen-piece band rehearsing in their living room two or three nights a week. Our sound may not have been the best, but it was ambitious. We ordered extensive big-band arrangements through the music store in Danville—"For Dancers Only" and "The Big John Special." I still couldn't read music worth a damn, but I knew my chord signatures, and when we unfurled one of our new arrangements, page after cryptic page of it, I put the music on the rack, followed my cues, and rolled along by ear. A couple of the musicians from Jimmy Raschel's disbanded New Orleans Ramblers were around town and would occasionally sit in at rehearsals, which was like manna from heaven. Clark Terry, for one, used to come over and play with us from time to time in the Morrises' living room.

The zoot suit, one of the more unfortunate men's fashions, was then at the top of its style—high-waisted trousers that ballooned out around the knees and were pegged in at the ankles; extra long jacket with heavily padded shoulders; gleaming watch chain that looped down to the knee and slapped against the thigh; a severely blocked felt hat with a wide brim, so wide, in fact, the hat usually had to be attached to the lapel by a narrow cord, in case of a sudden high wind. Shoes were preferably orange-tan, but black was acceptable. And a perfect shine was obligatory. A wide, garishly hand-painted necktie was the final, highly admired touch. This was big-city fashion, particularly in colored areas, and Billy Eckstine was the principal exponent of the "full drape" wardrobe; Billy Eckstine, who'd emerged as a star with his smooth singing versions of "Jelly, Jelly" and "I'm Falling For You."

Well, when the Dukes of Swing got their first big out-of-town engagement, a dance date in Springfield, there was a great to-do about what we should wear. The band's uniforms were almost as important as the music. Finally, after much discussion, it was decided the proper attire would be matching zoot suits, dark green with a pinstripe—the Dukes of Swing were going to come on as a big-city band. The suits could be bought in town for thirty-six bucks each. So off we went to Springfield, all the Dukes in green pinstripe "drapes" —except for me, the one holdout in the group. I *would* not wear a zoot suit, and I also just could not afford it. So I wore the white tails instead. They were pretty tight by now, the coat binding under the arms, the sleeves inching up my wrists, but I had nothing else. The wraparound camel's hair coat was also a shadow of its former glory, the hemline no longer flapping around my shins, but up to my knees.

Later on, I picked up steady work with a four-piece band. We were Louis Morris, bass; Bill Dupree, trumpet; Bobby Short, piano and vocals; and John Dyer, saxophone—Hooks Dyer, who'd been the first person to put me on stage, at the age of eight or nine, out at the Edgewater. The group played at the Dutch Mill, a nightclub on Main Street that had been opened by Gotch, one of the old owners of the Edgewater. "How High The Moon" was a hit that season, and we played it as a straight ballad; later, of course, it became a jazz classic. Along with our group, Gotch brought in special attractions —a singing bartender named George Wright, and exotic dancers imported from Chicago, young ladies down on their luck, who were encouraged to "mingle" with customers.

Monday was opening night for new shows, and a rehearsal would be scheduled for late in the afternoon when my classes were over. I recall lots of gypsy dances and florid arrangements of the "Hungarian Rhapsody" school. Half the time I didn't know what I was supposed to be playing, while the girl of the week was on the floor stomping and swirling and snapping her fingers, but I took my lead from the other instruments and faked it through. There were no complaints, though the young ladies found themselves dancing to a piano accompaniment they'd never heard before. But one afternoon, with the first run-through, the girl suddenly wheeled around in mid-shimmy. "Stop, stop," she cried. "There's a piano cadenza there . . . a cadenza!" A cadenza? I had no idea what she was talking about? John Dyer explained—I was to improvise for a couple of measures. Well, no problem there, I'd been improvising since the rehearsal began.

From the Dutch Mill, I went to the taproom at the Hotel Plaza, as a single. The taprooms at the Hotel Wolford and the Grier-Lincoln were considered the genteel bars in town, while the Plaza was the place to go for a whoopee evening, a whiz-bang good time. Jack Howard, who ran the taproom, always gave his performers a contract and good advertising. Ruth Arnold, an albino colored woman who came through Danville with her husband looking for work, played a fantastically good piano; she was the first Negro albino I'd ever seen, and Jack Howard billed her as Mademoiselle Blondie Arnold. Huila Gallez played and sang risqué off-color songs, which Jack Howard made the most of in his advertising. Mother, meanwhile, baffled by the French affectation of a name like Huila Gallez, always referred to her as Eula Gallezi. Jack Howard had a number of good ideas for me—some George M. Cohan songs, for instance, as well as several catchy tunes that had been popular in Jack's youth. One, a little waltz called "Absinthe Frappé," I sometimes slip into even now for a change of pace, a reminiscent interlude of my own.

XXV

Wade Cannon's soda fountain and candy store was the local hangout, where we all gathered to dance to the jukebox—to Ellington, Holiday, Lunceford, Andy Kirk and His Thirteen Clouds of Joy, and Waller. ("Don't love ya, cuz your feet's too big. Can't use ya, cuz your feet's too big . . .") Sometimes one of Lil Green's low-down songs would sneak on, or "Jive, Lover" sung by Bea Booze. Later, the new colored Elks Club on Main Street became the place to go dancing, lindy and jitterbug, but not the shag. Never the shag. That was the white kids' dance.

Lincoln Park was still in full swing with free movie nights, a WPA recreational program, and talent shows. They'd built a beautiful new sunken garden in Lincoln Park, with flower beds and a fountain, and on movie nights, if a couple strolled away toward the garden, everyone would call, "Look out for Blanche Hamilton!" Tall, thin Miss Hamilton had an official position with the city (probation officer, I believe) and was also a member of the colored elite. I never knew if it were true or not, but rumor persisted that Blanche Hamilton was sitting down in the sunken garden, watching to see which couples wandered away from the movie and into the dark. "Blanche Hamilton's down there with a pencil, and she's making a list. She's making a list. . . ."

The colored Community Center was another big gathering place, and from time to time a slight, close-cropped, middle-aged white lady, Miss Crist, who was in charge of entertainment at the Old Soldiers' Home, would round up a group of us from the center to put on a show for the veterans. We often spent an evening singing and dancing, helping Miss Crist take care of her boys, as she put it. The Home had a proper stage, with a proscenium, footlights, and a lighting booth at the back of the hall with a man to run the spots. Some of the veterans were sick and fading and senile and didn't know or care what was going on up on stage. But others got right into the music and hummed or sang along. Or went humming and singing off on their own set of songs. Some of them became unmanageable, to Miss Crist's distress ("Now, boys! Now, boys—*please!*"), and they'd shout for "My Buddy" over and over again. Nothing else would do but an evening of "My Buddy." Miss Crist, however, immortalized herself to me with a vivid lecture on the evils of syphilis, a lecture delivered when she was driving me home from a show; she was a medically-minded Christian lady, out to save us all from disease. She even named someone in town, a former musician, she told me darkly, who had been blinded by VD. And if I ever met that man and had to shake his hand, I must scrub my own hands immediately—thoroughly! —with yellow soap.

One summer Wayne Cook, the enterprising owner of Cook's Tavern (a jukebox and barbecued ribs) put together

a carnival, with the help of other colored merchants in town.
They set it up in a vacant lot down in the East End. Now
called Carver Park, in honor of the late Negro agricultural
chemist, the lot was then just an empty, red clay field that
turned to red mud after a rain. The sponsors turned this field
into a virtual fairground with booths and rides and games.
But the hit of the carnival was a revue. Talent was pulled in
from all corners, and people one hadn't even suspected of
having an itch to be on stage were suddenly up there audi-
tioning. My brother Bill, in one of his fey moods, got into
the revue along with his friend Beanie Riley, a colored man
around town. My cousin George Reid was also in the show
with jokes and skits; the Three Shades of Brown; Flossy Alexander singing "I'm Going to Lock My Heart and Throw
Away the Key"; and Bobby Short playing and singing "Tippy
Tippy Tin."

The revue was under canvas, and admission was charged.
At the end of the tent beside the stage was a platform with
wheels on which a piano sat. But after the first day, whoever
owned the piano took it back, which left us with no music.
After we'd scruffed around trying to borrow another one with
no luck, George Reid talked Aunt Rosie into allowing him
to take her nice old rosewood upright. So Aunt Rosie's piano
was carted down to the carnival and hauled up on the platform, and the show went on.

Everyone did their act with lots of make-up. One of the
side aspects of amateur theatricals is heavy make-up. People
bent on being as professional as possible often feel that
make-up is the key to a professional performance. Not just the
girls, but the men too. Beanie Riley and my brother Bill were
doing a Pigmeat Markham routine with a thick coat of black

cork on their faces. You'd see Beanie Riley in town somewhere at midday, in a bar or transacting a little business on a street corner. "Hi," he'd say. "How are you?" And you'd answer, "Hi, Beanie. How are you?"

"Well, I'm all right," he'd answer. And there he'd be, with most of the burnt cork still on his face, and two black eyes.

They also felt that part of being in show business was drinking a lot. The more you drank, the better the show. So before each curtain, while the third and fourth layer of cork was being applied, the drinking began. And by the end of the last show, they'd either be reeling or completely out on their feet. Beanie Riley would be propped up against Aunt Rosie's piano. Most of the time they drank their own mixture that they called "Stretch It"—gin and green Nehi soda pop—the cheapest gin you could find, because nobody had money for more than a half pint at something like sixty cents. "Getta half pint, man. Getta half pint." They'd mix it with green Nehi and take a good swig and another and another, and then swagger out to a thunderous reception.

But the sad ending, the bittersweet, comic ending.

The show ran for a week. Then the tents came down and every trace of carnival was removed—the rides, the booths, the strings of lights, everything, except the platform and my Aunt Rosie's upright piano.

The piano sat there for a month. One day would be pouring rain, the next would be ninety-five degrees hot, and there was Aunt Rosie's upright, being soaked by the rain and broiled by the sun, in the middle of the empty lot with all the mud puddles and the red dirt.

"Get my piano," Aunt Rosie kept saying. "You get my piano back here."

255

"Oh, *Mama.* We'll get it tomorrow. We'll get it tomorrow."

And of course by the time poor Aunt Rosie got her piano back, it had been damaged beyond repair.

Now, the Dozens. I was too young before leaving Danville to know about the Dozens, but in Chicago, in the rough area where I lived, I was aware of it instantly. The Dozens is a game that consists of an exchange of insults, the cruelest kinds of insults, usually having to do with your family—your mother is a whore, your brother is a pimp, and so on and on. It's a game of wits, the aim being to insult the other person as much as you can without coming to blows. It isn't a matter of someone saying let's play the Dozens. You would be *eased* into the Dozens, as the expression went. Someone who had it in for you might say, "Well, where was your mother last night? Out on the streets, wasn't she?" You'd realize the game was on, and might answer, "Yeah, with your old man." From there, the insults mounted higher and higher and higher, and though you were meant to spar without touching your opponent, the game almost always ended in a fight or, at the least, with tears of rage. I don't know how the name of the game originated, but I've read that the Dozens began back in those sunny old plantation days as an exchange of taunts between the field hands and the house servants, who often carried bitter antagonisms toward each other. They couldn't fight it out, so they talked it out, hurling insults back and forth from yard to kitchen door, and the crowning insults won the match.

When I got back to Danville, I ran across the Dozens again, this time from a kid in town, four years younger than I, who walked up to me one day, out of the blue, made the opening move with a filthy remark, then stood back and grinned, waiting for me to pick up the dare. But the Dozens was not my kind of game, and I knew I would have ended it by beating him up, so I let the challenge drop and stopped the game before it could begin. Later, though, when I mentioned this encounter at home, my mother, so naive about so many things, had no idea what I was talking about. "A game? What game?" she asked. Her friend Ella Primer screeched with laughter. Ella had been raised in the South and knew what that was all about. "Why, he was trying to ease Bobby into the Dozens." She laughed and laughed. "The Dirty Dozens! The Dirty Dozens!"

Another hangover from the old days was Dog Latin, or Tut Latin as I've heard it called. To the best of my knowledge, this was a secret language that began with the colored folks, and I've never seen it listed in any dictionary or book on American folklore. Mother taught us Dog Latin, and Barbara and I used it sometimes to say something secret in front of other people. It was more complicated than Pig Latin, for instead of rearranging syllables, entire words were spelled out in code. Vowels and the letter X remained the same.

A	a
B	bub
C	cack
D	dud
E	e
F	fuf
G	gug
H	hash

I	i
J	juj
K	kuck
L	lull
M	mum
N	nun
O	o
P	pup
Q	quack
R	rare
S	suss
T	tut
U	u
V	vuv
W	wack
X	x
Y	yack
Z	zuz

Double letters, such as the two b's in Bobby, were indicated by saying "square." Thus, my name in Dog Latin would be "bub-o-square-bub-yack."

Years later, I heard Dog Latin at the Parker House in Boston. The Parker House, once the epitome of elegance, had at one point fallen on bad times and become a second-rate commercial hotel. I had an appointment there and joined the crowd waiting in front of the only elevator running. The operator was a colored woman of about sixty—tough as nails and mad as hell because she was alone and her replacement hadn't shown up. She'd been on her feet for eight hours, and she wanted to go home. We packed ourselves into the car, and at each floor heard the whole story, with fresh embellishments. Someone in the car made a comment that was meant to be soothing, about the Parker House being known as one of the best hotels in Boston. To my astonishment and high delight, our driver mumbled to herself, "What you've heard is nothing but sus-hash-i-tut."

XXVI

I was now sixteen and making a living of sorts in Danville if I kept moving. I was beginning to put some clothes on my back, and I could put money in the kitty toward a ton of coal or groceries or some other pressing household expense of the moment. And I helped Barbara, also in high school, with her books and new clothes.

But the family had fallen too far behind. We'd reached the point of no return and could not keep up with the bills. Reg, who'd married the year before, was living in Evanston, and coping with his own financial slings and arrows, so the few dollars he'd been able to send home now stopped. Mildred, with her two little boys to support, was scuffling for whatever jobs she could find, picking up day work from time to time. Even Mildred succumbed to the despair that swamped the household and once snapped that I should get a steady job. A *real* job. I insisted that my marathons at the local gin mills seemed real enough to me, and that something "steady" would mean shining shoes or washing dishes or delivering groceries. I was going to stick with the piano. To add to all our difficulties, at the peak of our poverty I'd hocked the old Walworth upright and replaced it with a new Kimball spinet, which I was paying for on time.

Bill was in and out of the house, coming around when there was food to eat, but otherwise foraging for himself. He worked for a while in a barber shop and sometimes lived there. His morale was at ten below zero, and he became the bully of the household, gruff and short-tempered. And he had no use for me. I can only guess that nothing could have stuck in his craw more than the sight of little brother Bobby heading out for an evening at the piano, sure to have three or five dollars in my pocket at the end of the night. But Bill wasn't mad just at me, he was mad at the world, and was out to strong-arm the world. When our paths crossed, I couldn't fight him back; Bill Short would have dropped me with the flat of his hand. So we survived those bad times with silence. That was my only solution. No word exchanged, no conversation at the dinner table. All necessary communication passed on through a third person; and all of this to my mother's deep distress. Sometime in through here—I'm not sure just when—Bill went off and joined the CCC, as Reg had done earlier, and spent most of his free time in and around Evanston. After that we were friends again. Those were jam-packed years for all of us, the family growing out and away from each other in so many different directions, and all of us scratching for a living.

Then we lost the house. The fine new house on Oak Street that Mother so prized and loved. It wasn't a question of the sheriff coming to the door and saying, "Out. You're evicted." That had happened in our neighborhood, a family coming home to find all their possessions stacked on the sidewalk, the door locked behind them. In our case, it was the gradual accumulation of mortgage payments to be met, the debt at last too high and our income too low. Mother, the while, kept hoping for some sort of miracle, some way of saving the house, some sudden windfall that would put it all to rights again. Oh, she would say, how could Eli Brown do this to us? Eli Brown, a lodge brother, from whom Mother bought the house, because one should always do business with friends. But Eli Brown was an old man living in California, his Danville business affairs in the hands of an agent. Mr. Brown needed that monthly income, it was a matter of dollars and cents. And so the agent foreclosed.

We had a reprieve, however. While the house was up for sale, we were allowed to stay on at minimum rent. The family was at its lowest ebb. There simply wasn't another place big enough and yet cheap enough for us to afford. So there we sat, our days numbered, waiting for the final notice. And the days stretched out into weeks, the weeks into months, while we lived on the brink of eviction with no plan for the day after tomorrow.

Bad news travels fast in a small town. One day at the barber shop, I ran into Ray Chavis, who owned a moving and storage firm. "Hello there, young Short," he said. "How are you?"

I was fine, thank you, Mr. Chavis.

"So, I hear your family is about to move. Here's my card. When you get home, give it to your mother."

Oh no, I thought. I don't like that tactic at all. That was like the undertaker giving you his card because he's heard your father is home sick.

Mother, throughout all this, was steel and iron, hard-working, dogged in her belief that the Lord was watching over us, but never, I hasten to add, losing her addiction to dressing up and to having her hair just so, even in our bleakest days. Mother was an attractive woman with a trim little figure and good-looking legs; and after my father's death, she'd acquired a number of suitors. This could have been the solution to her financial despairs. Mother could have married again, but that wasn't her style. Perhaps she was still bound by the memory of my father, the witty and charming man she'd married when she was eighteen. Or perhaps she felt that life was toil and love was a trouble, and one marriage per lifetime was enough. Whatever her reasons, she did not remarry, though indeed she loved the attention and the flattery offered by her gentlemen callers.

One of them was Mr. Cross, a widower and a highly respected man in the church, who owned his house and had a pension. Many a Sunday after morning service we ate dinner at Mr. Cross's; a good, solid, square meal, often our only square meal of the week. There was Mr. Elias Lee, who was the administrator, I believe, for the colored children's home founded by his sister, Laura Lee. There was Mr. Scott and The Reverend Harry Stone, a young minister who was deeply fond of my mother and always arrived with the proper present—a box of chocolates, a bunch of flowers, a bottle of perfume, a pair of silk stockings. He was an attractive man, as well as being practical. I remember his coming to the house in work clothes to nail down the boards on the back porch or repair the cellar door, which impressed my mother tremendously. And there was Mr. J. L. Johnson, a retired postal worker whom she met at a lodge convention in Chicago. Mother loved to tell about the time she went to Evanston to visit Reg and his new wife. Mr. J. L. Johnson met Mother's train in Chicago and squired her out of the station and into a chauffeured limousine, which he'd hired for the occasion. In Evanston, there was some confusion about finding Darrow Avenue, where Reg and his wife were living, so the chauffeur stopped to ask directions from a group of young men on a corner. There among the group was my brother Bill. Mother rolled down the window and called, "Billy. Billy." But no one in Evanston called him Billy, or even Bill. His nickname was "Boot," Boot Short. So Bill paid no heed but went on talking to his buddies. "Billy . . ." Mother tried again. No response. "Charles William!" she commanded, and Bill spun around like a shot. "Charles William!" And there was Mama in the back of a limousine with a driver in uniform at the wheel!

One night, when I was working at the Dutch Mill, a man named Jack Burchet came in to see the show. Burchet, originally from Danville, owned the Club Caliente in Calumet City. He offered me a job on the spot. School was in session, so it would be a weekend job, twenty-five dollars a weekend, plus bed, board, and tips. Okay, I'd give it a try. So on Friday afternoon I rode the bus to Calumet City, and opened at the Caliente, wearing the remains of the tail suit, now so threadbare and outgrown that I was all hands and wrists and feet and ankles. But I was a hit, and business jumped from good to incredibly good.

Calumet City, on the outskirts of Chicago, like East St. Louis at the other end of the state, was wide open, with block after block of taverns and clubs and Anything Goes. And it usually did, until dawn—in sharp contrast to the pale night life just over the line in Indiana. Jack Burchet was a good businessman, a sporting character who was proud of his expensive clothes and his red Buick convertible and the success of his Club Caliente. Dining and dancing and entertainment, with gambling off the main room, which was large enough by itself to pack in a good-sized crowd, often quite a sophisticated crowd. I lived behind the club in a cabin—bedroom, living room, and a small stove. One of the waitresses had a cabin, too, as did Willy Wong, the Chinese chef. Joe Donovan, the bartender, took me on as his buddy and sidekick. Joe had a Victor recording machine, rare in those days, and I still have some of the records he made of Bobby Short at the piano at the Club Caliente.

With steady work in Calumet City, I now had credit, and the first thing I bought was a dinner jacket. I was no longer a small boy in costume. I had graduated to black trousers, dinner jacket, and black tie. At the same time I began evolving a new style, a new presentation—hard sell with all the tricks. I had become a full-fledged supper-club performer. And with the money that was now coming on a steady week-to-week basis, I could set about putting things in order at home.

The water bill, which had mounted up to something unthinkable like eighty-five or ninety dollars, was at last paid off; and we all sat there in the Oak Street house, waiting for the man from the water company. Mother, Mildred with her two little boys, Barbara and Naomi and me. It was a banner day. The water was coming on again, and we hadn't had water in the house for almost a year. Fine. The man from the water company arrived, and we were plugged back in to the city system. "Let's see how the hot water works," said I, walked over to the sink, and turned on the tap. Well, the hot water worked through the pipes in the monkey stove, the little stove we'd used for heating and cooking. And those pipes had been burned through. When I turned on the tap at the sink, there was a rumbling and bubbling from the basement, and the water came up into the kitchen, hit the monkey stove and gushed out through the burned pipes. I turned the tap off, but the pipes kept drawing. And the monkey stove, like the rock in the Old Testament, spewed water. The spring had been struck, and the kitchen was being flooded. We opened the windows to dump out the water as fast as we could. Mother, down on her knees with a dishpan, trying to stem the flood, began to laugh. She laughed till the tears ran down her face. "Oh, my Lord. My poor children. All this time without water. And now it's coming out of the stove!"

There was a valve in the basement, so we disconnected the hot-water line, but the valve, being brittle and rusty, broke off. For the rest of our stay in the Oak Street house, we were still heating water on the stove.

A white family named Kimball were our neighbors, Kenneth and Garnet Kimball. Mother and Mrs. Kimball talked over the clothesline. And we were friendly enough with their daughter Rita, but she was keen on country and western songs, which we thought were the worst in the world. "You Are My Sunshine" had made its great debut, and another that Rita used to sing was: "I want to be a cowboy's sweetheart, I want to learn to rope and ride. I want to drink my coffee from an old tin can . . ." Terrible stuff. We couldn't understand that kind of music at all.

Well, the rumor finally got to us that the Kimballs were

going to buy our house. They had a little money, enough to go down to the bank and borrow more, and the house was a good investment for them, two pieces of property side by side. But naturally Barbara and I didn't see it that way. We couldn't see that the house was up for grabs, and there was no reason why the Kimballs shouldn't swoop in and buy it. We began referring to the Kimballs as the Rats. The Rats had bought our house, the Rats were moving in. The Rats were throwing us out. On the day we left, as a last gesture, Barbara and I bought some chunks of cheese and hid bits of it in odd corners of the house, with signs saying "For the Rats."

The move was abrupt. We didn't have much warning, a couple of days or a week, but it was decisive and final. The family split up and scattered. Mildred found a room with kitchen privileges, down in the Bottoms near Aunt Rosie's, and moved in with her boys and Naomi. Mother found a large single room in a house on Washington Avenue, the street that marked the uppermost rise of the Bottoms. Right next door to Atticus H. Brown's rather grand funeral parlor. So the three of us—Mother, Barbara, and I—also set up housekeeping in a single room.

But Mother, too, had made a last gesture when we left the Oak Street house. She did not call Ray Chavis, but hired the best *white* moving firm in town to come for our furniture and put it in storage.

It was about this time that the Federal Housing Authority began to go into the backyards of cities across America, demolishing old buildings and putting up low-rent housing. In Danville, the site chosen was opposite us on Washington

Avenue. Our side, dominated by Atticus H. Brown's mortuary, had trees and lawns and a number of nice houses. But just across the street was the beginning of the slums, rows of wretched old shacks that would be pulled down and replaced with spanking new, two-story, brick apartment houses. Just as soon as this good news was published, both Mother and Mildred registered for apartments there.

Two housing complexes were completed the following year. The first, appropriately called Fair Oaks, was originally for whites, though now it's no longer segregated. The other complex, for colored tenants, was named Beeler Terrace in honor of the late Mr. Beeler, a colored man who'd served on the city housing authority.

When Beeler Terrace was completed, we were among the first to move in—out of the single room and into decent quarters, an apartment with living room, dining room, a large kitchen, two bedrooms, and a bath. It was a new life for all of us, and Mildred moved into her apartment shortly afterwards with her two boys and Naomi. But pets were not allowed in Beeler Terrace, so our dog Pal, by now quite an elderly gentleman, went to live with Mr. Cross. Pal came by to visit us from time to time, and then he was killed by a car on Jackson Street. Mother was in a state for several days.

XXVII

I'd been eleven when I left Danville with Len and Bookie, much too young to be fully aware of the arbitrary barriers between colored and white. I accepted them, those I'd fetched up against, such as at the movie theaters where only the balcony seats were open to us. But now, in high school, I was moving around on my own and could see how it was, first hand.

Restaurants in Danville were a problem. We were not welcome, not at all. Nor were we welcome at drugstore soda fountains—Walgreen's, Carson's (the high-school hangout) and so on. Even getting a hot dog at the dime store was a problem. We were a threat, the threat that Negroes might chase other business away. A couple of cafes would let us in late at night to get a plate of food—very late at night, if no one else were around. The only place we were sure of being served with the white customers was the Chicago and Eastern railway station, which had a restaurant that was open around the clock. We could eat there any time. The C. & E. I. was also a great late-night rendezvous for a couple having a clandestine love affair. They'd sit there in the small hours over cups of coffee. On the unfashionable end of Main Street some tacky old restaurants with steam tables were open to us, where we'd take out tenderloin sandwiches or fried fish sandwiches. And there was also a Chinese restaurant. We couldn't sit down to eat there, but they'd put up a bucket of chop suey to go.

The white-trade-only concept was tacitly understood in Danville—there were no signs to that effect anywhere in town, nothing that blatant. The first such sign I ever saw was at Kankakee Junction, on the bus route between Danville and Chicago. There, indeed, at the Junction restaurant was a sign: WE CATER TO WHITE TRADE ONLY. Which reminds me of a "whites only" policy I later ran across in Grand Forks, North Dakota, of all places; Grand Forks, where there were possibly two Negroes in the entire town. (I passed one of them on the street one day, and we stared each other up and down in wild surprise.) I'd gone out for lunch with six or eight white people on the staff of the nightclub where I was working, and we drove to a restaurant on the outskirts of town. The waitress knew someone in our crowd: "Gosh, I'm sorry, Maude," she said. "We just can't serve him. You saw the sign." Everyone at the table protested. The sign made no sense. What were they afraid of? Negroes weren't a menace in Grand Forks. Well, it seems the sign had been put there to keep out the Indian migrant workers who came through at picking time; hence, white trade only. No matter that I was not an Indian, I was the same color. No food, no firewater.

I don't know exactly when or how the segregation of restaurants was abolished in Danville. I think that, as in a lot of cities throughout the Midwest, it just stopped one day, without any pressure, without any demonstrations.

One day, all the movie theaters in Danville were open to us. And then one day, the Danville YMCA was open. High time, I might add. The YMCA, which had always proclaimed its dedication to (among other things) "social service and interracial conciliation."

And one day, colored physicians were allowed on the staffs of the local hospitals. That was about 1945, I believe, after a determined Negro doctor fought it through despite untold embarrassments and unpleasant reactions from his white medical colleagues. Up to that time, a colored physician with a patient in surgery, for example, could operate only if a white doctor were present. ("My medical degree is bigger than your medical degree.") No matter that they'd passed the same state boards and held the same state license to practice.

One day, the colored students in the Danville High School yearbook were pictured alphabetically, beside their white classmates, not clumped together in the back of the book, as they had been when my sister Mildred was graduated in 1932. And one day the Danville High School swimming pool was no longer out of bounds. This was after I'd left. The test case was the grandson of Reverend Tobias Hutchins, pastor of the Second Baptist Church. Reverend Hutchins had come to Danville from the deep South many years before and had hit town like a blast of dynamite. Along with Lawyer Allen, he was a real driver in the NAACP. When Reverend Hutchins' grandson signed on for the swimming team, no colored boy had ever been seen in that sacrosanct pool. The football team, the basketball team, the track team, yes. But not in the pool with white boys. The issue, therefore, was at last raised, forced, and resolved—the pool was open.

But when I was in high school, the swimming pool was the biggest *visible* discrimination. The situation was nothing like the state university, where colored students couldn't live in the dormitories or eat in the cafeteria. But at high school there were still the little things—teachers who had weak convictions or were afraid to buck authority. A teacher, for instance, who would nervously seat two colored students together when books had to be shared in the classroom. Maybe she was afraid some white child would go home and say, "I shared a book today with a colored kid," and the parents would raise hell. Who knows. The whole situation—no colored teachers in the high school, for example—was the fault of the Board of Education. They were an old-fashioned and stodgy group, and in my day they treated racial equality as unimportant. And as for any mingling of the races in a social way, like at a dance, that was considered intolerable. We could attend school parties, that was perfectly all right. But nobody would have dared cross the line to dance with a white girl. Nor would a white boy cross the line and dance with a colored girl. One did not overstep, from either direction. And this was understood by both sides.

All that's been largely done away with, now. Colored parents insist that their children join in everything. If your son is invited to a party, he goes. If there's a spring dance, he goes. If there's a field trip, he goes. No more fooling around.

Out there in the town, however—beyond the politely disciplined boundaries of our classrooms—Danville was sparked by an interracial scandal during my high-school years. I don't remember exactly how it began—some white girls from another town, or some colored men passing through. But suddenly, white girls and colored men were seen together, out in the open, in Danville, Illinois. First in the nightclubs and roadhouses, and then on the streets, in couples, for all the world to see. It caused a furor. Now, there have always been white women who have wanted to sleep with colored men, and vice versa. It's always gone on, and I knew about all that by the time I was nine years old, as I went from bar to bar, playing and singing and passing the hat. At a couple of low-down cafes you'd see white women snuggling up to colored musicians or a smart, gigolo-pimp type of guy. There were a few long-term love affairs between colored men and white women that were kept very *sub rosa*; they were never seen together in public. And some white men in Danville had colored mistresses, white men with lovely cars, who'd pick up their lady friends and zoom off to some hideaway for dinner or drive into the deep woods to a secluded spot.

Among the young people, one interracial romance, a secret, not-so-secret affair, was brought to an abrupt halt by the young lady's father. The young man was the family chauffeur. They had been warned; her father had tuned in on what was afoot and had read them the riot act, which had no effect. So one day he came home in the middle of the afternoon to check out his suspicions. It's the classic story—father slips into the house, tiptoes upstairs, bursts into daughter's bedroom, and there you have it. *In flagrante delicto*—a first-rate Latin phrase that literally means, "while the crime is blazing." The young man was banished from Danville by a legal order that allowed him to come home only on pressing business and only between sunset and sunup. The boy's family, however, with true American spirit, married him off within the month to a nice colored girl, and the crisis was over. But that legal order was ruthless and high-handed, and it took influence to put it through. Who knows whether the white community was aware of all this. But we were keeping score. However, we admit that in that day and age, if it had been in Mississippi or Alabama or Georgia, things might not have been handled so coolly. So, let us thank God, I suppose, for small favors.

Anyway, those black and white couples who had suddenly dropped from the clouds over Danville eventually went back to where they had come from or moved on, and the furor died down. But not without a final editorial in the Danville paper, which said, in effect, that we should all be thankful these outrageous goings-on had finally ceased, and for the sake of peace in the community we should forget that any of this had ever taken place. Meanwhile, those white men with colored girl friends went on as before—with discretion. And you still ran across the same few white women in the same few cafes, snuggling up to their colored paramours. The town was back to normal.

XXVIII

Colored students were in the minority at high school, and I truly mean The Minority. In my graduating class of about three hundred and fifty students, six of us were colored—five boys and one girl. We were absorbed into the system, as much as we could be. Harry Collier belonged to the Boys' Athletic Association and served on the Student Council. Joe Jackson was varsity football and track and sang in the A Capella choir. Junior Napier, a neighborhood pal from the days of our childhood theatricals, was in the International Club (for students interested in languages) and took part in Moments Musical, a yearly show put on by the music department. Henry Sayers had been on the Student Council and was an editor of the school paper. I was in the A Capella choir and Moments Musical, wrote for the Maroon and White, and had been president of the Boys' Glee Club. Elizabeth McMillan was a past president of the Phyllis Wheatley Club.

When I was a sophomore, several of us got together and founded our own club—the Triple A, which stood for All Around Activities. Clubs were painfully important in high

275

school; we too wanted a club, the male answer to Phyllis Wheatley. The Triple A gave picnics and dances and went on outings. When I was program chairman, I made a point of having speakers come in from other clubs—the Worth While Writers' Club, the Wrangler's Club (debating), the Science Club, the Radio Club, the Quill and Scroll, the International Club, and so on (there were some thirty-seven clubs in Danville High)—with the idea of getting colored students to join as many school activities as possible. I was a joiner myself, signing on wherever I could.

We were such snobs in high school, so club-conscious. Everything counted—our clothes, the saddle shoes and porkpie hats, the girls' pleated skirts and Shetland sweaters. Our slang—corny, mellow, solid, killer-diller, and creamy ("That fine creamy chick . . ."). Naturally it was the athletes, the football and basketball stars, who made up one camp. The band and choral groups were yet another, but the Dramatic Club was where the chic was. No bones about it. If you were really culture-bound, you moved with the Dramatic Club-English Department clique. And the elite course, taught by Mary Lee Miller, was Senior Grammar.

Mary Lee Miller was a marvel. She could enchant a roomful of students with a discussion on the use of the subjunctive or of correct pronunciations. Coupon, not "kewpon." Athlete, not "athalete." And put the "c" in arctic. I remember that she preferred adVERtisement over adverTISEment, and deCAdent over DECadent, because deCAdent preserved the sound of the root word, decay. And I also remember one day in Senior Grammar when we had our books out—Reed Smith was the book, our constant reference—and came to the section on words that were considered taboo in polite company,

276

including the word "nigger." But as Miss Miller read the list aloud quickly, she didn't say the word. We saw it, it was there in print; but she simply skipped over "nigger," as a courtesy to me—the only "nigger" in Senior Grammar.

It was an interesting situation in Danville High—we could join in to an extent, and then there would be the sudden, firm-but-polite "No." When I was a sophomore, for instance, I decided to join the Dramatic Club. I was already their musical pet, playing and singing at every get-together, so I told Miss Miller I'd like to try out.

She replied that she'd often thought of it. "But quite frankly, Bob, there is no reason for you to be in the Dramatic Club. You can try out if you want to. But you can never be in a play."

Why not, I asked.

Miss Miller explained without mincing words. The only roles for colored students were servants' roles, and she didn't think I should be limited to such parts. There were no alternatives; the Dramatic Club had no place for a colored actor. It didn't occur either to me or to Mary Lee Miller, who was always one of my biggest boosters, that this was sheer nonsense. It was simply a convention we both accepted, and nothing more was said.

But some conventions we would not accept. Once, in my freshman year, the colored students registered their protest. This had to do with a Negro boy named Landau Dufay, who played on the Champaign High School football team and whose father was a doctor, so he was never a poor boy. Champaign was one of our traditional rivals, and before a big game we always had a pep rally. The principal made a stirring speech, and the coach made a stirring speech, and the captain of the team got up and pledged victory. There were cheers and songs, and sometimes a full-scale pep parade through the main streets of town, the band in maroon jackets and white trousers, and the drum majorettes strutting along in their tasseled boots. And it was *Beat Champaign! Beat Irving! Beat Matoon! With a D. With an A. With a D-A-N. With a V. With an I. With an L-L-E . . . DANVILLE! DAN-VILLE! Rah, rah, rah!*

All right, here we are at the pep rally before the big Champaign-Danville game. After we'd heard the principal, the coach, and the captain, one of our science teachers made a speech. It was a funny speech. He went down the line-up of the Champaign team and caricatured each player, and when he got to Landau Dufay, he went right into the familiar Amos and Andy routine. Something like: "Lissen, boss, I doan give a nevah-mind if we's gwine have possum or sweet potatoes tonight. Ah'm gonna go ovah and whup de daylights outta dem Danville boys. . . ." And the crowd roared with laughter. Immediately after the rally, a small delegation of us went to this teacher's homeroom and explained in polite tones that we'd found his take-off on Landau Dufay objectionable and unsuitable. He was most apologetic. Indeed, he was very up-set, saying it would never happen again. And it never did happen again.

On the other hand, this time in my senior year, I had a teacher named Finley Hogbin. One day, out of the clear blue sky, Mr. Hogbin said to the class: "What if you had been born in this country and had gone to school here and got good grades in school. And you'd even gone on to college and got good grades in college. Then when you went to apply for a job you were told no, we don't care how well you did in school. We don't care if you do have a college degree. We don't like you. You're going to have to drive a truck. Or you can work as a janitor. Imagine if someone said this to you. What would you do?" I remember one boy saying there'd be some throats cut. Everyone had some indignant comment or other. Finley Hogbin went on to say that he was glad his students did not approve of such inequalities. Because, said Mr. Hogbin, a large percentage of American citizens were receiving exactly that kind of unfair treatment. And the reason? The color of their skin.

That's all he said, and class went on. I don't know if anybody else ever thought about that speech again, but I certainly never forgot it. No matter what my successes in a predominantly white high school, I always knew who I was and what I was, although my classmates never made me feel separate. Different, yes, but not separate. The difference remained, however, and I'd always been very keen on giving talks or reports about the Negro world—things they didn't know about at school. In American History, for example, when we were given a list of topics to select from for a report, I chose Plantation Life. (The cover of that report was dark brown, and the title and the only decoration, a banjo, were made of white yarn.) Another time I made a speech about Booker T. Washington, who was seldom mentioned in our history books. And I closed by saying: "To you, Booker T. Washington's rise from slavery to his position of eminence as a Negro educator may sound like just another American success story. But to me, it is a ray of sunshine and the prom-

279

ise of a better day. Thank you." Pure show business, but that's what speeches are all about.

Music, of course, was a school activity in which I always took part. I played and sang at all the major assemblies, usually at the end of the program. And the kids soon learned that the more encores I took, the shorter their morning classes would be. Until I joined the Boys' Glee Club, however, and the A Capella choir directed by Miss Pansy Avis Legg, no one had ever paid any attention to my vocal projection or singing techniques. Some early reviews, when I was on the road with Len, had described my voice as thin and forced. The classroom instruction I got from Pansy Legg was all new—scales, breathing exercises, enunciation; tonics and chromatics to warm up our voices, "La, la, la, la . . . Lo, lo, lo, lo . . ." Since those days I've been involved with vocal coaches two or three times, but, by and large, I still rely on the things Miss Legg taught me.

Every year the A Capella choir and the school orchestra took part in a state-wide choral meet called the Big Twelve Music Festival. Each high-school choir offered selections that were judged and graded by a panel of choral directors, and for the grand finale, all the choirs sang together—something like three hundred voices, accompanied by three hundred musicians.

Our big number for the Festival was a song titled "What The Flag Sings," with a dramatic, ringing tenor solo sung against a full choral background. "My people, ye who honor me . . . hear what my breeze-tossed ripples say . . . Oh, our own native faults lie bare. Point out the specious statesman's glare, whose words would hide with shout and prayer, his soul's sedition . . . Remember what I am to thee. I'm your sign of liberty . . ." These words were set to quite modern and sophisticated music, nothing like the usual school arrangements. I loved that song, and I was bowled over when Miss Legg asked me if I'd sing the solo at the Big Twelve Festival. I'd always felt that Miss Legg did not approve of the popular songs and the jazz I sang in assembly. I think she wanted me to put all that aside and devote myself to serious music, *good* music. Furthermore, after I'd sung half the night in a smoky club, it wasn't easy to be in tip-top shape early the next morning for A Capella choir. I remember her taking me to task one morning. "Bob Short, what's happened to your voice? You've been singing too many blues!"

Now, most of my teachers were interested in my singing career. But they were often divided over my choice of music. I'd be congratulated by one for a rendition of "None But The Lonely Heart" in morning assembly—"So much nicer than those ragtime tunes you sing." Then some other teacher would show up that evening at the Plaza Taproom and halloo to me from her table. "Bobby, Bobby. Play that song you played at school. That 'Tuxedo Junction' song."

Very well, Miss Legg had asked me to be her soloist. And the Festival was to be held in Pekin, Illinois, that year. The choir was to stay in the nearby town of Peoria. For me, this entire project was a disaster from the start. I asked Jack Howard, my boss at the Plaza, if I could have that weekend off, because I had been asked to sing the solo at the Festival. Jack said no, he flatly refused. I had a contract with him—I could not miss a Friday as well as a Saturday night. Out of the question. This I reported to Miss Legg, who expressed

281

disappointment. She'd wanted me to do the song, but there was nothing for it but to find a replacement.

My replacement was Elwood Farmer, who had been my musical rival since we'd started school together at the age of six. In the first grade, when I was singing "Trees," Elwood could get up there and sing "I'm flying high, but I have a feeling I'm falling," and sing the hell out of it.

I was wild. Elwood was an old friend, but "What The Flag Sings" was *my* song. A week later, of course, Jack Howard decided to let me have the weekend off. By then it was too late; the song belonged to Elwood now, and I would sing with the choir.

Miss Legg announced that we'd be staying at the Père Marquette Hotel in Peoria, where I'd stayed when I was twelve, for my weekend engagement in the Peoria Room. Each of us was to bring two dollars and fifty cents in advance to pay for our hotel room. The money was collected, and the big weekend at last arrived. After school on Friday, we left Danville in a chartered bus and sang all the way to Peoria. We were on top of the world. And we arrived, still singing, shortly before nightfall.

The next scene I will never forget as long as I live. There we stood in front of the Père Marquette Hotel, and Miss Legg said, "Now, children, come around. I'm assigning your rooms." She called off the names—Leggett, Johnson, and Farmer, Room 312. Connor, Karlstrom, and Reese, Room 314. . . . I stood waiting, as the sixty-odd names were called. But Miss Legg did not call my name. I'd never forgotten for one second that I was different from the others. I'd never forgotten that I was the only colored student in A Capella that year. But I wasn't prepared for this. My two-fifty had been taken along with everyone else's. Then one of my friends said, "Come on, Short. You're in our room."

I said I didn't think so. I hadn't heard my name.

"Where else would you be?" he said. "Come on, Short."

Just then, Miss Legg called to me quietly. "Bob. Bob Short. I want to talk to you."

Okay, I told myself. Here it comes. We all knew, she told me, there were certain things in this life that we could do and certain things we could not do. And when she'd told the hotel there was a colored student in the choir—well, they had made arrangements for me to stay elsewhere. It was a nice home, a lovely colored home, where Marian Anderson and all the other great colored performers stayed whenever they were in Peoria. The room in this lovely colored home would cost me the same amount of money, and in a few minutes the manager's own personal driver would take me over.

I protested. I told Miss Legg I'd worked in that hotel and had lived there when I was twelve. Was Jerry Gordon still the manager? Perhaps Mr. Gordon had forgotten me, perhaps if I spoke to him myself. And, through all this, I was trying to keep our conversation low so my classmates and friends wouldn't know what was happening.

We went into the Père Marquette. Jerry Gordon greeted me. "Hello there, Bobby. How are you?" But he was adamant. I might have stayed there when I was twelve, but that was then, and this was now; the car was waiting. I went to the desk, got my refund, and Mr. Gordon's driver took me off to the colored section of town. Indeed, it was a lovely house; I had a magnificent bedroom with a private bath. My host and hostess were charming people, and I'm sure that every big colored performer who'd come to Peoria had stayed there—not wishing to cause waves.

Of course, Jerry Gordon's driver, who was colored, understood the situation without a word being said. What was I going to do that evening? he asked. Nothing, I told him. Why, that would never do. He'd be off duty in half an hour. He'd come back for me and we'd take a tour of Peoria. So I spent the evening with Jerry Gordon's chauffeur, in Jerry Gordon's car, driving around Peoria. I remember passing small groups of Danville kids in the downtown area—sightseeing and buying cokes and clustered in front of a movie theater or store window or peering into a cafe, boys and girls sort of hugging each other and laughing and fooling. Should I yell hello, I wondered. I decided not to.

Miss Legg had told me to be at the hotel the next morning at eight. We were to have a quick run-through before the choral meet. When I walked in to rehearsal, my friends all gathered around. Where had I been? Where did I go last night? Why did I take off without a word? But I couldn't tell them what had happened. I was far too proud for that. I said I had some old friends in Peoria—after all, I'd worked there as a child—and these old friends had insisted I spend the weekend with them.

We rehearsed our program and then went on to Pekin for the Music Festival, and I bit my lip while Elwood Farmer sang my song. My solo. Looking back, I realize what a shrewd choice I was to sing that song in the first place—those star-spangled patriotic lyrics. And I'm not negating Miss Legg. But how perfect to select the one colored boy to sing that song. What staging! And what a feather in her cap, if she'd brought it off. But I stood in the bleachers that night while Elwood sang my song, and sang it very well.

The Triple A held a banquet my last year. There'd never been a colored students' banquet before. And since I was chairman of the program committee, I decided we'd put on a first-class party. We invited the superintendent of schools, the principal of the high school, the dean of boys, the dean of girls, our club adviser, and the Phyllis Wheatley girls. The banquet menu was worked out with Mrs. Crim, head of the school cafeteria, where the party was to be held. The dinner would cost thirty-five cents a plate, so it would be within the reach of all.

The dean of girls, Helen Thompson, suggested we have a speaker. That sounded fine, but who to ask? She had just the person for us, a man named Longbons, who lived nearby and often gave talks at young people's clubs. Miss Thompson offered to write him a note. Mr. Longbons replied that he would be honored to come to Danville and be the speaker of the evening at the Triple A banquet. And so on the night of banquet, this thoroughly pleasant white man arrived to sit at the head table and join in our festivities.

Before Mr. Longbons' speech, during dessert and while the tables were cleared, I played a few songs—nice square ballads for our guests—and it seemed that our Triple A party was a bright and merry success.

Then Mr. Longbons, speaker of the evening, rose to give his speech. He started graciously enough. But in minutes, I realized that that man, in a subtle way, was delivering an inside message. I listened and I sat bolt upright in my seat.

Your time is coming, he said. You have been held back too

285

long. There must be conditions in Danville that are unequal and unfair. There must be conditions in this very school that are unequal and unfair. It's time for Americans to see colored people as more than cotton pickers and shoe-shine boys and porters and cleaning women. Why, said he, today on the highway as you drive along, you'll see a fine car zooming by, all polished up and shining, and that car belongs to colored people. The image has changed. Colored people now have property and responsibility as well. And so on.

Mr. Longbons' speech was not a great speech. Far from it. But this was back in 1941. And he was indeed saying something. He'd been invited to speak to a group of colored teen-agers, and he was going to get a few things off his chest. This was certainly not what Miss Thompson had in mind when she invited him.

When he had finished speaking, half the kids hadn't understood. They hadn't been listening closely. They'd just heard a few words, like cotton pickers and porter and cleaning woman, and were made angry by these words. So there you have a crowd of angry, grumbling colored students. But also a crowd of angry, grumbling white teachers. I remember one, stirring his cup of coffee and stirring it again, and muttering down his shirt front, "The man is crazy. The man is crazy." And the school principal, whose Board of Education had forbidden him to have a Negro on his faculty all those years, and whose colored students were forbidden to use the school swimming pool, trembled to his feet, his voice almost incoherent with emotion. "I would like you to know . . . in this school . . . I have never . . . no one has ever . . . in this school . . . no difference has ever been made between any students . . . That man . . . I won't have that man leave this room tonight, giving the impression that anybody . . . anybody on my staff . . . has ever . . . in this school . . ." Then everybody was talking at once. Mr. Longbons had stirred up a hornet's nest. The evening was in shambles. I just sat tight —I loved it! Wow, I thought, this is one hell of a banquet. Well, we got through the rest of formalities somehow or other, and the party was over. The end.

Every spring, the high school staged the Moments Musical, a full-length review created by the music department and directed by Miss Legg. My senior year, two big scenes were planned for the A Capella choir. One would be set in a railroad station with a number of old World War I songs. The other would be in New Orleans, the boys dressed in top hats and frock coats, the girls in hoopskirts, bonnets, and parasols —a costume dear to American hearts. (Remember the line of high-yellow chorus girls back at the Apollo, in *their* crinolines and parasols.)

As the weeks rolled by, and plans for this extravaganza unfolded, Miss Legg told me that I was to be the key character in the station scene. Oh, I thought. Goody goody. What lovely part is in store? By now, I was as evil as I could be.

Miss Legg wanted me to be the conductor, and I would call out arrivals and departures. "Train for New Orleans! Track eight! Leaving in five minutes!"

Fine, I thought. That's honorable. That's better than being a porter.

"We have a marvelous song for you," she went on. "It's called 'When That Midnight Choo Choo Leaves for Alabam'.'"

I didn't know the song.

"It's a grand song. And with your rhythm, you'll do it beautifully."

That evening when I got home, I talked about Moments Musical and said I'd been given a part to play.

"What part?" Mother asked.

I told her I was to be a conductor, the key character in the railroad-station scene.

"Good for you," said Mother. "What are you going to sing?"

" 'When That Midnight Choo Choo Leaves for Alabam'.' "

"What? You're going to sing *what*?"

Was something wrong with it? I asked her. I didn't know the song.

"Well, I know it," she said. "And you're not going to sing that song as long as *I'm* alive." Mother grabbed my hat and snapped off around the room, doing a little dance step and singing, the hat cocked over one eye. "When the midnight choo choo leaves for Alabam', I'll be right there. I've got my fare. When I see that rusty-haired conductor man, I'll grab him by the collar, and I'll holler, Alabam', Alabam'. . . ." Now that song isn't necessarily a colored song, it could be anybody going down to Alabama. But for my mother, the song was Jim Crow. A little too much black-faced minstrel in it for her liking. "I'm sorry," she said. "You'll have to tell Miss Legg tomorrow that you cannot sing 'Midnight Choo Choo.' "

Miss Legg must have despaired of ever getting me out on stage, singing the solo of her choice. She explained to me how there are certain songs that only some people can really sing. When Marian Anderson closes her eyes and sings "Steal Away to Jesus," no one else in the world can sing it better.

And "Midnight Choo Choo" was the perfect song for me. No one else in A Capella could do it justice.

When I repeated this to Mother, her answer was still no. Oh, my Lord, I thought. What's going to happen this time. Well, the payoff was that I wound up singing "I'll Take You Home Again, Kathleen"—in my fine Irish tenor—and I stopped the show.

XXIX

The summer between my junior and senior years, Jack Burchet gave me a full-time job at the Club Caliente. He jumped my salary to forty dollars a week, and with tips my take-home pay averaged seventy-five dollars. Seventy-five dollars a week! Six months earlier, and we could have saved the Oak Street house. There wasn't an extra cabin for me at the Caliente, so Jack Burchet scouted the Negro neighborhoods in the area—Indiana Harbor, Hammond, East Chicago—for a place for me to stay. It was all part of the Chicago spillover, and the tenor of these neighborhoods was less than honorable—gambling, prostitution, petty rackets of one kind or another. Not communities that went to church.

In Hammond we found a very stylish colored lady, who said she'd love to have me as a boarder except she had no rooms left. However, there was a couple across the street. She didn't believe they were married, but she thought they had an extra room and could use the money. Indeed, the couple, Valentine Edwards and his common-law wife, Bernice, did have an extra room. It was nothing fancy, an alcove, with a curtain instead of a door. But it suited me and wasn't far from the club.

I never knew Bernice's last name. She was much younger than Valentine, about twenty-six or twenty-seven and quite handsome. Valentine was close to fifty, worked in the steel mills, and had a family just around the corner—seven or eight children and a hard-working respectable wife. But Bernice, the young girl friend, had pressured him until he'd left home and taken this little house where they could live together. He was still devoted to his children, and they often came around to visit.

Bernice adored Valentine and adored the security he gave her. She'd get dressed up and stand in front of the mirror. "Look at me," she would say. "I'm about as fine as I want to be. I've got everything a colored woman needs. . . ." But Bernice drank a lot, sometimes beginning with sherry flips at twelve noon, and there'd be impassioned lover's quarrels and impassioned reconciliations. He was mad about her.

But despite the quarrels and the sherry flips, Bernice followed her housewifely routine—that simple day-to-day pattern of small-town life. The husband leaves for work early in the morning and gets home around four. And when he comes home, his wife is ready for him. She has done her housework. She's had her bath and put on a clean house dress, oiled her legs so they won't look ashy. She's combed and dressed her hair and doused herself with Mavis talcum powder, a few sprinkles of talcum showing at the neckline on her brown skin. Then she sat on the front porch waiting for her man to come home. While he had his bath, they chatted back and forth, and she put the dinner on the table. The cornbread was mixed and all ready to slip into the oven. There would be boiled ham or fried chicken, fresh corn or green beans, and a salad. For dessert, she would have made a cake, a pie, maybe strawberry shortcake. If they didn't go out after dinner to visit friends or go to the movies, they sat on the front porch and had a couple of bottles of beer, played a few records or cards, on Saturday night perhaps getting drunk. And then they were in bed.

I was a real hotshot that summer. I worked in a nightclub, I always had money in my pocket, and every day the big red Buick convertible came to pick me up and take me to the Club Caliente. I sported a little wire-haired terrier—Tuffy was Jack Burchet's dog, but he was always at my heels, traveling back and forth from the club to the house and sleeping on my bed at night. I had some sharp new clothes, and I was a smash with the young ladies. My favorite was Ollie Mae Redd. Now until I arrived, Ollie Mae's beau had had been Manuel, the toughest, meanest boy in the neighborhood. But Ollie Mae and I had taken one look at each other, and that was it; so the whole summer was spent dodging Manuel. I'd go down to Ollie Mae's in the morning and spend the day with her, deep into our undercover romance and dancing to the victrola—Memphis Slim and Slim Gaylard, Ellington, of course, and Erskine Hawkins and lots of Lil Green, her recordings of "Ooh, My Mellow Man" and "Let's Be Friends" and "Why Don't You Do Right."

With all this hot music, high summer sun, and heavy romance, I suddenly realized that the people in the neighborhood did not see me as a cute kid who played the piano. They looked on me as a man—a young man, to be sure—but a very positive threat to wives and daughters and girl friends. I'd slipped over the line without knowing it. But they knew it, and the local housewives eyed me as a real rip and home-wrecker. Word got around that I was having an affair with Bernice—stolen moments while Valentine was off at the steel mill. And one day when I answered the back door in my swimming trunks, word flew from yard to yard that Valentine Edwards' boarder was walking around in his underpants. The scandal brewed, openly, noisily, from porch to porch, and a sharp-tongued neighbor named Sally, who lived back of us, polished off one backyard gossip fest with, "He ain't no baby, that boy. He got a rod this long. . . ."

Of course, the gossip reached Valentine. He was the man of the house, and the women wanted to make sure that he knew what was going on. But Vally never confronted me, so the harpies nagged on. Finally, one morning Vally hid under my bed, ready to wait out the day and settle his mind once and for all. It was Tuffy who found him there and darted around the bed, sniffing and whining and yipping. I heard about this later from Bernice. She'd wondered what was wrong with the dog, had finally gone in to see, and found Valentine.

"Valentine Edwards, what you doing under there?"

"Well, I was just . . ."

"Don't tell me! I know. You're waiting for me to come in here and get in bed with Bobby Short. . . ."

That was a bad morning. But it cooled the house. And we lasted out the next couple of weeks till the end of August.

There was a family of colored boys who also worked at the Club Caliente—the Crutcher boys—and as each brother got old enough to find steady work, a younger brother would take over, parking cars, sweeping up, carrying supplies into the kitchen. And Jack Burchet, a soft-hearted man, had also taken in a little white boy from Oklahoma, a fifteen-year-old on the bum, whose name was Howard. Howard had attached himself to Willy Wong, the cook, who was always handing out tidbits, a slice of ham or a piece of chicken.

One evening on my way into the club, I was met at the door by one of the Crutcher boys, his eyes wide, his face very serious, and he pointed into the kitchen. "Bobby! He just said it was black as a nigger outside." None of the Crutcher boys would have dared to protest such a remark. So he'd run to me, because I was older and had a certain status. I was a performer, not just kitchen help. Presented with this challenge, I marched into the kitchen. There was Willy the cook with a classic Chinese grin on his face.

"Tell me," said I, without wasting a minute. "Is there a moon out tonight?"

One of the Crutcher boys said yes, the moon was out.

"Well then . . ." I said, looking directly at Willy the cook, "Wouldn't you say that the moon is yellow as a chink?"

Willy blanched. The grin was gone. "What? What you say?" And like every Chinese chef worth his salt, Willy seized a butcher knife from the rack, charged across that kitchen as though all the dragons of the Manchu dynasty were after him, and chased me around the club, in and out among the tables and through the bar, brandishing his knife. He didn't catch me and finally retired to the kitchen, angry and unforgiving.

But it hadn't been Willy who had said it was black as a nigger outside. It had been little Howard, the boy from Oklahoma, who'd been saying things like that all his life. When I found out, I tried to explain this to Willy, but he wouldn't listen. I had insulted him gratuitously. I had offended him beyond any explanation. I had said those words, and Willy never spoke to me again while I worked at the Caliente. What's more, he refused to cook for me, even to make a sandwich, if he thought it were for me. I'd called him a chink, and that's all there was to it.

At the Caliente, I added a few of the classics to my repertoire, the most popular and most mutilated compositions by Debussy, Ravel, Rachmaninoff, Tchaikovsky, and Beethoven. The customers in a bar or a roadhouse thought nothing at all in those days of asking a saloon pianist to play Ravel's "Bolero" or Debussy's "Clair De Lune." Far from knowing how to play these pieces properly, I made an attempt to play them by ear, and I carried it off fairly well, considering the time, the place, and the audience. And some fans from East Chicago brought an old recording of Paderewski playing "Moonlight Sonata," so I could listen to it and then play the sonata as he had played it. But eventually my pride got the better of me. I decided never again to attempt serious music by ear, and I never did. But for a while, I was making hay at the Caliente.

Hazel Scott had enormous success swinging the classics, early in the 1940's. And with the music war, an interunion fight, between ASCAP (American Society of Composers, Authors and Publishers) and BMI (Broadcast Music, Inc.), many of the tried-and-true classics were forcibly brought to the attention of the radio-listening public. In the course of their squabbles, ASCAP, which held copyrights on all the standards, withdrew its entire library of songs from the air. So radio stations replaced the standards with stepped-up arrangements of familiar classics and workable arias from fa-

295

miliar operas. Connie Boswell's recording of "Martha" was the big hit in this field. Arrangers came up with jazzy variations on "Loch Lomond" and "Come Back to Erin" and "Jeannie With The Light Brown Hair." I worked out a gently swinging version of "I'll Take You Home Again, Kathleen" and a rather torrid "Merry Widow Waltz," both successes in Danville and at the Caliente. One day I was inspired to swing the "Anvil Chorus" from Verdi's *Il Trovatore*. I tried it out immediately on Leona Rouse, but from the moment she heard the first line, "God of our fathers . . . ," I could see it was no sale. I thought my changing tempos and crash ending were pretty swell. "No, no, no," said Leona. "It won't do." I shelved the "Anvil Chorus."

Another side effect of the ASCAP boycott was the new composers brought forward by BMI and given a chance to have their music played—Kramer and Whitney, Ernest Gold, Don McCray—and Ellington recorded "I Hear A Rhapsody" for BMI.

Goodman, Dorsey, and Miller were the big bands during my school years, and a fine new pianist was Mel Powell. Phil Moore, an outstanding arranger and composer, made his recording debut during this period, while Maxine Sullivan, an established singer, was doing some lovely things—"Brown Bird Singing" and "It Was A Lover And His Lass." Rodgers and Hart contributed their flawless score for *Pal Joey*—"Bewitched, Bothered, and Bewildered," and "If They Asked Me I Could Write A Book." And Vernon Duke wrote his brilliant songbook for *Cabin In The Sky*. Finally, the Hollywood musical *Kiss The Boys Goodbye*, with songs by Frank Loesser, introduced me to "Sand In My Shoes," a song that's become one of my standards.

I discovered Dwight Fiske's records in Calumet City—
"Why Should Penguins Fly," "Ida, The Wayward Sturgeon,"
and "Two Horses And A Debutante"—all written by Fiske
himself, half-spoken and half-sung in that wry, dry delivery to
his own piano accompaniment. I learned his "Mrs. Pettibone"
immediately. I was intrigued by Fiske, just as I was by Hildegarde, whose "Darling, *Je Vous Aime Beacoup*" I'd been singing since I was twelve. Both performers did their own arrangements and played and sang as singles, and every nuance
and trick of their techniques were salient to my routines.
Years later, we'd find ourselves working in Los Angeles
within two blocks of each other, Hildegarde at the Ambassador, Fiske across the street at the Chapman Park, and I at
the Haig. I've always remembered Fiske's advice to me,
when we first met. "As long as you can sit at the piano," he
said, "you'll never starve."

Those last years at school, two of my best friends were
Chuck Brown and Joe Berkowitz, both white boys and both
good musicians. Chuck played the drums and was under the
spell of Gene Krupa. Joe played slide trombone and tirelessly
rehearsed the latest Tommy Dorsey solos. On a Saturday
afternoon, the three of us would get together for a jam session and a couple of beers and we'd beat our way through
the hits of the moment—"Yes Indeed" and "Well, Get It" and
boogie-woogie. Although all of us were caught up in the
sounds and rhythms of the big bands, Art Tatum and Duke
Ellington remained my greatest influences. Art Tatum, the
musician's musician until the day he died. His arrangements
of "Get Happy," "Sweet Lorraine," and Dvorak's "Humor-

esque" have never been surpassed.

The Duke's orchestra had taken on a new luster with Billy Strayhorn, his protegé and arranger. Billy, who died a few years ago, devoted his whole career, his whole life, to working with and for Ellington. At the time, he was doing things like "Raincheck" and "Chelsea Bridge" and a melting arrangement called "Daydreams," written for saxophonist Johnny Hodges. Among Strayhorn's songs were "Lonely Coed" and "After All" and "Lush Life," which Nat King Cole recorded. But most of his music was known only to the jazz world. Possibly the most famous of his work was "Take The 'A' Train." Of course, in the Midwest, we couldn't figure out what the devil that title meant. We didn't know that the A train was the Eighth Avenue subway line to Harlem, and sometimes announcers on the radio, stumped by that New York lingo, would introduce the record as "Take Thee A Train."

After Pearl Harbor, the music industry did a complete about-face. We'd gone to war, and the war led to an assault of romanticized ballads and jump tunes about the old homestead, war production, rationing, the boys overseas, and even the shortage of men at home—the last immortalized by Bette Davis with "They're Either Too Young or Too Old." The Andrews Sisters were singing "Don't sit under the apple tree with anyone else but me . . . till I come marching home." Some of these tunes were unbelievably bad—"He Wears A Pair Of Silver Wings" and "Johnny Doughboy Found A Rose In Ireland." But some were quite good—"I'll Walk Alone" and "I Don't Want To Walk Without You."

From England came Vera Lynn's "We'll Meet Again" and Ivor Novello's "We'll Gather Lilacs." And from my friend

Eddie Seiler, with Marcus and Benjamin, "When the Lights Go On Again All Over The World." Duke Ellington recorded "A Slip Of The Lip Might Sink A Ship." And one of Ivie Anderson's last recordings with Ellington was "Hayfoot, Strawfoot," a rocking number that voiced the marching woes of the infantry.

Broadway contributed several exciting shows—Cole Porter's *Let's Face It,* and *Something for the Boys,* as well as Irving Berlin's *This Is The Army.* Even Lili Pons rapped out a fresh recording of "The Daughter of the Regiment."

With all these trends at work, my repertoire became a staggering melange of revived folk songs, arias from opera, scattered show tunes, contemporary ballads, boogie-woogie, and always my own watered-down versions of whatever Art Tatum had recorded. At the Caliente, I developed a following of fairly well-heeled people, a sophisticated audience accustomed to sophisticated night life. Chicago, after all, was just up the way. Devotees of Tatum, Maxine Sullivan, and Ella Fitzgerald were often in the Caliente crowd. What's more, this was wartime. Nightclubs and cocktail lounges were booming. Joe Donovan, our bartender, took me along Main Street to see the other entertainers in town. Christine Randall, a colored girl who sang and played the piano with great flair. The Four Black Cats, which included tenor Richard Montgomery, who later appeared in *Carmen Jones,* and Calvin Ponder, who later starred in New York with his wife Martha Davis. Howard Johnson, who also played and sang. The most popular entertainers were piano players, particularly singles, and sometimes a duo, like Ammons and Johnson, who played extraordinary boogie-woogie at their twin grands.

XXX

Early in the spring, Phil Shelley, a Chicago agent, showed up at the Caliente on an evening's tour of Calumet City. He expressed an interest in me and asked about my plans. I said my plans were simple. I would finish high school in June, and I was going to look into the possibility of college.

"What?" he said. "With your talent, why do you need college? What good will that be?" And then Mr. Shelley gave me his sales talk. He, Phil Shelley, was the manager for Maurice Rocco, and Maurice Rocco was the hottest thing in Chicago and was going to be a very big star. If I had any sense at all, I'd pursue my career, and I would pursue it under Phil Shelley's management. Furthermore, he had booked Maurice Rocco into the Capitol Lounge in Chicago, and if I wanted him to, he could book me into the Capitol Lounge, also.

A week later, I went off with some white friends from Hammond to see Maurice Rocco. Rocco, who was colored, was quite a talented showman. Rhythmical as could be, he played the piano and sang funny old songs and a lot of boogie-woogie. He'd jump up and play half-standing, then do a couple of dance steps, then back to the piano, and he'd shout, "Rock and roll with R-r-rocco! Rock and roll with R-r-rocco!" Mr. Shelley was indeed correct, Rocco would be a star someday. He had a fast-moving and amusing routine. But if that was what Phil Shelley had in mind for me, no thank you. I remember announcing very solemnly to my friend that Rocco's act was too undignified for me.

By now, Phil Shelley's steam is up—long talks on the phone, letters about opening at the Capitol Lounge. Our agreements are made and the job is set to begin after I graduate in June. Eddie South had worked at the Capitol Lounge, Walter Fuller and Wild Bill Davison. It's a good spot. Everything is just fine.

But one day the phone rang. Calling from Chicago and ready for a scrap, was Bookie Levin.

"What's this I hear about you going to the Capitol Lounge with Phil Shelley? You have a contract with me till you're twenty-one, kid. You can't sign on with Phil Shelley."

Yes, I told him. There had been a contract once, but I hadn't heard a word from him in four years. So he'd damn well lost the right to butt into my life after all this time.

"We'll see about that," said Bookie.

He called back a few days later. He was going to be down in Danville on business, and he wanted to talk to me. So down he came. Well, times have indeed changed. We are wearing beautiful clothes. Custom-tailored shirts and elegant shoes. And driving a silver-gray La Salle convertible. I took all this in, and being only seventeen years old, I thought, wow, Mr. J. J. Levin looks mighty good.

Bookie persuaded me to go off to Chicago with him for ten days, see the town and settle our business contretemps.

301

In terms of school, my rushing away for ten days of hoopla in Chicago was insane. Final examinations were coming up soon. My schedule was heavily overloaded: I was carrying six and a half subjects, instead of the usual five. And I'd developed a kind of weariness with the whole thing that made studying difficult. I wasn't pushing anymore, I was coasting. I had become impatient to put school behind me, to put aside all that kid stuff and move along.

I'd given college serious thought—I could have worked my way. Junior Napier, with finances only slightly more secure than mine and no sure means of helping himself along, had enrolled at Tuskegee. It was a time for someone to tell me what to do. Had my father been living, he could have been that person. If he had lived, perhaps Bill and Reg would have finished high school and gone on to college. But it was so easy for me to glide into a full-time show business career, when school was over. I was already self-supporting and I was paying Mother's bills at home. College suddenly seemed an uphill battle. And I'd begun skipping school when there was no real excuse. I remember Mrs. Funk, the truant officer, an attractive lady who checked immediately if you weren't in class. When she couldn't reach the house by phone, she'd get in her Ford and drive over before the morning was out. Many a time she'd knock on our door. "Bobby isn't in school this morning. I came by to check. Is he ill?"

It hadn't been hard for Bookie to persuade me to take off. It was spring, the weather was perfect, and I couldn't wait to escape the last plodding weeks of school life, to be whisked away in the silver-gray La Salle.

In Chicago, I am further impressed by Bookie's large, plush office—with a staff. And I'm treated to a round of red carpet nights on the town, the best bars, the best restaurants, and meeting everyone, including Cleo Brown, at long last.

And out in Evanston, where I was staying with Reg, I met all the new girls and was the big star and danced on the front porch to Coleman Hawkins' recording of "Body and Soul." I was pretty pleased with myself. When it came down to the wire, Bookie got what he'd been after. He was still my agent. There was a showdown with Phil Shelley, raised voices, lots of elbowing, and Bookie flashing the old contract signed when I was twelve, telling everyone that he'd known this kid since he was eight years old. Very well, I would open at the Capitol Lounge, as planned, and Bookie and Phil Shelley would split the commission.

After my ten days of glory in Chicago, I returned to near disaster. I was about to flunk in Spanish, because I hadn't been handing in my homework. But I dug in and managed to scuttle through. I was flunking typing, a course I'd taken in emulation of Mildred, just as I took French because she had taken French. I was a fast typist, and I enjoyed that class because we practiced touch typing in time to a ricky-ticky old march that was played on a wind-up phonograph. But I had not completed my assignments. Even after my teacher offered to let me make up the work, I let it slip. Miss Brown said she was sorry. The deed was done. I'd flunked. Still I passed all my academic courses, thanks to my helpful and endlessly tolerant teachers.

Junior Napier gave a big party at his house to celebrate our graduation, and commencement exercises were held on the football field on a hot June evening. This being wartime, the program had a strong military flavor. The school band played martial songs, and I had three rousing solos—"Keep

'Em Flying" and "Arms For The Love Of America" and one other. I remember there was a problem in synchronization, because the band was at one side of the field and I sang from the other, which left me just about a half beat behind. And Mildred said afterwards, not understanding the problem and trying, of course, to say the right thing, "Well, after all, you had three songs to sing. They couldn't expect you to sing everything perfectly."

We wrote our farewell message in each other's yearbooks. Good-bye and Good Luck. Luck and Joy. You're the tops. Here's to success. Remember the fun we had. Remember the good times. Remember me. Best wishes, always and always.

And when the time came, I left Danville.